THE POA

THE HISTORY OF THE ROYAL LINC   ⌐MENT
1685 – 1969

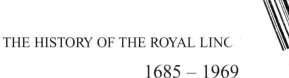

DAVID NALSON

PUBLISHED BY THE TRUSTEES OF
THE ROYAL LINCOLNSHIRE REGIMENTAL MUSEUM

This book is dedicated to all those who served in The 10th Foot, The Royal Lincolnshire Regiment 1685-1969.

The author wishes to acknowledge with gratitude the substantial contribution made by The President of The Royal Lincolnshire Regimental Association, Major-General R. E. J. Gerrard-Wright, CB, CBE, DL, towards the publication of this book. He has ensured that the reputation and traditions of a fine County Regiment will be carried forward into the future.

The author also wishes to acknowledge the assistance of Miss Alix Baker, Dr. Ronald Barr, Mr. Simon Craven, Mrs Tamasin Craven, Mr. John Elms, Colonel Brian Foster TD, DL, Mr. Robert Griffith, Mr. Vincent Kehoe, Captain John Lee, BEM, Mr. Martin Middlebrook, The Reverend John Moon, Lieutenant Colonel Trevor Veitch and Colonel Peter Walton but most of all Mrs Wendy Nalson, whose contribution has been invaluable.

The illustration on the front cover, showing a Private of the 10th Foot at Sobraon on the 10th February 1846, was specially commissioned from Miss Alix Baker, F.R.S.A., A.F.A.S., whose grandfather, Lieutenant Colonel Cecil Norris Baker, served in The Lincolnshire Regiment from 1888 to 1891.

First published in Great Britain in 2003
By the Trustees of The Royal Lincolnshire Regimental Museum,
Sobraon Barracks, Lincoln, LN1 3PY.
Copyright © 2003 by David George Nalson

David George Nalson is hereby identified as the author of this work in accordance with Section 77 of the Copyright, Designs and Patents Act 1988.

ISBN: 0-9546539-1-2

Printed and bound by CIT Brace Harvatt 01437 772200

John, Earl of Bath, First Colonel of the 10th Foot.

THE POACHERS

THE HISTORY OF THE ROYAL LINCOLNSHIRE REGIMENT.

ILLUSTRATIONS

Frontispiece John, Earl of Bath, First Colonel of the 10th Foot. The Trustees of The Royal Lincolnshire Regimental Museum.

Between pages 128 and 129

16. The 2nd Battalion The Lincolnshire Regiment crossing Modder River on chains circa 1900 during the South African War. The Trustees of The Royal Lincolnshire Regimental Museum.

17. Breakfast at Riet River, South Africa circa 1900. The Trustees of The Royal Lincolnshire Regimental Museum.

18. Some of the Grimsby Chums 1914. Imperial War Museum Negative Number HU37006.

19. The death of Lieutenant Colonel George Burbury McAndrew at the battle of Neuve Chapelle, the 10th March 1915. The Trustees of the Royal Lincolnshire Regimental Museum.

20. The battle of Epéhy. The Lincolnshire Regiment holding a captured reserve trench beyond Epéhy, the 18th September 1918. Imperial War Museum Negative Number Q. 11,327.

21. The 1st Battalion The Lincolnshire Regiment on Ramree Island, Burma, February 1945. Imperial War Museum Negative Number SE2213.

22. A 3 inch mortar of the 6th Battalion The Lincolnshire Regiment going into action at Faenza, Italy, December 1944. The `Trustees of The Royal Lincolnshire Regimental Museum.

23. A party of the 4th Battalion The Lincolnshire Regiment who went out on a patrol across the islands seen on their return, Holland 1945. Imperial War Museum Negative Number B 15001.

24. Members of the Mortar Platoon The Royal Lincolnshire Regiment on a jungle landing zone near Chemore, Perak, January 1958. Left to right Lance Corporal Rogers, Lieutenant John Wooddisse, Guyang (Eban tracker), Corporal Alan Bond, M.M., Corporal Gooch and Blauan (Eban tracker). M. Tointon, Esq.

MAPS Drawn by JOHN ELMS
Between pages 48 and 49

FOREWORD BY MAJOR GENERAL R.E.J. GERRARD-WRIGHT, CB, CBE, DL, PRESIDENT OF THE ROYAL LINCOLNSHIRE REGIMENTAL ASSOCIATION

As part of the major reorganisation of the British Army that took place in the 1960s the infantry suffered a significant reduction in size. The Royal Lincolnshire Regiment, whose history dated back to 1685, was amalgamated with The Northamptonshire Regiment and later became part of The Royal Anglian Regiment. The latter still carries the history, customs and traditions of The Royal Lincolnshire Regiment.

From 1960 to 1985 the Lincolns' Regimental Museum, which had been in Sobraon Barracks in Lincoln, was closed – remaining unseen and uncared for. In 1985, Lincolnshire County Council took on the display of the collection within the Museum of Lincolnshire Life. However, by 1995 it was in need of major refurbishment and, thanks to the generosity of many hundreds of people and organisations both within and without the County, and with invaluable support from the Heritage Lottery Fund, this was done. The Museum was re-opened by H.R.H. the Duke of York to wide acclaim in 2000 – earning a Museum of the Year Award from the Association for Heritage Interpretation in 2001.

All of this led to a resurgence of interest in the Regiment, not just from military historians and researchers but from the public at large and, particularly rewarding, schools – for the Museum has an educational bias and caters for the young visitor with video displays, interactive screens and other facets of modern museum technology.

At the same time there emerged a requirement for an up to date history of the Regiment. There are some nine different books, many other published references and several thousand mentions of the Regiment on the internet covering various periods of its history but what became clear was the demand for a short, affordable, readable book covering the whole history of the Regiment. This has been provided by David Nalson, a history graduate of Nottingham University with a long-standing interest in the Regiment. I commend the book to all those both inside and outside the County who, for personal, family or any other reason, are interested in the history of this famous county Regiment.

PROLOGUE: SOBRAON 10TH FEBRUARY 1846

'Nearer and nearer they came, as steadily as if they were on their own parade ground, in perfect silence. A creeping feeling came over me; this silence seemed so unnatural. We Sikhs are, as you know, brave, but when we attack we begin firing our muskets and shouting our famous war-cry; but these men, saying never a word, advanced in perfect silence. They appeared to me as demons, evil spirits, bent on our destruction, and I could hardly refrain from firing.

'At last the order came, " Fire", and our whole battery as if from one gun fired into the advancing mass. The smoke was so great that for a few minutes I could not see the effect of our fire, but fully expected that we had destroyed the demons, so, what was my astonishment, when the smoke cleared away, to see them still advancing in perfect silence, but their numbers reduced to about one half. Loading my cannon, I fired again and again into them, making a gap or lane in their ranks each time; but on they came, in that awful silence, till they were within a short distance of our guns, when their colonel ordered them to halt and take breath, which they did under heavy fire.

'Then with a shout, such as only angry demons could give and which is still ringing in my ears, they made a rush for our guns, led by their colonel. In ten minutes it was all over; they leapt into the deep ditch or moat in our front, soon filling it, and then swarming up the opposite side on the shoulders of their comrades, dashed for the guns, which were still defended by a strong body of our infantry, who fought bravely. But who could withstand such fierce demons, with those awful bayonets, which they preferred to their guns – for not a shot did they fire the whole time – and then, with a ringing cheer, which was heard for miles, they announced their victory.'

> Hookum Singh, a gunner in a battery on the right wing of the Sikh army directly opposed to the advance of the 10th Foot at the battle of Sobraon, the 10th February 1846.

Chapter 1

THE RAISING OF THE REGIMENT.

The Tenth Regiment of Foot was raised in 1685, the year of the accession to the throne of Great Britain of King James II, a staunch Roman Catholic, who was suspected by many of his fellow countrymen of wishing to impose his religion upon them. Shortly after his reign commenced, the Protestant James, Duke of Monmouth, had invaded England, Parliament convicted him of high treason and a reward of £5000 was offered for his capture. A supply of £400,000 was voted to enable the King to cope with the situation, allowing the Monarch to raise cavalry and infantry forces. The unit which was to become The Royal Lincolnshire Regiment was the tenth of the infantry regiments raised. Ten companies, each of 100 men, formed the Regiment in 1685 and a further company was added on the 17th March 1686.

The Counties of Derbyshire and Nottinghamshire were the districts drawn upon for recruits and a Commission dated the 20th June 1685 gave the rendezvous as Derby, and the Colonel as John Granville or Grenville, Earl of Bath. At this time, regiments bore the names of their colonels, so the 10th was known as the Earl of Bath's Regiment. John Granville had fought for King Charles I in the Civil Wars in the 1640s and had made a stubborn defence of the Scilly Isles. When King Charles II went to war with the Dutch in 1672, the Earl of Bath organised the militia of Devon and Cornwall and improved the fortifications of Plymouth.

After the defeat of the Duke of Monmouth, the 10th was one of the regiments kept in being. However, it was reduced to ten companies of not more than fifty men in each. The records state that the 10th's uniform was blue until 1691 and it was the only infantry regiment wearing that colour. The men wore single-breasted coats, with long full skirts, the edges of which were turned up revealing red linings. Their waistcoats, knickerbockers, stockings and garter ribbons were also red and their hats soft, broad-brimmed, black beavers with red bands and, round the brims, white lace. Although the brims of the hats were turned up on one side or the other, it is uncertain whether this had any significance.

The soldiers were either pikemen, musketeers or grenadiers. The pikemen wore red worsted sashes, while across the left shoulder of the musketeers was a bandolier of leather containing the charges of powder for the musket. In the bandolier belt was a ball-bag with 25 bullets. A soldier in the Earl of Bath's Regiment was armed with either a pike, a musket or a straight-bladed sword. The latter was carried in a black leather scabbard with steel mountings. The eventual adoption of the bayonet, which had been invented in 1640, made the pike obsolete early in the Regiment's history. Grenadiers were first established in the British Army in about 1678 and threw small shells or grenades. They were the tallest and finest men in a regiment and wore tall caps rather than broad ones, so as not to impede the slinging of their grenades.

The Regiment was equipped with the flintlock musket which had a range of 100 to 200 yards. It required twenty-four separate movements to load and the average rate of fire was two rounds per minute. Sergeants and the escort to the colours were armed with pikes or halberds. Each Captain had a colour which was yellow with the red cross of St. George.

When the 10th Regiment was raised, there was no statutory authority for the enforcement of discipline, however in 1689 the Mutiny Act was passed. This laid down harsh punishments, for example mutiny or sedition would result in death if nine out of thirteen officers, who constituted the Court Martial, agreed. The private soldier's pay was 8d (about 3p) a day of which 6d (just over 2p) was taken to cover the cost of his quarters. The remaining 2d paid for clothing, equipment and other deductions. There were no barracks and the men were billeted in victualling houses, taverns and ale-houses. This and the lack of organised recreational pursuits encouraged drunkenness.

The cost of maintaining his large army, the influx of Roman Catholic officers, the suspension of Parliament and especially his attempts to establish Roman Catholicism made King James II increasingly unpopular. In 1688, overtures were made to the King's Protestant elder daughter, Mary, who was married to Prince William of Orange, the ruler of Holland and a prominent opponent of King Louis XIV of France, whose power at this time menaced the rest of Western Europe. William landed at Torbay, in Devon, with an army in November 1688. The 10th at this time was in garrison at Plymouth with the 13th Regiment, commanded by the Earl of Huntingdon. The Earl of Bath, still commanding the 10th Regiment, was an assentor to the invitation to the Prince of Orange but his Lieutenant Colonel, Sir Charles Carney, was loyal to King James II. Furthermore, the Earl of Huntingdon was a supporter of the King but his Lieutenant Colonel, Ferdinando Hastings, was in favour of the Prince. The Earl of Bath, however, ascertained that the men in his own Regiment and those of the 13th supported Prince William, as did the townspeople of Plymouth. The Earl, therefore, as senior officer and governor of the fortress, arrested Huntingdon and four Roman Catholic officers, assembled the 10th and 13th Regiments on parade and, almost without demur, they declared for Prince William.

King James II, incensed by the Earl of Bath's desertion and the loss of Plymouth, cancelled the Earl's commissions and replaced him as Colonel of the 10th with Sir Charles Carney. However, the defections of soldiers and civilians from the King's cause led to James fleeing to France, throwing the Great Seal of England into the Thames on his way. Before the end of 1688, William of Orange reinstated Bath as Colonel of the 10th and Carney left the army. James was determined to regain his throne but the 10th were not engaged in the fighting in Scotland and Ireland. However, William III's accession involved England in European affairs as an ally of Holland. Louis XIV wished his grandson to succeed to the throne of the King of Spain, who was thought to be dying. Alarmed that this would upset the European balance of power, the Austrian Empire, Prussia, Holland and England formed an alliance. War began against France which, with only a brief respite between 1697 and 1702, lasted until 1713. In this conflict the 10th Regiment acquired its first Battle Honours of Blenheim, Ramillies, Oudenarde and Malplaquet.

At first, the 10th remained in Plymouth except for six companies who were posted to Jersey and Guernsey. The presence of a strong force in the Channel Islands was deemed necessary to oppose any French threat. However, a French move on the Spanish Provinces in the Netherlands led to an English contingent, including the 10th, being sent to Flanders in 1691. The Earl of Bath was still Colonel of the Regiment but it appears from a note in the English Army List that he was kept away from Flanders where he might have made contact with supporters of King James II in the French army. The note read 'His anxiety to be on the winning side at the [1688] Revolution lost him the confidence of the two masters he pretended to serve, and though reinstated in the Colonelcy on the abdication of James, he only retained the command of Plymouth Garrison until 1691.' It should be added that if the Earl of Bath was undecided as to the relative merits of Kings William III and James II, he was far from being the only man in that position! In any event, the Regiment was commanded on the Continent by Lieutenant Colonel Sir Bevil Granville, the nephew of the Earl of Bath, who, two years later, became the 10th's Colonel.

The Regiment did no fighting in 1691 and, as was the custom of the time, went into winter quarters, emerging in 1692. The French army was commanded by an able general, the Duke of Luxembourg. Namur fell to the French forces, which threatened Brussels, causing King William, with a numerically inferior force, to pursue them. Luxembourg placed his troops in a strong position at the small village of Steenkirk. The French were on high ground, protected by a river, woods and ravines. The 10th received orders during the night of the 2nd August to advance to a position in the Bois de Xoulmont which involved a laborious march through narrow defiles. Sir Bevil Granville's men were positioned at the extreme left of the Bois. At first, the 10th were not involved in the battle but Lunenberger troops on their right were thrown into disorder and Granville's men and the 3rd Regiment were sent to their support.

Sir Bevil gave orders that not a shot was to be fired 'until they were muzzle to muzzle with the Frenchmen.' The 10th went forward steadily, with the 3rd. The musketeers and the grenadiers were on either flank and the pikemen in the centre. It was a fearful advance, the enemy's artillery and infantry fire making great gaps in the ranks. The 10th proceeded 'as coolly as if on parade' and when they did open fire the French were shattered and the Lunenbergers saved.

Two sergeants of the 10th rescued a wounded Allied general, the Baron of Pibrack, and then the Regiment advanced again and held their ground until recalled. The vanguard of the English army, of which the 10th formed part, won admiration from both sides. The historian, Sir John Fortescue, said that British troops never fought a finer action than Steenkirk. Unfortunately, the remainder of the Allied army was too slow to reinforce the British success and King William had to retreat. It is not known what losses the 10th suffered in this battle but they were considerable. The Regiment was commended by the Prince of Nassau for gallantry when under fire for the first time.

Their 'bearing proved a presage of future renown.'

The men of the Regiment endured hard fighting and gruelling marches and counter-marches during the remainder of the War; however, events proved that while Regimental officers and men of the English army were courageous and disciplined, the generals were often poor. Neither the Allies nor the French achieved a decisive result.

In 1693, the 10th were in action under the Duke of Wurtemberg in an attack on the enemy lines between the Scheldt and the Lys. The Duke was so impressed with their all-round conduct, he gave every man a ducat. Two years later they fought valiantly at Kenoque. Fear of French invasion and a rising by the supporters of King James II (the Jacobites), saw the 10th, with nineteen other battalions, return to England in 1696. They remained in London for a short time and then moved to Suffolk and Essex. The following year the Regiment returned to Flanders, however there was no fighting, only skirmishing, as peace negotiations were taking place and the War ended with the Treaty of Ryswick later that year. William III was acknowledged as King of England by Louis XIV and the 10th departed to garrison duty in Ireland, where they remained from July 1698 until 1700.

With the end of the War the House of Commons reduced the army. Memories lingered of Cromwell and his major generals and there was fear that a King might use the army as an instrument of despotism. Moreover, the Commons were desperately short of money. Accordingly, they reduced the army to 7,000 men for the English establishment and 12,000 men for Ireland. Sir John Fortescue considered this 'an act of criminal imbecility', and it says much for the efficiency of the 10th, that they were one of the few regiments retained.

In 1700, the King of Spain died and in his Will left his throne to King Louis XIV's grandson. After some deliberation, Louis accepted this in spite of it being contrary to the second Treaty of Partition in respect of the Spanish dominions to which he had been a party the year before. William reconstituted the Alliance with the Austrian Empire and Holland, but Parliament was reluctant to embark upon war. However, in 1701, with the death of James II, Louis acknowledged James' son as King James III of England in violation of the Treaty of Ryswick. In addition, the English business community was fearful that Louis' ordinances against their manufactures would lead to widespread ruin. Accordingly, a War-Parliament was returned in September 1701, the army increased to 40,000 men and a force of 10,000 sent to the Low Countries. The 10th were part of this expedition. King William III died in March 1702, being succeeded by Queen Anne, and John Churchill, Earl, later Duke, of Marlborough, was appointed 'Captain-General of all the English Forces at home and in Holland and, in addition, Master-General of the Ordnance'. Thus, when war was declared that same year, the 10th served under one of Britain's finest generals, being with him in all of his great battles.

At the beginning of the War of the Spanish Succession the 10th were encamped at Cranenberg on the Rhine, forming part of the covering force during the siege of Kaiserswerth. As French forces, about 60,000 strong, advanced the British and their allies withdrew to Nijmegen, with the 10th forming part of the rearguard. Desperate fighting enabled the Allied troops to reach the fortress.

Successful onslaughts drove the French from the borders of Holland. The 10th was part of the covering force at the siege of Venlo in September 1702 and in the attacks on Ruremunde and Liége the next month. The following year they were in action at Huy and Limberg under a new commanding officer: Colonel William, Lord North and Grey, a young man of about twenty-five. He was a competent soldier but was removed as Colonel of the Regiment when suspected of Jacobite sympathies during the Rebellion of 1715.

In 1704, the 10th, as part of Marlborough's army, participated in one of the most heroic marches in the history of the British Army. The French and their Allies, the Bavarians, threatened Vienna and there was a danger that Britain's Ally, Austria, would be defeated. Marlborough persuaded the Dutch that it was necessary to concentrate on the Moselle to relieve pressure on Austria. Having arrived at the river, he marched east and, covering 250 miles in six weeks, reached the Danube near Ulm. Despite the distance involved, the march was a masterpiece of organisation, with commissaries appointed to furnish supplies for the men. Captain Robert Parker of the Royal Irish Regiment stated, that after marching, the soldiers 'had nothing to do but to pitch their tents, boil their kettles and lie down to rest. Surely never was such a march carried on with more order and regularity and with less fatigue'. The 10th began marching at 3 a.m. and halted six hours later. Every fourth or fifth day was given over to rest. Marlborough ensured that money was available to purchase supplies and forbade plundering with soldiers hanged if caught. The British regiments proceeded in good order and when the Elector Palatine inspected the infantry at Mainz, he was so impressed with their clothing and appearance, he commented 'all these gentlemen are dressed for the ball'.

Once the British army had arrived on the Danube, Marlborough, aware that French reinforcements were on their way, attacked without delay, resulting in the bloody battle of the Schellenberg. The Bavarians were entrenched on a bell-shaped hill, some two miles in circumference at the base, and with a flat top about half a mile wide. It was a difficult position to take and not all Marlborough's forces had arrived. The Foot Guards, Royals and the 23rd Regiment were in the first wave: they advanced into a murderous fire of musketry and grapeshot. Out of 50 grenadiers in the attack, about 40 were killed. The 10th went forward with the second wave and marched up a hill strewn with dead, dying and mutilated men. When they came within range, the tremendous fire of the enemy disordered their ranks. However, a further charge, supported by cavalry and Marlborough's German Allies, saw the Bavarian entrenchments taken. Each side lost about 5,000 men. In spite of the fire the Regiment faced, the 10th lost comparatively few in the battle; 1 officer and 15 other ranks killed, 3 sergeants and 36 men wounded. The Allied army was further depleted by the Margrave of Baden departing to besiege Ingolstadt. Marlborough joined forces with Austrian troops under Prince Eugene of Savoy and French reinforcements arrived from the Upper Rhine to bolster the enemy, who took up position at the village of Blenheim.

At this time, the usual organisation of an infantry regiment was one grenadier and twelve line companies, each having a strength of about sixty men. In battle, a regiment would be drawn up in three ranks, with the colours in the centre and rear, grenadiers would be on each flank. A regiment was usually split into four divisions each of four platoons, which in turn were then divided into 'firings' so that a regiment could produce a volley of fire all along its front. The French fired by lines rather than platoons and contemporary accounts state that the British weight of fire was heavier. The aim of the infantry then, as in the First World War, was to wear the enemy down in preparation for a decisive cavalry charge.

Marlborough planned to attack the enemy on both flanks so as to make him reinforce the threatened areas at the cost of weakening his centre. The decisive assault would then be made on the middle of the enemy's forces. Marlborough had 52,000 men and 60 guns against the enemy's 56,000 and 90 guns. This contrasted with many Twentieth Century battles when the attacker outnumbered the defender, as for example at El Alamein..

At dawn on the 13th August 1704, the 10th and 21st Regiments led the attack on the French right flank at the village of Blenheim itself. The 10th advanced under their Colonel, Lord North and Grey, with orders not to fire until the enemy palisades were reached and that the village 'must be carried with the steel'. These orders were carried out although the 10th were assailed 'at thirty paces distance by a deadly fire from the French'. When the palisades were reached, a volley was fired and the survivors then strove to remove the obstacles. Unfortunately, losses due to enemy fire were so severe that the Brigade, including the 10th, had to retire. A second attack on Blenheim also failed. The losses of the 10th and other regiments were so terrible that Marlborough ordered them to retreat. However, they were not defeated and checked the French forces on their side of the battlefield as Prince Eugene's men did on the far side. These gallant actions enabled Marlborough to make his decisive assault on the French centre.

The 10th and their brigade then attacked the village of Blenheim again. Lord North and Grey, with his right hand shot off, bravely led his men. When news arrived that Marlborough's troops had decisively won in the centre, and that the forces of Prince Eugene had successfully advanced on their side, the enemy in Blenheim tried to retreat. However, they were enveloped by the British troops and twelve squadrons of cavalry and twenty-four infantry battalions surrendered. The French lost 20,000 men killed and wounded, with a further 14,000 taken prisoner, 60 cannon, 300 standards and colours and the contents of their camp. The Allied casualties were 13,000.

The losses of the 10th at Blenheim were heavy, and The Blenheim Bounty List records 12 of the Regiment's officers killed and 9 (including the Colonel) wounded. It is not known how many casualties there were amongst the non-commissioned officers and men. The Blenheim Bounty was money given by Queen Anne to her troops in March 1705 in recognition of this victory. The amounts received were on a sliding scale, ranging from £144 to Colonel Lord North and Grey to £1 each for privates and drummers. It is interesting to note that while the Regimental surgeon got £12, the Chaplain received £20!

Blenheim was one of the decisive battles of history and one of the greatest events in the life of the Regiment between its foundation and the First World War. The victory almost destroyed the French and Bavarian armies in Central Europe. Louis XIV found the fear of French arms shattered and turned his mind to ending the War. England rose to a position, in the eyes of Europe, previously unknown. In the greatest English feat of arms on mainland Europe since Agincourt in 1415, the 10th had played a notable part.

In 1705, when the Regiment, fortified by new recruits, left winter quarters, 'its appearance was much admired'. However, the campaign that year was disappointing. The 10th captured two places near Landen, Neerwender and Neer-Hespen, but that was all. The next year, by contrast, was marked by another of Marlborough's great victories— Ramillies.

Marlborough received intelligence that the enemy was resolved to protect Namur and he encountered the French on the 23rd May. He began his attack on the enemy's left, which led to the transfer to that flank of troops from the French centre and right. Certain British forces, including the 10th, were left on high ground, while others were moved, unseen by the enemy, behind the hills to attack the weakened parts of the French line. Notwithstanding that the French left wing was paralysed and awaited an attack, the slaughter in the centre of the battlefield was enormous. Eventually, the Allied cavalry rode down the French centre and the time arrived for the 10th and its Brigade to sweep forward on Ramillies itself. The Allied killed and wounded totalled some 3,600 men. The French lost 13,000, 80 standards and colours, 50 guns and a vast quantity of baggage. More than this, Belgium was lost to Louis. Many fortresses fell and Brussels and Antwerp passed into Allied hands. The results of Ramillies were even more outstanding than those of Blenheim. In recognition of the 10th's services, its Colonel, Lord North and Grey, was promoted to Brigadier General.

While Prince Eugene assaulted France along the Riviera in 1707, Marlborough gave himself the role of fighting a holding campaign. There was, therefore, much marching, involving the 10th; but Marlborough was not strong enough to make a direct attack on the French army or undertake a major siege. Fears that the Pretender (James II's son) was about to invade England in 1708, led to the 10th and other regiments being allocated to home defence. However, the French invasion force was dispersed in a great storm and, when it was known that the Pretender had returned to France, the 10th and the other troops went back to Ghent. The next French plan was to besiege Oudenarde, a fortress on the Scheldt. Marlborough and his army marched to the town's relief.

By a skilful advance, the British Commander placed his men between the French forces and the frontiers of France. The enemy raised the siege of Oudenarde and took up a defensive position to the north, protected by high ground. The ensuing battle saw the 10th, under the command of Brevet Colonel Henry Grove, engaged on the Allies' right. Marlborough made two co-ordinated attacks on the enemy's flanks which encircled the French. Around the 10th the fighting was hard but by great efforts the front line of the foe was broken and the second line engaged. The French lost 15,000 men including 7,000 prisoners. The Allies' casualties were 3,000, those of the British 175.

The 10th then played a conspicuous part in the siege of Lille. Initially, the Regiment escorted supplies, furnished outposts and provided part of a covering force. Later, its grenadiers took part in the siege operations. Before the successful culmination of these, the 10th was included in a triumphant march resulting in the French raising the siege of Brussels. Subsequently, the Regiment engaged in heavy fighting which led to the fall of Ghent on 2nd January 1709.

Appalling service awaited the 10th at the siege of Tournai, where they, with the 8th, 15th and 16th Regiments, took part in underground fighting. The Daily Courant of the 20th August 1709, stated: - 'Now, as to our fighting underground, blowing up like kites in the air, not being sure of a foot of ground we stand on while in the trenches. Our miners and the enemy very often meet each other, when they have sharp combats until one side gives way. We have got into three or four of the enemy's great galleries, which are thirty or forty feet underground, and lead to several of their chambers; and in these we fight in armour by lanthorn and candle, they disputing every inch of the gallery with us to hinder our finding their great mines. Yesternight we found one which was placed just under our bomb batteries in which were eighteen hundredweight of powder besides many bombs; and if we had not been so lucky as to find it, in a very few hours our batteries and some hundreds of men had taken a flight into the air'. The 10th, despite the hazards of being buried alive or suffocated, stuck to its unpleasant task though many soldiers who bravely faced visible dangers, recoiled from the subterranean ones. There was great relief when Tournai capitulated on the 3rd September.

Marlborough then advanced on Mons and as the French moved to prevent this, the armies met at Malplaquet on the 10th September 1709. The 10th was in the centre of the line and many bodies of the enemy were in entrenchments making the battle a siege. The 10th advanced courageously; they penetrated the entrenchments and forced the French back into an adjacent wood where every tree was disputed. The French centre and right were defeated and the entrenchments captured after a terrific fight. The tenacity of the British regiments involved rather than tactical subtlety had brought victory, but at the cost of 25,000 men. The French lost about 13,000. It was not until the 29th April 1882 that Queen Victoria commanded that the victories of Blenheim, Ramillies, Oudenarde and Malplaquet should be inscribed on the Colours of the Regiment.

The 10th formed part of the covering force at the successful siege of Mons in 1709, and they encountered the French, while similarly situated, at the siege of Douai the next year, coming under severe fire until the French withdrew. They lost heavily at the siege and capture of Aire where they were singled out for commendation by their Commander, the Prince of Anhalt. The 10th's last action under Marlborough was in the operations leading to the capture of Bouchain in 1711.

After this, the Duke of Marlborough became a victim of political machinations and court cabals and was replaced as Commander of the British forces by the Duke of Ormonde, with orders not to fight. The War ended with the Treaty of Utrecht in 1713 which propelled Britain further along the road to Empire with the acquisition of

Gibraltar, Minorca, Nova Scotia and Newfoundland. The grandson of King Louis XIV, however, retained the Spanish throne, contrary to the aim of the War.

The 10th was recalled to England in August 1715 to supplement the forces in the United Kingdom in view of the threatened Jacobite Rebellion, but the Regiment took no part in the campaign which quelled the insurrection. Indeed, the 10th was to see no further active service until the War of American Independence in 1775. Until 1730, the Regiment remained in England apart from a short spell in Scotland. From 1730 to 1749, it was based in Gibraltar and then spent the years 1749 to 1767 in Ireland. On the 1st July 1751, the Regiment ceased to be known by the name of its Colonel and officially became the 10th Foot.

It was during these years of garrison duty that three officers of the 10th reached the rank of Field Marshal. George Wade (1673-1748), who was commissioned in the Earl of Bath's Regiment in 1690 and fought with it at Steenkirk, was responsible for opening up the Highlands of Scotland to trade and commerce by constructing roads and bridges in the area. The 10th served under him in Scotland in the 1720s. Wade was appointed a Field Marshal in 1743. John, Earl Ligonier (1680-1770), purchased a captain's commission in Lord North and Grey's Regiment in 1703. He borrowed the money for this, repaying the lender from winnings at the gaming table. He was wounded in twenty-two places at Malplaquet but lived to become Commander-in-Chief of the Army (1757-1763) and a Field Marshal in 1757. James O'Hara, 1st Baron Kilmaine and 2nd Baron Tyrawley (1690-1773), was Colonel of the Regiment from 1746 to 1749. He commanded the British troops in Portugal in 1762 during the Seven Years' War (1756-1763) and became a Field Marshal in 1763.

Chapter 2
THE REGIMENT ON THE WORLD STAGE

When the War of American Independence broke out in 1775, the 10th were already in North America. They had arrived at Quebec in August 1767, moving to Boston in October 1774, after two years of frontier fort duty. The situation in America was not a happy one. On the one hand, there was the discontent of the colonists who resented the British Government's taxation and, on the other, the regiments serving as a garrison were in a bad state. The troops were unpopular with the townspeople of Boston, where most of the British garrison was stationed. In March 1770, a riot had been caused by local ruffians snowballing the British sentries; shots were fired and there were casualties, but the soldiers were acquitted. The Commander-in-Chief, General Thomas Gage, received notice that a large amount of military stores was being collected at Concord and a force of light infantry and grenadiers under Lieutenant Colonel Francis Smith of the 10th and Major John Pitcairn of the Marines was sent to destroy them.

News of the troops' departure leaked out. Smith found the area through which his force was advancing disturbed by the ringing of bells and firing of guns; he therefore ordered Major Pitcairn, with six companies of light infantry, to secure two bridges in Concord. At about 4 a.m. on the 19th April 1775, intelligence was received by Pitcairn, when he was within two miles of Lexington, that around 500 men were assembled ready to oppose his force. A colonist attempted to shoot a British officer but his musket misfired, by "flashing in the pan".

As the British troops approached the village green at Lexington at 5 a.m., they found the local militia, about 70 strong, drawn up. A British officer ordered the rebels to disperse and the militia commander agreed. The colonists' leaders were anxious not to fire the first shot and orders had been issued not to get into open warfare with the British army, but, in the confused situation, shots were fired wounding a man of the 10th and hitting Major Pitcairn's horse. This was the first British soldier casualty of the War. The troops returned fire, killing and wounding several colonists. The British advanced to Concord but the bulk of the stores had been moved.

Lieutenant Colonel Smith, in a letter dated the 22nd April 1775 to General Gage, described the retirement from Concord. 'On our leaving Concord to return to Boston, they began to fire on us from behind walls, ditches, trees, etc., which, as we marched, increased to a very great degree, and continued without intermission of five minutes altogether, for, I believe, upwards of eighteen miles; so that I can't think but it must have been a preconcerted scheme in them to attack the King's troops the first favourable opportunity that offered, otherwise I think they could not, in so short a time, as from our marching out, have raised such a numerous body, and for so great a space of ground. Notwithstanding the enemy's numbers they did not make a gallant attempt during so long an action, though our men were so very much fatigued, but kept under cover.' This detachment was relieved by a large force under Lieutenant General Earl Percy, who then took command of the retreat to Boston.

By the time the British soldiers reached the safety of the causeway over which the Cambridge highway entered the Charlestown peninsula, they were exhausted and thirsty and had expended almost all their ammunition. Fortunately, they were under the protection of the guns of the British ships. If the rebels from Marblehead and Salem had arrived an hour earlier, the whole British force would have been cut off from Charlestown peninsula.

The opportunity for the British to exact retribution for their harrowing experiences on the retreat from Concord soon occurred. It was discovered that the rebels were on Breed's Hill and Bunker Hill, which dominated the town of Boston. The rebels had erected a redoubt and dug themselves in. Gage, who had a great contempt for his opponents, resolved on a frontal assault, which included the flank companies of the 10th. On 17th June 1775, General William Howe, in command of the force, addressed his men: - 'You must drive these farmers from the hill or it will be impossible for us to remain in Boston. But I shall not desire any of you to advance a single step beyond where I am at the head of your line.'

The rebels are said to have been more than twice the number of the attacking British force. Moreover, the King's soldiers had to carry the weight of knapsack, cartouche box, ammunition and musket. It was, also, a very hot day. After a brief bombardment by cannon, the British troops advanced up Breed's Hill. The rebels held their fire until near enough for a volley to take an awful toll and the British came under a terrible fusilade. An eyewitness wrote: 'Most of our grenadiers and light infantry, the moment of presenting themselves, lost three-fourths, and many nine-tenths, of their men.' Before the battle was over, every officer of the 10th who took part was wounded.

The British retreated, advanced a second time and were again repulsed by heavy fire. Reinforcements were brought up, artillery was placed so that it could sweep the rebels' position and the soldiers removed their knapsacks. A third advance was made up the dreadful slope. At first, the rebels' fire was fierce but they were running out of ammunition. The persistence of the British force was eventually rewarded by the capture of Breed's Hill. In October however, Gage was recalled and replaced by General Howe, who, with few reinforcements from England, reasoned Boston was untenable and he evacuated the town on 17th March 1776.

When Boston was evacuated, the 10th moved to Halifax and were part of General Howe's force which took Staten Island, in an unopposed landing on 3rd July. The flank companies (light infantry and grenadiers) were formed with some from other regiments into separate battalions while the other eight companies operated as a unit. This split the 10th into three different forces while Colonel Smith acted as Brigadier of the 5th Brigade in Rhode Island. The next operations which involved the 10th took place on Long Island where they were in the 3rd Brigade under Major General Jones in Lieutenant General Earl Percy's Division. A night attack was made on 26th August and first Lieutenant General Henry Clinton's Division, then Percy's, were able to outflank the Americans through an unguarded pass. A successful action was fought in which American losses exceeded 3,000 whereas the King's forces lost fewer than 350. The British troops fought well and by 30th August the Americans had quit Long Island. Howe now turned to capture New York.

General Washington, commanding the American army in the city, advised that it be abandoned. Congress disagreed. Washington, therefore, left 5,000 soldiers in New York, saying it was better to lose a quarter of his army than the whole. He stationed most of his forces in a strong position to the north of the city. The 10th were one of the first regiments to enter New York after a sharp skirmish with the enemy, who retired after losing 300 dead and wounded. The British casualties were under 100; 67 guns and some military stores were captured. Shortly afterwards, fires broke out in New York and, despite the efforts of the 10th and others, a third of the city was ruined.

In an attempt to get on the flank and rear of the enemy, Howe sent part of his forces, including the 10th, up river to Westchester, which was reached on 12th October. Howe advanced so slowly that his troops did not get to White Plains, thirty miles on, until the 26th. Before the general advance, the 10th had a victorious little action at Pell's Point. Later, on the 28th October, they were involved in heavy fighting at White Plains whilst attached to General Clinton's column. Howe failed to follow up his advantage and Washington escaped with the bulk of his army. Possibly the memory of the attack on Breed's Hill had made the British Commander more cautious.

The 10th formed part of the force under Earl Percy sent down to Harlem Creek to attack American entrenchments at Fort Washington on the 16th November. After bloody fighting, the 10th and other troops captured the enemy position. The advance involved a precipitous climb in which the soldiers pulled themselves up by tree roots and bushes while in heavy marching order. This was followed by hand to hand combat. The American losses were 3,300 men but the British casualties were 458, including Captain Mackintosh and 8 rank and file of the 10th.

In June 1777, the 10th were in the army which Howe took to attack Philadelphia. On the 5th July, they embarked for Chesapeake Bay but the ships did not leave Sandy Hook until the 23rd. As it was the hottest time of the year, the conditions for the soldiers and horses cooped up in the transports were bad. The weather then worsened and it took a week for the ships to reach the Delaware. The army landed unopposed at the mouth of the river Elk on the 24th August.

The American army under George Washington was encountered on the 11th September at Brandywine River. At 15,000 strong they slightly outnumbered the British. Washington's forces were in a strong position with cliffs preventing an attack on their left flank, where the militia were posted. Washington was in the centre of his army at Chad's Ford. Howe decided to turn Washington's right flank and, accordingly, distracted the Americans by attacking their centre. The 10th were part of the forces sent against Chad's Ford. After desperate fighting, Washington was defeated, losing 1,300 men and numerous guns. However, it was too late in the day for effective pursuit and so the American forces escaped annihilation. The 10th who succeeded in crossing the river, lost only 2 men killed and 6 wounded. The total British casualties were between 400 and 500.

The British advanced towards Philadelphia. On the 13th September, the Regiment was at Ashtown, and by the 25th they were at Germantown. The 10th and the 42nd Regiments were then detached to attack gun positions which the enemy had constructed to prevent ships of the Royal Navy sailing up the Delaware. A surprise attack by these two Regiments at Billing's Fort led to the destruction of guns and barracks. After their return from this foray, Howe sent three regiments, including the 10th, to escort a large convoy of supplies, which was heading for the British base at Germantown. Washington learned of this division of enemy forces and resolved to attack. Howe received intelligence of this and drew up his army; the 10th, coming back after a forced march, were positioned on the right flank.

The battle of Germantown began in a fog on the 4th October and the 10th were not at first engaged. Heavy fighting took place in other parts of the battlefield, in which Colonel Musgrave, with a force holding Chew House, was prominent. Part of the right wing of the British forces, including the light company of the 10th, was then directed on to the enemy's left. Their irresistible onslaught led to this portion of the American army fleeing in disorder. It appears that some of the 10th did not play an active role in this battle but those who did fought with great valour. The rest of the American army stood their ground but, with losses mounting and their ammunition running out, they retreated. Again, the British Commander failed to follow up his victory and Washington regrouped his scattered troops. Total American losses were estimated at 2,200 whereas the British had 100 killed and 400 wounded. It is not known how many of the 10th became casualties, but the Regiment merited its share in Howe's despatch which said: - 'The fatigues of a march exceeding one hundred miles, supported with the utmost cheerfulness by all ranks, without tents, and with very little baggage, will, I hope, be esteemed as convincing proofs of the noble spirit and emulation prevailing in the army to promote his Majesty's service.'

On the 22nd October, some of the 10th failed in an attack on Mud Island Fort near Philadelphia but the mauling inflicted upon the defenders led to them abandoning the position. A similar story took place at Red Bank Fort, where, after two days of battle, the Americans retired. The 10th were engaged in successful skirmishes, notably at Edge Hill, well into December 1777. Intense cold and snow, added to the lack of tents and baggage, made the later stages of the campaign especially harrowing. The 10th spent what was to be their last American winter in quarters at Philadelphia. Sir Henry Clinton replaced Sir William Howe as Commander of the army in which the Regiment was serving in May 1778. Clinton began to move his forces to New York on the 18th June. The Americans were given a prolonged breathing space to re-equip, train and replenish their ammunition and stores. This failure of the British Command contrasts with the courage and fighting prowess of the regiments engaged in the campaign. It was in this War that the 10th earned the nickname of 'The Springers', by reason of their readiness at any time for duty, whatever the emergency. It should be mentioned, however, that another story has it that the soubriquet derives from the Regimental March, 'The Lincolnshire Poacher', a springer being one who sets traps or springs.

Clinton left Philadelphia to avoid being starved out. American forces 'swept the more remote townships clear of food and fodder, and left a bare larder for the British commissariat'. Farmers were prevented from taking food into the city, ships and barges on the river were intercepted and war stores were captured. The British moved to New Jersey. The weather aided the Americans. Fourteen consecutive hours' rain drenched the British clothes, food and ammunition. Then came 'the most terrible heat which had afflicted the province within the range of human memory'.

Amidst a hostile population and harassed by the enemy, Clinton's army reached Monmouth Court House on the 27th June. The British forces were divided into two divisions, one under General Wilhelm von Knyphausen and the other under General Earl Cornwallis. The 10th were originally with Knyphausen but were sent to aid Cornwallis when his division was threatened and he decided to attack the Americans to protect the army's baggage train. The Regiment took a leading part in the battle which followed. Despite tremendous heat, the British troops routed the first and second lines of the enemy and would have pressed them further, but Clinton, his baggage saved, and his army weary, did no more.

Knyphausen's division had routed American attackers and the British army had the distinction of defeating an enemy twice their strength. Fortescue said that 'the action cost the British 358 officers and men, of whom no fewer than 60 fell dead from sunstroke, owing to the overpowering heat of the day. The loss of the Americans was almost exactly the same, but Clinton's army was considerably reduced during this march by the desertion of some six hundred men, three-fourths of them Germans, who had contracted attachments of one description or another to the town of Philadelphia'. As well as desertion, the British army under Clinton also suffered serious lapses of discipline and the Commander-in-Chief complained that 'Marauding had been unbridled'.

Clinton moved his forces to New York, anxious to reach there before the arrival of French troops, who were coming to aid the Americans. The 10th were in such a depleted state that the Commander-in-Chief recommended that the Regiment be disbanded and returned to England. Apart from battle casualties, many of the 10th's men were worn out with privation and fatigue. A large number who were fit for active service volunteered for other units leaving for the expedition to St Lucia in the West Indies. Late in October 1778, the rest of the 10th embarked for home, arriving there at the beginning of December. The Regiment had fought well in America and had, in addition, avoided the disastrous campaigns of Saratoga and Yorktown. However, losses were great: the monthly return of the 1st January 1779 showed a mere 39 of the Regiment present and fit for duty, on Command, Recruiting, and on Furlow, with 901 required to bring the 10th up to full strength. By the 1st December of the same year, 577 were still needed.

However, the army was not an attractive career. The pay of a private soldier was 10d (about 4p) a day. There were still no barracks. Diseases were rampant, especially those induced by lice which infested the soldiers' white powdered wigs. Military discipline was harsh and punishments, as in civilian life, severe. Moreover, in the Army flogging was common.

The 1778 Recruiting Act empowered Justices of the Peace and Commissioners of Land Tax 'to raise and levy all able-bodied, idle and disorderly persons, who cannot, upon examination, prove themselves to exercise and industriously follow some lawful trade and employment, for their support and maintenance, to serve his Majesty as soldiers... and all persons convicted of smuggling, to the value not exceeding forty pounds, may be raised and levied in like manner for soldiers, in lieu of the present punishments they are liable to. Able-bodied men only to be enlisted, and none under 17 or above 45 years of age.' In due course, the 10th's ranks filled up but the Regiment did not return to America as the Government retained it at home due to a feared French invasion.

Before the end of the War, the 10th acquired their territorial association with Lincolnshire. The Colonel of the Regiment, Major General Sir Robert Murray Keith, received the following Order from General the Honourable Henry Conway, Commander-in-Chief of the Army: -

'London, 31st August 1782

His Majesty has been pleased to order that the 10th Regiment of Foot which you command should take the County name of the 10th, or North Lincolnshire Regiment, and be looked upon as attached to that Division of the County. I am to acquaint you it is His Majesty's farther pleasure that you should in all things conform to that Idea, and endeavour by all means in your power to cultivate and improve that connection, so as to create a mutual attachment between the County and the Regiment which may at all times be useful towards recruiting the Regiment...'

The 69th Regiment was designated the South Lincolnshire Regiment. It had been recruited in Lancashire, Derbyshire and Nottinghamshire in 1756. A second battalion was raised in Lincolnshire in 1803. This unit later became the 2nd Battalion The Welsh Regiment. The 81st Regiment was raised as The Loyal Lincoln Volunteers, a territorial designation confirmed in 1832. It became the 2nd Battalion Loyal North Lancashire Regiment.

There was a drastic reduction of the Army at the end of the War of American Independence in 1783, the year the 10th were posted to Ireland. At that time, their total strength, with officers, was 463. After three years quelling riots, the Regiment embarked for Jamaica. The Government suspected that the French or Spanish might wish to seize the island and so a strong military presence on Jamaica was deemed necessary. However, the soldiers suffered more from diseases, such as yellow fever, than any enemy. The 10th remained on the island for nine years due to fears of a native uprising. These were the years of the French Revolution in 1789 and the outbreak of war between Great Britain and France in 1793. The authorities in Jamaica worried that

French natives from St. Domingo would invade but, in fact, it was Maroons in Jamaica who rebelled. The 10th played its part against the rebels but had so many sick that it was ordered back to England in 1795 to recruit. When they landed, only 147 ordinary soldiers were fit for duty. However, by the 1st March 1796, the effective rank and file numbered 371. The establishment of the Regiment was completed by drafts from other corps since, in spite of the 10th now belonging to Lincolnshire and being able to appeal to that County's loyalty, recruiting remained slow. Knowledge of the Regiment's imminent return to Jamaica did not help.

Having had experience in the West Indies, four companies of the Regiment were sent to the Caribbean under Lieutenant Colonel John Wemyss at the end of 1795. The reduction of the British fleet in those waters had enabled the French to regain Islands previously lost. Hence, Major General Sir Ralph Abercromby commanded a new expedition to the West Indies, with the four companies of the 10th forming part of the 5th Brigade.

Surviving storms and fever-ridden ships, the 10th were part of a force sent to Grenada to crush a native uprising. The rebels were strongly entrenched on a steep ridge, crowned by a fort, armed with four field guns and several swivels, and covered by a strong abatis. It took two attempts to storm the ridge. The losses of the British force were 6 officers and 105 men killed or wounded but enemy casualties were estimated at five or six times that number. The insurgents were not crushed and a strong force of French troops came to their assistance. A pincer attack by British forces secured the surrender of the French and the natives took to the hills. A night attack crushed the uprising, the rebel leader hurling himself over a precipice. The Regiment then returned home. Some men had been killed in action but far more had been slain by yellow fever. Sir John Fortescue estimated that half of Abercromby's forces were lost to this scourge. Nearly 2,500 British soldiers died between the 1st April and the 1st October 1796: the 10th bore their share of this misfortune.

Back in England, the Regiment was stationed on the Isle of Wight as part of the forces to oppose a threatened French invasion. Encamped at Sandown Bay, the 10th consisted of 79 officers and 950 rank and file. The descent of the French on Egypt, however, led to fears for Britain's position in India, on the part of the authorities in both London and Calcutta, and, accordingly, the 10th sailed on the 28th August 1798 for Madras, arriving on the 13th April 1799.

The 10th landed in India during the campaign against Tippoo Sahib, the ruler of Mysore. They formed part of the Reserve Corps and so did not take part in the storming of Seringapatam on the 4th May, missing out on a share of the £1,100,000 prize money. The 10th's time in India was filled with garrison duty: they stayed in Madras for almost four months and then, on the 6th August, moved to Bengal. Here, they were part of a defensive force intended to protect Oude from the Afghans. The records show that the cost of pay, clothing and allowances of the 10th for one year while in India in 1799 and onwards was £24,031.5.11.

The continued presence of the French forces in Egypt led to a British army of

15,000 men, under Sir Ralph Abercromby, being sent across the Mediterranean to co-operate with a Turkish force from Syria, in operations designed to evict them. In support of this, the Governor-General of India, the Marquess Wellesley, planned to send troops, under Major General David Baird, to the shore of the Red Sea. The 10th were to be part of this expeditionary force. As the country to which they were to proceed was too impoverished to support them, supplies had to be collected and the time which this took meant that the 10th, 1,000 strong, did not reach Bombay until the 1st April 1801. Meanwhile, Abercromby defeated the French near Alexandria on the 13th and 21st March, being mortally wounded on the latter occasion.

Baird's instructions from the Marquess were to take Suez if possible and deprive the French of the trade and resources of that area and to 'employ every proper method to conciliate the inhabitants of the coasts of the Red Sea or of Egypt to our interests, and to induce them to make common cause with us against the enemy.' Unfortunately, due to north-east winds, progress up the Red Sea was almost impossible. The ships, on which the 10th and the other troops sailed, were in turn becalmed, suffered violent gales and a high-running sea. The result was that the force landed on the 15th June, at Quseir, well south of Suez. The fleet was dispersed during the stormy passage up the Red Sea and only eight of the ten companies of the 10th landed at Quseir. One ship, the *'Cavern'*, sank with all the Regiment's baggage.

Baird received a letter from Major General Sir J. Hutchinson, who had succeeded Abercromby as Commander of the troops in Egypt, stating he would not leave the vicinity of Cairo until the force from India had crossed the desert to join him. Baird, accordingly, began to march, with the troops who had landed, across the desert to Qena on the Nile. The remaining two companies of the 10th, and other detachments delayed on the Red Sea, arrived at Quseir on the 23rd June, and set off after the main body without delay. This second body of troops joined the main force at Girgee on the 20th July. The 10th had never been on such a march. The country to be crossed was desolate, with intense heat, the glare from the blinding sun and blistering sand, swarms of insects, dysentery and well-nigh intolerable thirst with wells few and far between. In addition, there was the danger of hostile arabs attacking the force or killing stragglers.

The march was undertaken in eight stages. Baird's plan was to pass his army over the whole distance in small divisions, of which the first was to send its camels and water-bags back to the fifth stage; the second, on reaching the fifth stage, was likewise to send its camels back to the third stage; and the third division, on reaching the third stage, was to send back its camels to the first stage, enabling the remaining divisions to come forward in succession on the same principle.

The first part of the march, taking three days, was along a ravine and rocks. The 88th Regiment went first, followed by the 10th and some sepoys. There was red rock everywhere, reflecting the heat of a blazing sun; however, the sense of duty and loyalty of the 10th were equal to the strain.

After 11 miles, water was found at the New Wells, but when the troops arrived at a spot half-way to Moilah, a further 17 miles on, no water was to be had. The situation was saved by the return of soldiers sent on in front by Baird, who came in with their camels laden with water-skins. Unfortunately, the skins leaked and the exhausted men could only partially slake their thirst. A further advance of 17 miles brought the 10th to Moilah where water and dates were found. Another 9 miles saw the Regiment reach Advanced Wells where, again, there was water as a reward after the awful march. There was, however, a disappointment after a further 19 miles' march, to a stage half-way to Legiatte, as no water was found. A supply was brought back by camel from Legiatte itself, 19 miles on. The landscape changed to a boundless waste of sand, which tried the nerves, depressed the spirits and sapped the strength of the men.

At Legiatte conditions improved – the troops found water and provisions, and at Baromba, 18 miles nearer the Nile, there was not only water but also cornfields and sugar-cane plantations. The 10th was able to buy milk, eggs and fowls. A final 10 miles' tramp and the Nile was reached at Qena. The horrific march had seen 120 miles covered in twelve to fifteen days, and the Regiment lost 24 men in their journey across the desert.

After leaving garrisons at Qena, El Giza and Damietta, Baird and the rest of his troops reached Cairo on the 23rd August, en route to Alexandria, but were halted by Major General Hutchinson as the garrison there had capitulated. The strength of the 10th at Cairo was 930, including 269 sick. There was a Vote of Thanks by both Houses of Parliament to show their high approval of the 'zeal, discipline and intrepidity uniformly displayed during the operations, so arduous and memorable, of the army in Egypt, by the non-commissioned officers and private soldiers… and that the same be signified by the commanders of the several corps, who are desired to thank them for their exemplary and gallant behaviour'. The Vote went on to say that 'the honour of the British nation had been so signally upheld, and additional lustre reflected on the British arms'. The importance of the operations, in which the 10th had played a most gallant part, was that 'if the French had succeeded in their project of obtaining and keeping possession of Egypt, their views would have been next directed to India which might, to say the least, have put our territories in that part of the globe to some hazard, inconvenience and danger'.

The 'Journal of the Secret Expedition' to Egypt stated that both men and officers had submitted to the march from the Red Sea to the Nile ' with the greatest patience, and have manifested a zeal for the honour of his Majesty's arms which is above all panegyric. The conduct of the soldiers has been orderly and exemplary. A discipline has been observed which would have done honour to any troops'. Major General Hutchinson wished to retain the 10th with other troops in Egypt even after the fall of Alexandria.

The services of the 10th in Egypt were recognised by a letter from Colonel Harry Calvert, the Adjutant-General, to Lieutenant General The Honourable Henry Edward Fox, the Regiment's Colonel, dated the 6th July 1802.

'Sir,

I have the honour to acquaint you that His Majesty has been graciously pleased to grant permission to the several regiments of His Army which served during the late campaign in Egypt, to assume and wear in their Colours a Badge as a distinguished mark of His Majesty's Royal approbation, and as a lasting Memorial of the glory acquired by His Majesty's Arms, by the Zeal, Discipline, and Intrepidity of His Majesty's Troops in the arduous and important campaign.

His Royal Highness, the Commander-in-Chief, has directed me to make this communication to you in order that the 10th Regiment of Foot, under your command, may avail itself of the honour hereby conferred by His Majesty, and I am commanded at the same time to apprize you that a pattern of the Badge approved by His Majesty is lodged at the Office of the Comptrollers of Army Accounts there to be had recourse to as circumstances may require.'

This led to the Sphinx over the word 'Egypt' being placed on the Regiment's buttons, tunic collars, helmet-plates, waist-plates and forage caps. The British Government did not see fit to issue a medal to the surviving soldiers for Egypt until 1850, and only sixty veterans of the 10th received this belated award—the Military General Service Medal, with the bar, 'Egypt'.

A man of the 10th Foot at this time had plenty to carry. In his knapsack he had a shirt, a greatcoat, spare socks, 3 pairs of shoes, an extra pair of soles and uppers and a blanket. Every 6 men had a camp kettle, which they took it in turn to carry strapped to the knapsack. At the hip the soldier had a haversack containing a fork, clasp knife, spoon, tin mug and other personal items, together with 3 days' rations amounting to 3lbs of beef and 3lbs of biscuit. He also had a filled water bottle, hatchet, Brown Bess musket, bayonet and 80 rounds of ammunition. The officers, of course, were better off and, at this period, some are said to have arrived at their regiments with up to 10 baggage animals for their belongings.

The long War with France ended with the Treaty of Amiens in 1802 but due to plague, the Regiment only left Egypt for Malta on the 7th March the following year. However the troops were not permitted to land for six weeks lest they introduce the disease there. The Regiment was not in Malta long before war with France broke out again on the 18th May, and they were sent to reinforce the garrison at Gibraltar. They reached the Rock on the 20th June and stayed there from 1803 to 1807. While they were at Gibraltar, the town and garrison were beset with Bulam fever, similar to one of the diseases from which the 10th had suffered in the West Indies. At one stage, 7 out of the Regiment's 16 officers died.

Even if they remained healthy, the private soldiers' life was far from pleasant. They were discouraged from marrying, but many had wives when they enlisted. Soldiers at this time were quartered in barracks and their wives lived with them. Blankets were used to partition off the barracks to provide a modicum of privacy. Only 6 women per company, chosen by drawing lots, were allowed to follow their husbands abroad. In camp, the women did washing, mending and cooking for the soldiers in return for a small payment. If a married man was killed, most wives married another soldier without delay to avoid being sent home. The women were under the same harsh discipline as the men.

On the 6th September 1807, the 10th embarked for Sicily due to concern over a possible French invasion. Napoleon's forces were in Naples and the 10th remained in Sicily in readiness for any emergency, however the Regiment's next major action was further north. The Austrians were fighting the French in 1809 and the British Commander in Sicily, General Sir John Stuart, resolved to create a diversion by capturing the city of Naples. Stuart's expedition, which attacked Ischia, at the entrance to the Bay of Naples, was successful in causing the French to divert troops to Italy who would, otherwise, have been engaged on the Danube. The 10th's part in the Ischia operation was limited to helping to capture a line of posts at the Straits of Messina. The formation of a large corps of National Guards by the French led to Stuart abandoning his project to take Naples in favour of an attack on the castle of Scylla, in which the Regiment was to participate with the 21st Regiment and Chasseurs Britanniques.

Fighting commenced soon after the 10th landed and they had to advance through difficult, strongly defended country. The troops, commanded by Lieutenant Colonel Smith, reached Mela overlooking Scylla on the 14th June 1809. However, the time Smith took making his dispositions caused a fatal delay, which allowed large French reinforcements to arrive. This led Smith to retire to Messina, abandoning the besieging train, though he lost no men. However, on the night of the 2nd July, the French blew up the castle of Scylla and retreated themselves, leaving the British an immense quantity of ammunition and stores.

In his despatch of the 9th July 1809, Stuart stated:-
'The conduct of Lieutenant-Colonel Smith during the course of this service, although attended by a momentary reverse, has been reported to me by Major-General Mackenzie in terms of great approbation, with every praise to the zeal and perseverance of the troops employed under his orders.'
In this operation, the 10th were fortunate to lose only 2 men, who were reported missing.

The Regiment remained on garrison duty in Sicily until 1812, when they were sent to Eastern Spain. The object of this expedition was to hold the French army under Marshal Louis Suchet in Catalunya and so prevent him from joining the French who were opposing Lord Wellington's forces further west in the Peninsula. The army, which was 8,813 strong, left Palermo on the 25th June 1812, commanded by Lieutenant General The Honourable Thomas Maitland, Colonel of the 10th. The Regiment numbered 902 plus their commissioned officers.

Having collected a Spanish force of 4,000 infantry, 250 cavalry and 200 artillery under Major General Whittingham, at Majorca, Maitland's troops arrived off Palamos in Catalunya on the 31st July. In a letter to the Prime Minister, the Earl of Liverpool, Maitland stated that his army consisted of the 1st, 10th, 58th, 81st and foreign forces, that its first object was the safety of Sicily, and its employment on the coast of Spain was temporary. Maitland and his officers decided that, as the French appeared to be too strong at Palamos and possessed all the coastal fortresses, the army should go to Alicante. Accordingly, the forces landed there on the 10th August and, apart from a short-lived advance to Elda, a little to the North-West, stayed where they were.

The Spaniards were difficult allies, haggling over supplies although their own situation, after a recent defeat, was not encouraging. Moreover, Maitland found his commissariat was inefficient and his field artillery had been so badly prepared in Sicily that it was almost useless. He had hired mules at great expense for the transport of his guns, and of provisions from Alicante, but the owners of the mules soon declared that they could not fulfil their contract unless they were fed by the British, while many of the muleteers, after receiving their money, deserted with both mules and provisions. On the first day's march a convoy with six days' supply was attacked by armed bandits and the convoy was plundered or dispersed. On landing, Maitland was reinforced by Major General Ross with 700 men of the 67th Regiment and De Watteville's Regiment but the British-led force was greatly outnumbered, King Joseph Bonaparte's Army of the Centre, Marshal Soult's forces from Andalucia and Suchet's having combined. Maitland concluded that the French numbered at least 60,000 men and asked Wellington's permission to withdraw to Sicily.

Wellington directed Maitland to remain and further fortify his camp at Alicante. He did what he could, but was compelled to strengthen his defences with as little outlay as possible owing to shortage of funds. Happily, reinforcements, including the grenadier company of the 2nd battalion of the 10th*, arrived from Sicily. Maitland, however, had to leave his troops on account of illhealth, his replacement being Major General William Clinton, who took over on the 26th October. Clinton, lacking a strong force of cavalry, had to adopt a defensive policy. Whether this counted against him is not known, but he was replaced by Major General Campbell, who arrived from Sicily with another 4,000 men, on the 2nd December.

Campbell, like his predecessors, had doubts about the abilities of his Spanish troops, and wrote in a despatch:- 'The two British Corps and one German are all that I can or ought to place any reliance upon.' However, the presence of the army at Alicante prevented Suchet from taking active steps against Wellington and, thus, made a significant contribution to the Allied cause in the Peninsula. On the 25th February 1813, Lieutenant General Sir John Murray took over command of the army of which the 10th formed part. Murray set out to drive the French from the mountains in front of him. He assembled four columns of troops, placing the 10th in the one which was to seize Alcoy. This force travelled by a bad road over a very steep, rugged ridge, and along a narrow mountain pass. The French saw them and there was severe fighting before Alcoy was occupied. One of the other columns was supposed to co-operate in trapping the French but arrived too late. A further problem was that due to difficulties in Sicily, 2,000 of Murray's best troops, including the 2nd Battalion of the 10th, had to return there, leaving forces that included many in whom little reliance could be placed.

Suchet, ascertaining that Murray's forces were weakened, prepared to advance:

* Raised in 1804 see page 32

Murray had to retreat. On the 18th March, the 10th were sent to Castalla via Ibithe. The Regiment entrenched on a rugged sierra and on the 11th April, the French attacked. A Spanish corps on the left of the Allied front was put to flight. Then, on the 12th April, Suchet advanced on Castalla in great strength. The 10th made a determined stand but, overwhelmed by numbers, they and the 27th with two Italian regiments fell back in good order. The next day, Suchet attacked again but, during the night, Murray had entrenched his forces, making his right wing practically impregnable. After a demonstration in this area, Suchet advanced on the entire Allied line, two and a half miles long, but was beaten back, in many places with the bayonet.

The French withdrew to where their reserves were and Murray, leaving his own reserve to hold his original position, advanced in two lines. Suchet's rearguard made a desperate stand but were defeated and, if Murray had pressed his advantage, defeat might have become a disaster. As it was, the French withdrew and reformed. However, Suchet lost 2,500 men and much prestige, while the Allies' casualties were small. Furthermore, the French were obliged to remain in the east of Spain instead of being able to concentrate against Wellington. It is to the credit of the 10th that they had formed part of the most reliable section of Murray's force.

Wellington diverted Murray, in May 1813, to attack Tarragona, on the assumption that Suchet would assist the defenders and so weaken his army in Valencia which might then fall to the Spaniards. The 10th formed part of Murray's force of 14,000 men, who left Alicante on the 31st May and proceeded by sea, disembarking on the 3rd June. The siege of Tarragona, in which the 10th took part, needed to succeed quickly before Suchet's relief force arrived. Unfortunately, Murray had no sense of urgency and, moreover, the ship carrying the most crucial siege equipment had not arrived. At the outset, the army had not one gabion or fascine.

Information came in that Suchet had 46,900 men and the larger part of these were so near, Murray decided to abandon the guns and stores in his most advanced batteries. He re-embarked his force, on the 8th June, despite the local Admiral and his own officers imploring him to save the guns. In support of Murray's decision, a storm threatened, which could have made the embarkation impossible. During the evacuation, a man of the 10th was killed by a cannon ball while the Regiment was marching to the beach.

On the 9th June, the 10th and another battalion were landed at Col de Balaguer possibly to threaten Tarragona; however, a new Commander, Lord William Bentinck, arrived and moved all his forces back to Alicante. Bentinck's troops, including the 10th, then advanced to Valencia and Tarragona. As usual, there were supply difficulties and problems with the Spanish officers. Valencia was abandoned by the French, but the 10th were engaged in hard fighting at the siege of Tarragona until the advance of Suchet, with substantial forces, led to the abandonment of the operations. However, Bentinck's activities kept Suchet occupied in eastern Spain and prevented him attacking the forces under Wellington, who, having won the battle of Vittoria, advanced towards the Pyrenees.

On the 22nd August, a fire destroyed four hundred stand of arms, and about the same number of suits of clothing, knapsacks and sets of accoutrements belonging to the 10th. Hence, the Regiment was rendered unfit for the field until the 5th September. On the 13th, however, they took the brunt of the fighting involved in covering the retreat of a force under Colonel Adam from Ordal. In the course of the operations, the 10th, under Colonel Robert Travers, defeated a French cavalry charge and saved the Allied army. An officer stated that the Regiment's conduct 'cannot be too highly praised.' The senior Major of the 10th, Brevet Lieutenant-Colonel Otto Beyer, met Marshal Suchet later (during negotiations for an exchange of prisoners), and he said, with regard to the Regiment, that he had never before in his life seen any troops behave so beautifully or with such steadiness.

Dangers in Sicily led to Lord William Bentinck returning there on the 23rd September 1813. Lieutenant General William Clinton became the Commander of the army in eastern Spain and the 10th, who were quartered at Villafranca, suffered, with the rest of the army, from confusion as to who should furnish their supplies: Gibraltar, Sicily or Wellington. Food became scarce and footwear was worn out with the marching. Fresh meat in sufficient quantity was not obtainable in Spain, while money was so scarce it was impossible to buy other necessaries. A fever in Gibraltar complicated matters, though eventually food was obtained from the navy victuallers.

An attack by Clinton's troops, including the 10th, at the Llobregat, was rendered abortive by the lack of co-operation from the Spaniards. Napoleon's retreat from Moscow, however, led to Suchet retiring towards France. He was aided in this by the tardiness of the Spanish troops. Nevertheless, an advance was made to Barcelona, which was besieged on the 7th February 1814. Unfortunately, the commissariat of Clinton's army had broken down and the men of the 10th and their comrades in other units had to endure the hardships of life on campaign with reduced rations and, frequently, no pay. The foreign troops that had come from Sicily returned there owing to the threat from Italy and a fierce sally from Barcelona had to be beaten back. This event took place after the official end of the war as neither side was aware of the situation.

The Marquess (later Duke) of Wellington, in a despatch from Toulouse dated the 19th April 1814, praised the conduct and merit of the troops under Clinton's command and wrote:-

'Circumstances have not enabled those troops to have so brilliant a share in the operations of the war as their brother officers and soldiers on this side of the Peninsula; but they have not been less usefully employed; their conduct when engaged with the enemy has always been meritorious; and I have every reason to be satisfied with the General Officer Commanding, and with them.'

In 1816, the 10th received Royal Authority to bear on their Colours the word 'Peninsula'. The Regiment had performed an arduous and most useful function in keeping French forces in the east of Spain and away from Wellington's great advance from the Portuguese frontier to the south of France. It was a similar role to that of the

31

Allied armies in Italy during the Second World War, in relation to the main front in North-West Europe.

The threat of an invasion of England by Napoleon had led to The Additional Force Act being passed on the 20th July 1804. This provided for home defence and gave the Government power to send the men raised on foreign service. In accordance with this Act, the 2nd Battalion came into being on Christmas Day that year. The men for this new unit were raised in Essex and its headquarters were at Maldon.

For five years, the 2nd Battalion were based at home. Then, on the 9th November 1809, they were sent as reinforcements to the ill-fated Walcheren Expedition. This campaign followed the British Government's decision to strike at French naval resources in the Scheldt and destroy the arsenal at Antwerp and the ships of war stationed between there and Flushing. An Officer of the Battalion later recounted his experiences on arrival. There were no tents for the men, and 'towards morning we found ourselves wrapped in that chill, blue marshy mist rising from the ground, that no clothing can keep out, and that actually seems to penetrate to the inmost frame. And this we always found the morning atmosphere of Walcheren—the island covered with a sheet of exhalation, blue, dense and fetid…The venom of the marsh-fever had a singular power of permeating the whole human frame. It unstrung every muscle, penetrated every bone, and seemed to search and enfeeble all the sources of mental and bodily life. I dragged it about with me for years.' By the end of December, the army had had to be evacuated from Walcheren. Fever rather than the enemy was the cause of the Expedition's failure. However, General Don, in his despatch, stated that 'the conduct of the troops has in every respect merited my warmest approbation'.

The 2nd Battalion was sent to Jersey, where it arrived on the 17th January 1810, to Gibraltar in April and to Malta in August; then it joined the 1st Battalion in Sicily in August 1811. It was while based there that the 2nd Battalion took part in the capture of the island of Ponza in February 1813. With the return of the 1st Battalion from Spain in 1814 the two battalions of the Regiment remained together in Sicily until 1815, when they were posted first to Naples and then to Malta.

In 1814, for parades, the officers of the 10th wore long scarlet-tailed coats with yellow lapels, buttoned back by ten silver buttons and narrow, yellow silk buttonholes. The collar was yellow with one silk buttonhole, the cuffs and cross-pockets each had four buttons and buttonholes. The skirt was ornamented with silver, and turned back to show the white lining. It is believed the breeches were white. Officers carried a long, straight sword in a gilt-mounted, black leather scabbard with a gold and crimson shoulder belt, in the centre of which was the regimental breastplate.

In 1826, the shape of the private soldier's coat was altered. The chest loops of regimental lace, worn at equal distances across the chest, were made broader at the top, tapering downwards to the bottom, and the lace taken off the skirts. At this date, officers' coats were long-tailed and lined white, with skirt ornaments. The flank companies had silver embroidered grenades or bugles and the gorget was gilt, with 'G.R.' engraved on it. The dress trousers were very full, cossack shape, of light bluish grey cloth. A blue greatcoat, otherwise a frock coat, was authorised for undress, with a crimson sash and a sword hanging from a black waist-belt. In undress, a shako was worn, without a feather, and covered with oilskin.

At this time the barrack room in which a soldier of the 10th Foot lived was oblong in shape with a door at one end and a fireplace at the other. The room would have a row of iron bedsteads along each side. It served not only as a dormitory but also as a dining room with tables and chairs and a wash house for the soldiers' wives. By the 1817 Regulations, 4 married women in each company of 60 men were permitted to live in the barrack rooms, usually in a curtained-off corner. The other families had to manage in lodgings, but only in 1851 was a lodging allowance paid. The barracks were often badly overcrowded with a soldier having only 200 – 300 cubic feet of air whereas a convict had 600! No wonder sickness rates were high.

In 1816, after the conclusion of the Napoleonic Wars, the two battalions of the 10th were amalgamated and the invalids and limited service men were sent to England. This was part of the usual reduction of the British army at the end of a major campaign. The Regiment was posted to Corfu in 1816 due to fear of an insurrection and the possibility of Russia taking the Island under her protection. The Commander-in-Chief in the Mediterranean, Lieutenant General Maitland, the Colonel of the 10th, kept down sedition through a display of force rather than fighting. The Russian threat failed to materialize. Colonel Robert Travers with the headquarters and five companies of the Regiment went to Cephalonia and Zante on the 31st August 1817, and then to Malta in March 1819. The other companies, under Major Thomas Trickey, sailed for Malta on the 28th March 1818. The 10th was stationed there for three years, after which they were recalled to England. In 1823, the Regiment moved to Ireland, where there was considerable unrest. As the Insurrection Act had been renewed and Habeas Corpus suspended, a strong military presence was necessary. From the returns, the 10th, which had numbered 1,093 excluding Commissioned Officers, when in Malta, was, by 1823, down to 480 all told. However, in 1826, it had increased to 736.

That year the Regiment was sent back to the Iberian Peninsula. A threatened invasion by Spain led to the Princess Regent of Portugal requesting British aid. Six Service Companies of the 10th formed part of a corps of 5,000 men under General Sir William Clinton, which landed at Lisbon on the 3rd January 1827. The Portuguese, emboldened by the British presence, largely dealt with the crisis themselves and none of their ally's troops were much under fire. Clinton fought a sharp action on the border of Douro Minto where the enemy retired in disorder. On the 11th March 1828, the 10th went on board transports to carry it to Corfu. Zante became the headquarters of the Regiment, detachments going to Paxo and Cerigo in 1829. Three years later, the 10th was back in Corfu. In 1838, it was, again, in Ireland, moving to Liverpool the next year. The Regiment had its first experience of railway travel when it went to Manchester on the 24th May 1839; previously, movement had meant marching, whatever the weather. In 1842, the 10th was in Glasgow and, while there, orders came for it to proceed to the East Indies.

The Regimental Colours were left at the 10th's depot in Winchester but disappeared. The King's Colour was later found in the possession of an Irish family named Garvach and the Regimental Colour came to light in the house of an old man in Scrivelsby, Lincolnshire. The man said he found it in a cottage in Ireland. It was much reduced in size and fastened to a broomstick with tintacks. It became known as the 'Broomstick Colour'. At the beginning of the Twenty-first Century it was preserved in the Regimental Galleries of the Museum of Lincolnshire Life at Lincoln.

Chapter 3
THE REGIMENT IN THE VICTORIAN ERA.

The 10th left Gravesend with a strength of 30 Officers and 1,210 NCOs and men, together with 135 women and 174 children. The Regiment spent a quiet period in India between 1842 and 1845. However, the Sikhs in the Punjab had been in a state of anarchy since the death of Ranjit Singh in 1839 and these disorders forced the British to strengthen their frontier posts. This was interpreted by the Sikhs as being preparations for invasion and they crossed the river Sutlej on the 11th December 1845. The 10th, serving at Meerut, was despatched to the seat of war, 130 miles away, under Lieutenant Colonel Thomas Franks on the 16th, leaving 100 men at the depot. Franks had with him, besides officers, 743 NCOs and men. At that time, British infantry still used the Brown Bess of the Peninsular War (1808-1814), which had an effective range of 300 yards; field artillery could fire about 800 yards with round shot and shell and 300 with grape. Sikh muskets and artillery were as good as those of the British and they had more guns.

After difficult forced marches, the troops from Meerut—the 10th, 3rd Light Cavalry, the 9th & 16th Lancers, and some native regiments—joined the Commander-in-Chief, Lieutenant General Sir Hugh Gough, and his forces at Sultan Khan Walla on the 6th January 1846. The Sikhs had constructed a strong position at the village of Sobraon, to cover a bridge of boats across the Sutlej just below the fort of Hurrekee. The defences consisted of several half-moon bastions, connected by curtains, with a ditch in front and both flanks on the river. The works, manned by about 20,000 Sikhs, were two and a half miles long and protected by around 70 heavy guns and many camel swivel-guns. The British forces, under Gough, were 15,000 strong, of which one third were Europeans. The 10th was in the first line of Major General Sir Robert Dick's Division, on the left of the British front.

The British fell in, silently, at 2 a.m. on the 10th February. It was not only dark but foggy. Gough intended to attack with Dick's Division and, having penetrated the Sikh right wing, to roll the enemy up. The battle began at 7 a.m. with an artillery duel. However, the British guns made no great impression on the Sikh fortifications, so Gough sent word to Dick to advance. He in turn sent Lieutenant Colonel Lane's horse artillery and Captains Fordyce and Horsford's batteries forward to within 300 yards of the Sikh position. These covered the advance of the Brigade under Brigadier Stacey consisting of the 10th and 53rd Regiments with the 43rd and 59th Native Infantry. The Brigade advanced in line as if on parade, as ordered by Dick. Had they advanced in open order, many more would have lived. However, yet again, a general's mistake resulted in supreme gallantry on the part of his command.

Lieutenant Colonel Franks was a terrible martinet – hated by all ranks under him and so harsh it was said no officer in the Regiment would accept the position of adjutant. Field Marshal Wolseley related:- 'Just before the battalion moved into action the day of Sobraon [Franks] said to his men: " I understand you mean to shoot me today, but I want you to do me a favour; don't kill me until the battle is well over." It was quite true; they had meant to shoot him, but the coolness with which the request was made, the soldier-like spirit and indifference to death it denoted, the daring and contempt for danger he displayed throughout the battle, so won their admiration that they allowed him to live. But history tells us he never reformed.'

Despite deadly fire from muskets and swivels and enfilading artillery fire, the Brigade went forward, silently with not a shot fired. Men fell at every step, yet still the survivors advanced. The 80th Regiment followed up gallantly. The right wing of the Sikh army was broken into and driven towards the enemy centre. Further assaults by the British on the Sikh left and centre broke their resistance and they retreated to the river. A heavy rainstorm two days earlier had made the fords across the Sutlej impassable and there was only one bridge. The fugitives, jammed on this, were pounded by cannon and rifle fire, while other Sikhs flung themselves into the river and were drowned. The Sikh losses were estimated at 10,000 men, 67 guns and all their standards and military stores. Sergeant Major James Murphy of the 10th captured two Sikh colours. He was given a commission, became Paymaster and served in the Regiment for another 30 years.

The British had 2,383 killed and wounded. The 10th's Divisional Commander, Sir Robert Dick, was killed and Lieutenant Colonel Franks was wounded, having his horse shot under him. Surprisingly, the Regiment suffered fewer casualties than might have been expected: 29 dead and 135 wounded.

The Commander-in-Chief's despatch praised the steady courage of the 10th: the way they marched with the precision of a field day, holding fire until they were within the enemy's works. Brigadier Stacey wrote to Lieutenant Colonel Franks: - ' the gallantry of H. M.'s 10th, and you, their gallant leader, will never be effaced from my memory. The glorious conduct of the 10th at Sobraon is beyond any praise that I could give. They were the *corner stone* of the victory. I have seen much service, but I *never* saw anything to equal their cool and resolute courage on that day. You will do me the favour to offer my explanations, how I left without calling, and allow this, my testimony of the steadiness and gallantry of the corps to be placed on the mess table.'

The Regiment was awarded the Battle Honour 'Sobraon', Franks was appointed a Companion of the Military Division of the Most Honourable Order of the Bath and the troops received the special thanks of Parliament. At this time, there were no gallantry awards for Regimental Officers, NCOs and men. The Battle of Sobraon was followed by the Treaty of Lahore on the 8th March 1846 which ended the War. Sobraon was the decisive battle of the First Sikh War and helped secure British rule in India, with momentous consequences. In this great victory, the 10th had played a crucial part.

Greetings were still exchanged on Sobraon Day in the 21st Century between The Royal Anglian Regiment, the successors of the 10th Foot, and The Worcestershire and

Sherwood Foresters Regiment, the successors of the 29th Foot, to commemorate the comradeship forged in the battle.

The murder of two Englishmen at Multan, in 1848, ignited the simmering discontent of the Sikhs and, on the 10th July, Major General W. S. Whish was ordered to march on the city. The British force contained a battering train and 6,000 men, including the 10th and 32nd Regiments. The 10th, commanded by Lieutenant Colonel Franks, had a strength of 29 Officers and 767 NCOs and men when it joined Whish's force on the 12th August. Its grenadier and light companies were in action on the 17th when they beat off a night attack on their camp. The British troops reached Multan the next day, but the siege train had not arrived.

Major General Whish summoned the city to surrender. The Sikhs refused. Accordingly, siege operations began on the 7th September, when the enemy were driven into their defences. On the 9th, the right wing of Whish's army, including the 10th, assaulted the Sikh outposts. The attack was repulsed with the Regiment losing 1 Officer and 6 men killed and 37 rank and file wounded. The 10th formed part of the Right Column, under Franks, which took the strongly entrenched position of Dhunam Sallah, on the south of Multan, on the 12th September. The Regiment attacked at 8.30 a.m. and carried the first enemy position in half an hour, and, also, stormed a further section. Out of six companies engaged, the 10th lost 4 men killed and 27 wounded, Lieutenant John Herbert fatally.

The unexpected defection from the British side of Shere Singh (a Sikh leader who had been thought loyal) with 900 infantry and 3,800 cavalry, on the 14th September, led to the British retiring from Multan. The 10th, who formed the army's rearguard, had to be alert for enemy attacks for a whole day in sweltering heat. Shere Singh was successful in raising the Sikhs against the British, and the conflict thus grew from the siege of Multan to a Second Sikh War. This led to the formation of the Army of the Punjab, under Lord Gough, with the 10th being in the 2nd Brigade of the 1st Division, under Major General Whish.

On the 7th November 1848, Whish returned to besiege Multan again. Franks commanded a successful attack on Sangkund, where the 10th's headquarters, grenadier company and left wing, under Lieutenant Colonel George Young, captured all the enemy's guns by a bayonet attack, with no shot fired. The Regiment's losses were 11 wounded. A three-pronged attack on Multan took place on the 27th December. The left wing of the 10th with the headquarters, under Captain Henry Longden, were in the Right Column which took some heights before the city after severe fighting but with small loss. Although all three of the prongs of the attack made progress and the principal magazine was destroyed, Multan held out. On the 2nd January 1849, the 10th formed part of the forces which captured the Bohur gate, despite a stubborn defence. This was followed by the collapse of resistance in the city, many Sikhs retreating through the only gate open on the west of Multan. Fighting, however, continued, for the Sikh commander, Moolraj, retired to the fort and did not surrender until the 22nd . Longden of the 10th had worked hard in preparing galleries for three mines which made a big contribution to the Sikh surrender.

After thwarting Sikh plans to cut them off and occupying the fords of the Chenab, Whish's division joined Gough's army on the 17th February. The acquisition of additional forces was most welcome to the Commander-in-Chief. He had just fought an indecisive but costly battle at Chillianwallah. He now had 20,000 men and 94 guns. Gough followed the Sikh army to Gujerat and attacked them on the 21st February at 7.30 a.m. The 10th was in Brigadier Hervey's Brigade with the 8th and 72nd Native Infantry. This was one of the brigades in the 1st Division under Major General Whish.

For the first time, Gough made full use of his artillery. He quickly discovered the position of the Sikh guns, halted his own infantry and advanced his artillery. A fierce artillery duel took place, lasting nearly two and a half hours, before the Sikhs retired with their guns. Gough ordered a general advance and there was desperate fighting, in which the Regiment was prominently engaged. An Officer who survived stated that the 10th was the centre regiment of its brigade. 'They were drawn up in line when the alarm of cavalry was raised. The two native regiments on our flanks at once formed square. Colonel Franks ordered the 10th to remain steady with the front rank kneeling. On came the cavalry, a fine body of men, Sikhs and Afghans, many of them in chain armour, and made a furious charge on our left wing. The men stood like rocks, till the cavalry came within 80 yards of them, when they opened such a heavy fire, as speedily drove off the enemy with heavy loss. Immediately after we charged and swept away the Sikh infantry.'

Through hard fighting, the 10th, gallantly led by Franks, captured Chota Kabra, a Sikh strongpoint. In this exploit, the Regiment was aided by the British artillery repulsing a body of enemy cavalry who threatened to overwhelm them. The 10th, however, still had to engage the troops in their front. This was carried out so successfully that the Sikhs retreated and the Regiment pursued them for four miles. Leaving the cavalry and horse artillery to continue the pursuit, the 10th returned to the battlefield to find that the victory had been won. Lord Gough told Lieutenant Colonel Franks that 'I have to thank you and your gallant regiment for the splendid way in which you have aided me in winning the battle of Gujerat.'

In his despatch, the Commander-in-Chief wrote 'A very spirited and successful movement was also made… against a heavy body of the enemy's troops, in and about Second or Chota Kabra, by part of Brigadier Hervey's Brigade, most gallantly led by Lieutenant-Colonel Franks, of Her Majesty's 10th Foot.'

Major General Whish, in his despatch to the Adjutant General, also praised the achievements of the Regiment and Hervey's Brigade. 'In the flank movements by the 1st Brigade, already adverted to, and which, under a heavy fire from the enemy of round grape and matchlock, with the reformation to line (in discovering that the enemy did not make the anticipated attack) was effected in the most steady and orderly manner…The 1st Brigade on halting [at the town gate] detached a sub-division of H.M.'s 10th Regiment, and the grenadier company of 52nd Native Infantry, to expel a party of 200 of the enemy in occupation of the temple and a garden in rear…which was effected with trifling loss on our side, but the enemy had 30 or 40 killed and wounded and a great number taken prisoners.' Lieutenant Colonel Franks was mentioned in the list of officers named for thanks 'for the intelligence and zeal with which they carried out their orders, and to all the officers and men under their command for their steadiness and prompt obedience.'

The battle of Gujerat ended the Second Sikh War and completed the British conquest of India within its natural boundaries. The Regiment was awarded three Battle Honours, more than for any other campaign between Marlborough's battles and the First World War: ' Mooltan', 'Goojerat' and 'Punjaub'. The 10th remained in the sub-continent and was there at the outbreak of the Indian Mutiny in 1857.

Dissatisfaction in the Bengal army ignited into open insurrection by the belief that the cartridges of the Enfield rifle were greased with cow and pig fat, thus defiling both Hindus and Muslims when they bit off the ends before loading. There were deeper causes such as the prohibition of native customs and fears that the Indian religions were to be undermined.

When the Indian Mutiny broke out, the 10th were stationed at Dinapore, which was not immediately affected. Major General Stansfeld wrote that 'the native regiments here funk the 10th, as they have seen them fight in the Punjaub, and they are certainly the finest regiment in the Country.' Captains Henry Norman and Stephen Annesley, Ensign Henry Donald and 167 men of the Regiment were sent to Benares, where it had been decided to disarm the 37th Native Infantry who were showing signs of discontent. When the disarming began, fighting ensued on the 4th June 1857. Two men of the 10th were killed and eight mortally wounded. The men of the Regiment went out to bring into the lines any Europeans they could find.

Private John Kirk (1827-65), a Liverpool man, of Captain Annesley's 7th Company, heard that Captain Brown, a Pension Paymaster, his wife, small child, servants and others were in a detached bungalow surrounded by mutineers. Kirk with Sergeant Major Rosemond of the 37th Native Infantry and Sergeant Major Gill of the Loodiana Regiment volunteered to try to rescue the Paymaster and his party. The three soldiers fought their way into the bungalow despite hostile fire and drove off the mutineers. Captain Brown, his family and associates were conducted to the British lines. Kirk, Rosemond and Gill all received the Victoria Cross, which had been instituted in 1856. Three members of the 10th were to earn this award in the Mutiny Campaign.

On the 16th July 1857, Lieutenant Henry Marsham Havelock of the 10th (later Lieutenant General Sir Henry Havelock-Allan 1830-97), who was born at Chinsurah in Bengal, won the Victoria Cross at Cawnpore. The 64th Regiment had suffered severely from artillery fire and were ordered to advance on a 24-pounder gun. Lieutenant Havelock placed himself, on his horse, in front of the centre of the 64th, opposite the gun, and led the troops forward despite enemy fire. The gun was captured.

On the 25th July, the 4th, 7th, 8th and 40th Native Infantry mutinied but retreated when confronted by the 10th supported by artillery. The Regiment's next action against the mutineers was an advance to relieve Arrah, a civil station which had fallen to rebel sepoys. The Europeans had barricaded themselves in a detached two-storey house and the 1st, 5th & 8th Companies of the Regiment (about 150 men) and some 50 Sikhs were sent up the Soane River by steamer to relieve them. However, the force was too small for the task it had to undertake.

The men of the 10th and the Sikhs disembarked and marched towards Arrah. On approaching the village, at nearly midnight, they came under fire, suffering several casualties and were unable to advance. After holding their position during the night, a retreat was ordered in the morning. The mutineers harassed the retiring column, causing further casualties. Ensign Erskine was wounded but saved from capture by Private Denis Dempsey who carried him to safety, latterly with the help of Privates Denis Allen and W. Wallace, both of the 10th's grenadier company. This was one of two actions by which Dempsey (1826-96), who came from Rothmichael, Bray, County Dublin, won the Victoria Cross. Erskine was brought back across the river but died the next day. The survivors rushed to the boats, some of which stuck in the mud, causing soldiers to swim the river. The Commanding Officer of the Sikhs may have been killed by a crocodile, as there were plenty of them about! The attempted relief cost 47 killed and 30 wounded. Subsequently, the defenders at Arrah were saved but the Regiment played no part in this.

At one stage, only 150 men of the 10th were fit for duty but, by the 7th August, 200 NCOs and men of the grenadiers and the 4th and 6th Companies with 2 Officers and a surgeon, were able to march to Arrah to join the troops who had carried out the relief. On the 11th, the force defeated the mutineers at Sugderpore, capturing two guns. During August and September, in view of the need for mounted troops, 24 men of the Regiment were clothed and equipped as Light Cavalry, using horses from the 5th Irregular Cavalry, a regiment that had mutinied.

Numbers 2, 3, 4, 6 and 7 Companies of the 10th formed part of a field force, under Brevet Lieutenant Colonel Longden, of the Regiment, which was employed, from the 3rd November 1857, in holding the frontiers of Jaunpore and Azimghur against the rebels from Oude. On the 9th November, the men of the Regiment played a gallant part in the capture of two forts at Attrouka in the Azimghur district where one member of the Regiment was killed. At the end of the month, Colonel Franks was appointed Brigadier General in command of three British battalions, three batteries of British artillery and 3,000 Nepalese, to ensure the safety of Benares. The serious state of affairs in India led to the Government increasing the size of the army. Accordingly, the 2nd Battalion of the 10th was re-formed on the 2nd September 1857 but no Officers were gazetted to it until the 12th January 1858.

Longden's force was added to occasionally, and, on the 7th December 1857, Franks took command, bringing with him two regiments of Gurkhas. For the next few weeks, the 10th moved from post to post, sometimes burning villages where the inhabitants were suspected of having aided the rebels. On the 19th February, the Regiment, with the assistance of some artillery, captured Chandah, which was garrisoned by 4,000 mutineers. In the ensuing pursuit, over five or six miles, the 10th took 7 guns and then repulsed a horde of 20,000 rebels, who attacked the British camp from 4 p.m. to sunset. The defences must have been effective as there were only 3 men of the grenadier company wounded.

On the 21st February, the 10th moved to assist in the capture of Lucknow. They dislodged an enemy force at Badshagunge, on the 23rd, when 19 guns, tents, baggage and munitions were captured. Only 3 men of the Regiment were wounded, but one died. More fighting followed. Although a fort opposite Douraha remained uncaptured after two hours' struggle, a body of 20,000 enemy under Mahomed Hussein Nazim was defeated. A further victory was won on the same day and another two days after. In these last three actions, Franks had 2 killed and 16 wounded. The enemy casualties were heavy and 21 guns were captured.

At Lucknow, the 10th, under Brevet Lieutenant Colonel William Fenwick, were in the 7th Brigade of the 4th Division under Franks. Operations commenced on the 9th March but the 10th were not engaged until the 14th when the attack on the Imambarrah took place. A breach was made in the walls by artillery and then the Sikhs, some of the 90th followed by the 10th, advanced. There was little fighting and rapid progress was made by the Sikhs with men from the 10th. When the remainder of the Regiment came up, both the Imambarrah and the Kaiser Bagh had fallen.

It was during the fighting on the 14th that Private Dempsey carried out the second action that earned him the Victoria Cross. The advance of the Regiment was halted by a battery of guns. A volunteer was called for to blow them up. Dempsey volunteered, and despite heavy fire and sparks from burning houses, successfully accomplished his mission. He was wounded but recovered. By the 21st March, Lucknow was captured.

At the end of the month, the 10th were in a force under Major General Lugard which marched to relieve Azimghur. On the way, they encountered 3,000 rebels who fled. On the 15th April, the 10th defeated 600 sepoys and captured a bridge, despite heavy fire from the enemy. The Regiment lost 1 man killed and 3 wounded in this action. They reached Arrah on the 6th May, having marched nearly 700 miles since Christmas, crossed 24 rivers and seen much fighting in difficult climatic conditions.

The force continued its advance. The 2nd and 4th Companies, under Captain Henry Norman, fought a small action on the Buxar road on the 8th May and the 10th were involved in heavier fighting at Jugdespore, which was captured, and at Chitourah, where 1 man was killed and 1 officer and 5 men were wounded. Although neither received the Victoria Cross, Corporal James Maher and Private Edward Walsh carried despatches from the column to Buxar, a distance of about 40 miles, travelling through hostile territory. The intrepid pair muffled their horses' hooves and the jingling parts of their accoutrements. They cut down sentries and were chased by a troop of Sowars but accomplished their mission. On the 26th May, eight companies of the 10th attacked mutineers in the jungle near Jugdespore, driving the enemy before them and doing great damage to the rebels and some villages. Further loss was inflicted on the enemy on the 4th June when the 10th were in action near Chitowrah with the 84th and two companies of Madrassees. The mutineers' losses would have been greater if cavalry and horse artillery, who moved round the jungle, had blocked the escape route.

The major part of the 10th returned to Dinapore on the 19th June. On the 3rd September, the Regiment's headquarters and one company, under Lieutenant Colonel Longden, moved to Bulliah in North Bihar. The 10th's final active service in India, in 1858, was when mounted troops from the Regiment and the 1st and 10th Companies formed part of a field force under Brigadier Douglas in operations in the Shahabad district.

The day before the Regiment began their journey back to England, with the departure of 31 sick with the women and children from Dinapore on the 8th February 1859, Brigadier Christie, the Station Commander, issued an Order in which he said he desired 'to express his unqualified approbation of the high state of discipline which the Regiment has always maintained since it has been under his command, now off and on upwards of 15 months, and begs to assure every individual composing it of the high estimation in which they are held by him.

Brigadier Christie further desires to express to Lieutenant Colonel Longden, the officers, N.C. officers and soldiers, his admiration of their gallant conduct in the Field, as well as the orderly and steady conduct of the men in quarters. It is thus they have sustained their reputation for gallantry and high discipline which Brigadier Christie is happy to believe has ever distinguished the 10th Foot whenever and wherever employed.

It is impossible but to regret the departure of such a magnificent Regiment from the Dinapore Brigade. Brigadier Christie assures both the officers and the men that he will always entertain the warmest interest in their future welfare, and that they will ever bear with them his hearty good wishes.'

On leaving India, the 10th parted from Brigadier General Franks, a rigorous and uncompromising officer. He was, also, brave and competent and much of the praise received by the Regiment was due to Franks' leadership in the preceding years, which included the two Sikh Wars.

The Regiment was further honoured by both the Commander-in-Chief, Lord Clyde, and the Governor-General, Lord Canning. When the 10th were about to embark at Calcutta, Lord Clyde issued a General Order, in which he alluded to several regiments, including the 10th. After sketching the Regiment's services from Sobraon to Shahabad, he continued ' that in the opinion of those best qualified to judge, they have well maintained the reputation which was committed to their charge by those who went before them… the Commander-in-Chief considers that he can pay no higher or heartier compliment to the Regiments of which he is now taking leave than to assure them in all sincerity that they have on all occasions during their Indian career proved themselves worthy of the approbation won in former days by men wearing the same number and badges as themselves.'

On the 18th March, the Governor-General issued a General Order in which he said: 'Her Majesty's 10th Foot is about to embark for England.

His Excellency the Governor-General, in Council, cannot allow this Regiment to pass through Calcutta without thanking the officers and men for all the good service they have rendered in the last two eventful years, first in the outbreaks at Benares and Dinapore, next as a part of the column under their former Commander, Brigadier-General Franks, and more lately in the harassing operations conducted by Brigadier-General Sir E. Lugard and Brigadier Douglas on either bank of the Ganges.

The Governor-General in India desires, in taking leave of the 10th Regiment, to place on record his cordial appreciation of their valuable services.

The Regiment will be saluted by the guns of Fort William on leaving Calcutta.'

The Regiment was awarded the further Battle Honour 'Lucknow'.

The 10th served in England and Ireland until 1864, when the 1st Battalion proceeded to South Africa, where the 1st, 5th and 7th Companies were detached to St. Helena. The Battalion then moved to Japan, arriving at Yokohama on the 4th April 1868. At that time, the Japanese were hostile to all foreigners. In consequence of this, various European Powers stationed troops in that country. The 10th replaced the 20th and 11th Regiments, these being the only line regiments that served in Japan during the Victorian Era.

It was during this time in Yokohama that an American, Charles Austin, befriended the Regiment and celebrated his association with a generous endowment, which continued into the Twenty-first Century.

The Regiment was commanded in Japan by Brevet Colonel Henry Norman, who maintained a high standard of efficiency. There were often threatened outbreaks of violence and the Regiment was frequently called to arms at night. There were also typhoons, smallpox epidemics and earthquakes. The end of the posting on the 8th August 1871 was therefore a relief. Part of the Regiment, consisting of three companies, the band and drummers, went to Hong Kong, while the remainder proceeded to Singapore. A detachment from Dublin was to have gone to Hong Kong but was detained at Singapore where it was joined by the Hong Kong detachment at the end of 1872. On the 21st December, 'A' and 'B' Companies were sent to Penang and 'C' Company to Malacca.

In 1874, a disturbance in Simghur Ujong led to two detachments from the Regiment, one of 2 officers and 28 N.C.O.s and men from Malacca and the other of 1 officer and 56 other ranks from Singapore, occupying Kapayong and destroying Rassa, a fortified town, and several smaller places, without loss to themselves. The following year there was further unrest due to the immigration of tin miners from China and a dispute over the succession to a local throne. The British Resident in Perak, Mr. Birch, was murdered and a contingent of 2 officers and 60 men was sent from Penang to punish the culprits. On arrival, they raised the siege of the Residency. However, attacking a stockade, higher up the Perak river, they were defeated, 1 man was killed and both officers and 8 men were wounded. One of the privates died of his wounds and another, who was missing, was later found dead. More troops were sent from Singapore and, on the 15th November, a combined attack under Captain Stirling R.N.

and Captain William Whitla of the 10th destroyed two stockades and a village without loss to the British. A strong force, including a Gurkha battalion from Calcutta, and a naval brigade, under the command of Major General the Honourable F. Colborne, captured Kinta, without loss, on the 17th December. In his despatch, Colborne made mention of 'the zealous and gallant conduct of the 10th Regiment serving in Perak'.

The disaffection spread nearer to Malacca. Part of the Regiment was in action at Rassa on the 27th November and the 5th and 7th December. Following these episodes, Lieutenants Henry Hinxman and Charles Peyton, Sergeant Oven, and Privates Adams and Haynes were commended by H.R.H. The Duke of Cambridge, the Field Marshal Commanding-in-Chief of the British Army.

On the 21st February 1876, the Major General Commanding issued an Order on 'the approaching departure of the 1st Battalion 10th Regiment' thanking all troops for 'the assistance he has received from them during the late operations in the Malay Country…his appreciation of the gallantry they have displayed on every occasion of the attack on the position of the enemy, as well as of his sense of the general good conduct of the men, the unvarying good spirit and cheerfulness with which they have encountered considerable exposure and deprivations consequent on arduous marches through a very difficult country.'

The 1875-76 troubles in Malaya ceased in March after operations conducted by Colonel Clay of the 1st Gurkhas. Meanwhile, the 2nd Battalion of the Regiment, which had been re-formed in 1858 at Mullingar, Ireland, reached a strength of 852 all ranks by the following March. The 2nd Battalion received their first Colours on the 11th August of that year. They were ordered to South Africa, arriving on the 10th March 1860, and then to India, disembarking at Calcutta on the 28th December 1865. In 1871, the Battalion moved to Rangoon and returned to England in 1873. While stationed at home, in April that year, authority was given for NCOs and men to wear a 'Sphinx' as a collar badge, and in December, approval was given for officers to wear a badge with the Sphinx at the base on their forage caps instead of 'X'. These were belated honours for the Egyptian Campaign of 1801. These changes were followed on the 14th November 1874 by the introduction of the Martini-Henry rifle.

In view of possible hostilities with Russia in 1877, the 2nd Battalion was raised to war strength by recruiting and transfers from the 1st Battalion. On the 15th May, the 2nd Battalion comprised 1,095 officers, NCOs and men, however the crisis passed and the Battalion enjoyed peaceful postings in Malta 1878-81, Gibraltar 1881-82, India 1882-92 and the Straits Settlements 1892-95.

The 1st Battalion arrived in England from the Straits Settlements in April 1877, having been delayed in transit by measles and scarlet fever. A General Order dated the 11th April 1881 stated that the Infantry of the Line and Militia would be organised in territorial regiments of four battalions for England, the 1st and 2nd of these being Line Battalions and the remainder Militia, with Volunteer Battalions, originating from 1859, still existing. The Order continued that the Regiments would bear a territorial designation corresponding to the localities with which they were connected, the words

'Regimental District' replacing 'Sub-District'. Accordingly, the 10th became 'The Lincolnshire Regiment' and the '30th Brigade Depot', the '10th Regimental District'. Happily, this preserved the old number of Foot.

'The Poacher' had been used as the quick march of the 10th North Lincolnshire Regiment for many years before being officially adopted in 1881. Rudyard Kipling, having heard the song in a cholera camp in India, noted that it restored 'shaken men back to their pride, humour and self-control'. Latterly, the Lincolns were often nicknamed 'The Poachers' reflecting the Regimental march. As mentioned before, the Regiment has also been called 'The Springers'. However, the best-known nickname is 'The Yellowbellies'. The origin of this is not known. Yellow waistcoats were never worn so the idea that the name derives from them cannot be substantiated. It has been claimed that the Lincolns crawled through yellow mud on some battlefield, thus staining their waistcoats. Unfortunately, this suggestion, like the theory that yellowbellies derive from the tint of a Lincolnshire lizard, has never been proved true.

The Victorian private soldier was paid 1 shilling (5p) a day but, from 1870, free food was issued, so the pay was received gross. From 1876, he was awarded an additional 2d (1p) per day, payable as a pension, and good conduct earned him a further 1d a day. A daily ration of 12 ounces of meat and 1 pound of bread was issued but groceries and vegetables had to be provided by the men themselves. In the field, tea, sugar, pepper, salt, rice and fresh vegetables were issued. Flogging was abolished in 1881 but discipline was still harsh.

During this period, three officers of the Regiment reached the pinnacles of their distinguished careers. Honorary General Sir Henry Longden had the distinction of being the only officer during the Victorian Era to serve in the Regiment in every commissioned rank: Ensign, Lieutenant, Adjutant, Captain, Major, Lieutenant Colonel and Colonel. He was appointed Colonel of the Regiment in 1888 and held the office until his death just over a year later. Longden fought at Sobraon, Multan and Gujerat and was heavily engaged in the Indian Mutiny. He was mentioned in despatches for his services in both the Punjab and Mutiny Campaigns. Sir Frederick Haines (1819-1909) served as a Captain in the 10th from 1846 to 1847 and fought in both Sikh Wars as well as the Crimea. He was Commander-in-Chief in India from 1876 to 1881 and received the thanks of Parliament 'for the ability and judgement with which he directed operations' in Afghanistan 1879-80. Haines was appointed a Field Marshal in 1890. The best-connected officer in the Regiment's history was Prince Edward of Saxe-Weimar (1823-1902), a nephew of Queen Adelaide. He was Colonel of the Regiment 1878-88, Commander-in-Chief in Ireland 1885-90 and became a Field Marshal in 1897.

On the 1st April 1894, the Regiment adopted the field service cap which was made of water-proofed black cloth. On the left side of this was 'The Sphinx with Egypt' badge of white metal. The cap was three and a half inches high at the front and two and a half inches at the back with a cloth peak, and sides which could be lowered in cold weather.

The 1st Battalion was ordered to Malta in November that year, arriving in February 1895. In April they met the 2nd Battalion, who then arrived there. This was their first meeting for many years although there had been considerable interchange of personnel between the battalions. At this time the 1st Battalion took on 375 men from the 2nd. In January 1898 the 1st Battalion, which had been in Egypt since February of the previous year, received orders to be ready to go on active service as part of Major General Sir Herbert Kitchener's army in the re-conquest of the Sudan, where Major General Charles Gordon had been murdered thirteen years earlier. The Lincolns proceeded via Aswan, Wadi Halfa and Abu Hamed to Gurheish, the worst part of the journey being in open trucks from Wadi Halfa to Abu Hamed. Corporal George Skinner of the Medical Staff Corps, who travelled with the Lincolns, stated they 'were packed like sardines... the dust making everyone look like nigars (sic).' Skinner also records that Sergeant Haines of the Lincolns cut his throat from ear to ear. At Gurheish they were joined by the 1st Battalion the Royal Warwickshire Regiment and the Queen's Own Cameron Highlanders. These regiments formed a brigade under Major General William Gatacre. A rapid advance was made to attack a Dervish army under Mahmoud, and to forestall any danger of the enemy disrupting Kitchener's railway and cutting off detached British troops. This entailed leaving the tents and baggage behind as there was difficulty with transport. In six days, including one on which there was a halt, 140 miles were covered, in great heat, and with each man carrying 100 rounds of ammunition and his greatcoat. Beset by flies and exhausted, the Lincolns of 1898 were worthy successors to the men of the 10th who marched across the desert in 1801. At Kenur, a draft of 64 N.C.O.s and men joined the Regiment and the Brigade was augmented by the arrival of the 1st Battalion Seaforth Highlanders.

On the 30th March, Kitchener's army reached Ras-el-Hudi on the Atbara River. It was reported that the Dervishes were at Nakhila on the right bank. Accordingly, the army moved against them, each brigade advancing in square formation; the British Brigade, including the Lincolns, leading. At 6.15 a.m. on the 8th April, the enemy position was bombarded by the artillery for just over an hour; then the order to advance was given.

The British Brigade was on the left of the army and the Lincolns were on the right of the Brigade. The Regiment was in column to the rear of No. 1 Company of the Camerons and its left flank was on the edge of a deep khor. The enemy was entrenched behind a zariba but the Lincolns had a small knoll in their front which gave some cover to within 30 yards of the enemy's position. The Dervishes opened fire at about 300 yards and the Lincolns did not have room to deploy as the 11th Sudanese kept closing in on them. Colonel Thomas Verner, who commanded the Regiment in the battle, stated in his report to the General Officer Commanding that 'Owing to the restricted front available, I was never able to deploy more than...two Companies, but the Officers commanding the rear Companies led them independently through the zariba, and assisted wherever required.' A tremendous burst of fire hit the Lincolns as they reached the top of the knoll but, passing through No. 1 Company of the Camerons, they rapidly plunged into the enemy position. The fire which assailed the Regiment came from their left front and the trenches immediately ahead were found to be empty apart from dead bodies. The Lincolns overlapped the left wing of the Sudanese and, it appears, that as well as attacks from more Dervishes coming out of hiding, the Regiment suffered casualties from friendly fire as the Sudanese shot wildly. However, the superior discipline and fire power of Kitchener's forces were too much for the Dervish army, which was driven from its position. 'We went over the palisade wall into the middle of them firing and using the bayonet, dead dervishes, donkeys, ponies, camels and in places women and children lay dead and wounded in indescribable confusion – the smell was like a slaughterhouse', wrote Captain Samuel Fitzgibbon Cox of the Lincolns. There was more scope for the bayonet in the pursuit.

The Lincolns lost 1 sergeant killed and 3 officers, including Colonel Verner, and 13 men wounded. The Dervish army was destroyed as a fighting force, its losses estimated at 2-3,000 killed in the battle and the pursuit, with 1,000, including Mahmoud, taken prisoner. Kitchener's army spent the summer in various camps along the Nile. The burning heat caused the death of 14 men of the Lincolns and 80 had to be invalided back to Cairo.

The British received reinforcements: notably, more artillery, a second British infantry Brigade and the 21st Lancers. On the 25th August, the march on the Dervish capital, Omdurman, began. The Lincolns were in a brigade commanded by Brigadier General Andrew Wauchope. The Dervish army came out of Omdurman and battle was joined at 5.57 a.m., according to Corporal George Skinner, on the 2nd September. Foolishly, the Dervishes, in massed formation, attacked the British position and were mown down by artillery and rifle fire from the 1st Egyptian and 1st British Brigades. The fire from the newly issued Maxim guns was devastating. Eventually, Kitchener ordered his forces to attack, moving in echelon of brigades to the south from the left to prevent the enemy retreating into Omdurman. It was essential to avoid having to gain Omdurman through house to house fighting which would entail many casualties.

The order of march from left to right was Lyttleton (2nd British Brigade), Wauchope (1st British Brigade) followed by the Egyptian Brigades under Maxwell, Lewis and MacDonald, then the Camel Corps and Egyptian Cavalry. MacDonald's Brigade became dangerously isolated and was attacked by an enemy force who emerged from behind some hills called Jebel Surgham. MacDonald requested assistance from Lewis but the latter did not respond as he had been ordered by Kitchener to keep up with Maxwell. Fortunately, MacDonald broke up his assailants by heavy rifle fire before another Dervish attack, from the Kereri Hills to the north, fell upon him. Meanwhile Kitchener had ordered Wauchope to move his Brigade into the gap between Lewis and MacDonald's left. However, the latter now needed help on his right flank and asked Wauchope to come round to this side. Wauchope, while moving the bulk of his Brigade to MacDonald's left, detached the Lincolns to his right at the double. MacDonald's Brigade was saved by the lack of co-ordination of the two Dervish attacks but the arrival of the Lincolns, who were renowned for their marksmanship, completed the destruction of MacDonald's attackers.

By 11.30 a.m. the Dervish army was shattered and Kitchener's forces made a triumphal entry into Omdurman. The death of Gordon had been avenged. The city was found to be in a very unsanitary state with dead animals in various stages of decomposition lying around 'in hundreds and thousands'. No doubt the Lincolns were glad to leave for Dakheila after the Memorial Service for Gordon on the 4th September. The Regiment had suffered 18 casualties and for its services was granted the Battle Honours 'Atbara' and 'Khartoum'.

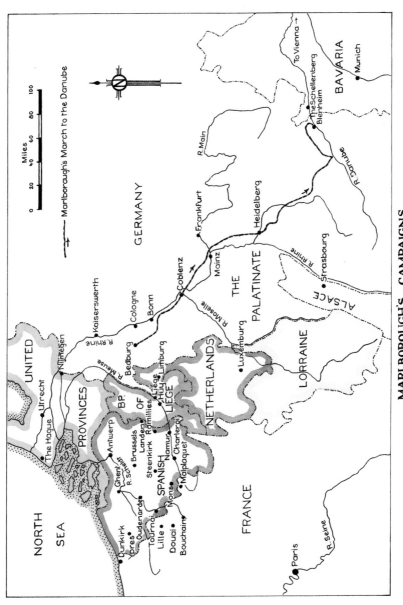

MARLBOROUGH'S CAMPAIGNS

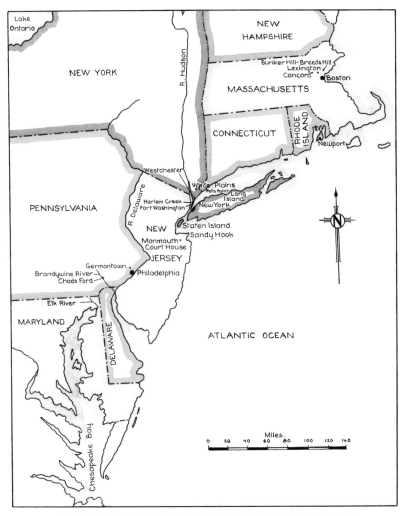

THE WAR OF AMERICAN INDEPENDENCE

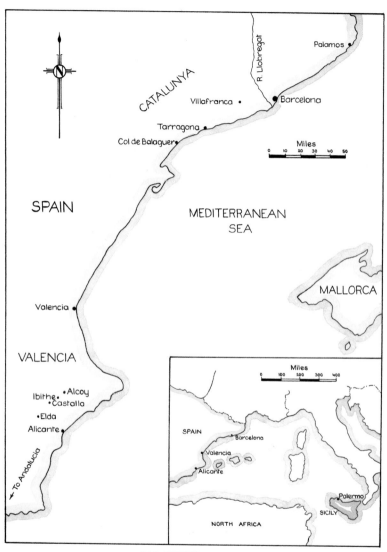

EASTERN SPAIN

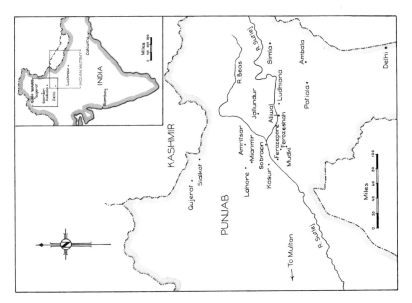

SIKH WARS

Calcutta

INDIAN MUTINY

INDIA

Lucknow

Bombay

Miles
0 100 200 300

SIKH WARS
Gujerat
Sobraon
Ambala
Delhi

KASHMIR

R. Beas

R. Sutlej

Simla

Ambala

Delhi

Jallundur

Amritsar

Miānmir

Lahore

Sobraon

Kasur

Ludhiana

Aliwal

Ferozepore

Ferozeshah

Mudki

Patiala

PUNJAB

Sialkot

Gujerat

To Multan

R. Sutlej

Miles
0 20 40 60 80 100

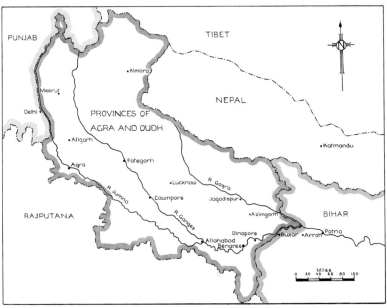

PUNJAB

TIBET

•Almora

Meerut

Delhi

NEPAL

PROVINCES OF
AGRA AND OUDH

•Aligarh

•Katmandu

Agra

•Fategarh

•Lucknow

R. Gogra

R. Jumna

Cawnpore

Jagadispur

•Azimgarh

BIHAR

RAJPUTANA

R. Ganges

Dinapore

Buxar •Arrah Patna

Allahabad
Benares

Miles
0 20 40 60 80 100

INDIAN MUTINY.

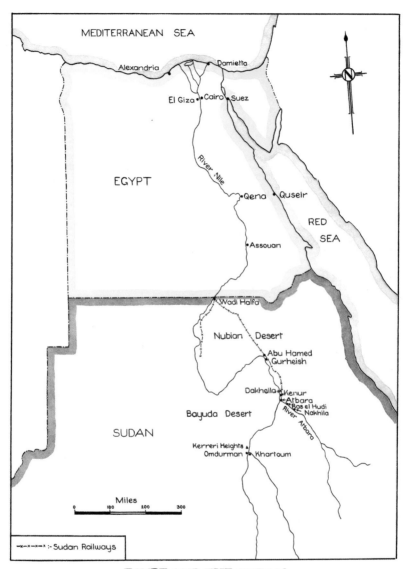

MEDITERRANEAN SEA

Alexandria

Damietta

El Giza• •Cairo •Suez

EGYPT

River Nile

•Qena •Quseir

RED
SEA

•Assouan

•Wadi Halfa

Nubian   Desert

•Abu Hamed
Gurheish

Dakheila •Kenur
•Atbara
•Ras el Hudi
Nakhila

River Atbara

Bayuda Desert

SUDAN

Kerreri Heights •
Omdurman • •Khartoum

Miles

0   100   200   300

—x—x—x—x :- Sudan Railways

EGYPT AND THE SUDAN

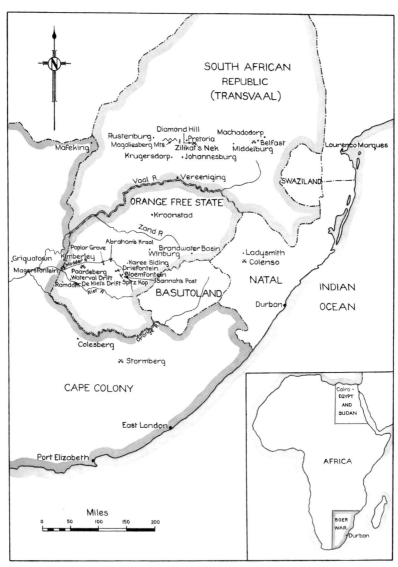

BOER WAR

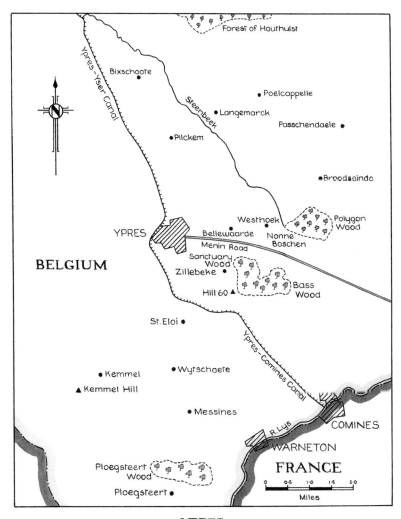

Forest of Houthulst

Bixschoote

Poelcappelle

Langemarck

Steenbeek

Passchendaele

Pilckem

Broodseinde

Westhoek

YPRES

Bellewaarde

Polygon
Wood

BELGIUM

Menin Road

Nonne
Boschen

Sanctuary
Wood

Zillebeke

Bass
Wood

Hill 60

St. Eloi

Kemmel

Wytschaete

Kemmel Hill

Messines

COMINES

R. Lys

WARNETON

Ploegsteert
Wood

FRANCE

Ploegsteert

0   0·5   1·0   1·5   2·0

Miles

Ypres-Yser Canal

Ypres-Comines Canal

YPRES

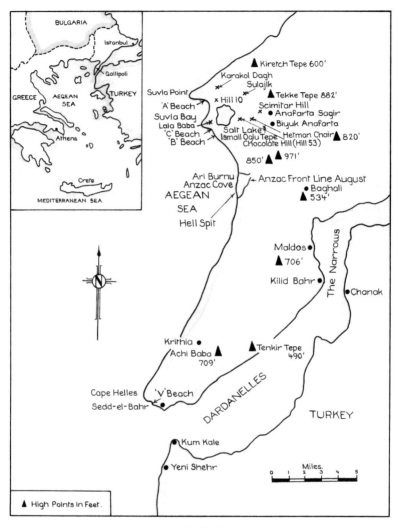

GALLIPOLI

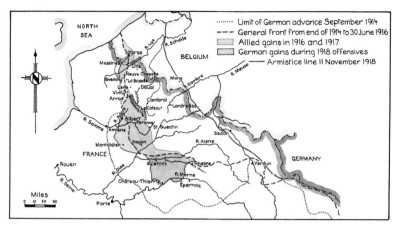

THE WESTERN FRONT

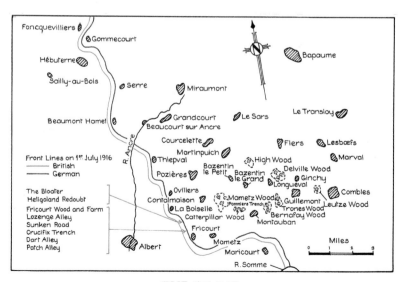

THE SOMME

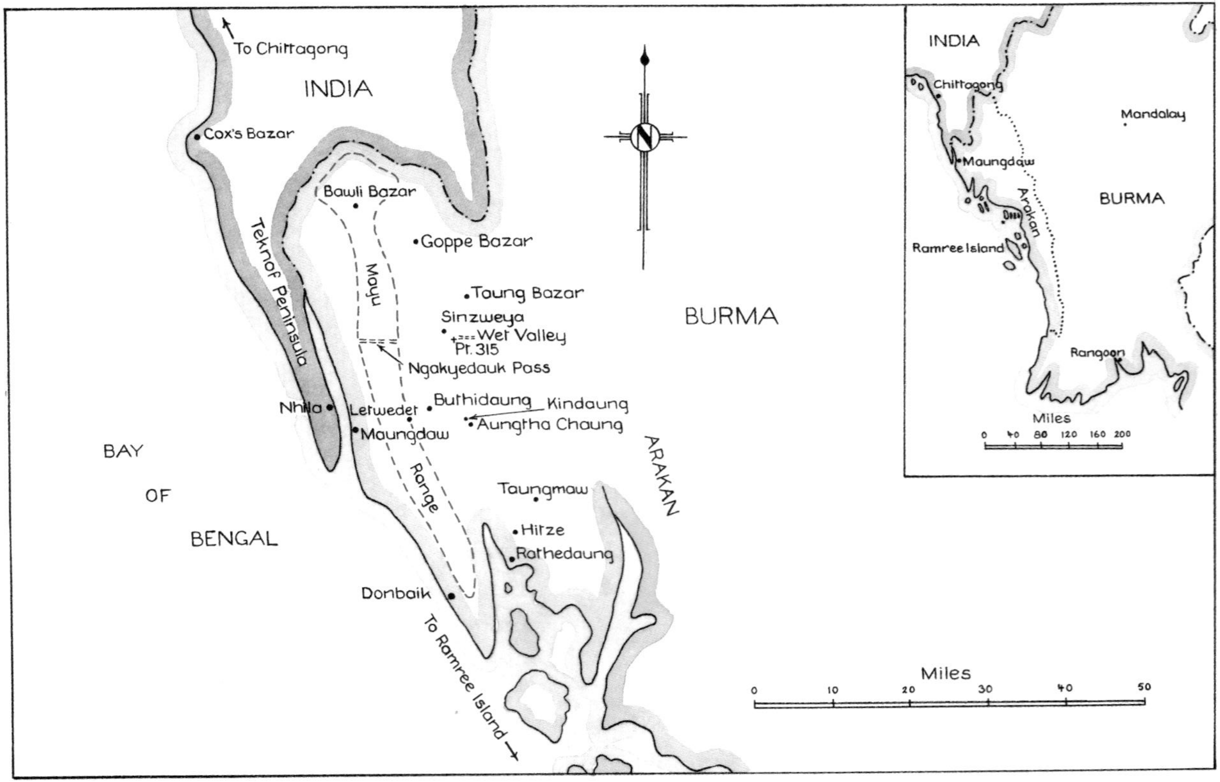

BURMA

BAY
OF
BENGAL

Cox's Bazar

To Chittagong

INDIA

Teknaf Peninsula

Nhila

Bauli Bazar

Mayu

Goppe Bazar

Letwedet

Toung Bazar

Maungdaw

Sinzweya

Range

Wet Valley
Pt 315

Donbaik

Buthidaung
Ngakyedauk Pass

Kindaung

Aungtha Chaung

BURMA

To Ramree Island

Taungmaw

ARAKAN

Htize

Rathedaung

N

0   10   20   30   40   50
Miles

INDIA

Chittagong

Ramree Island

Maungdaw

Arakan

BURMA

Mandalay

Rangoon

0   40   80   120   160   200
Miles

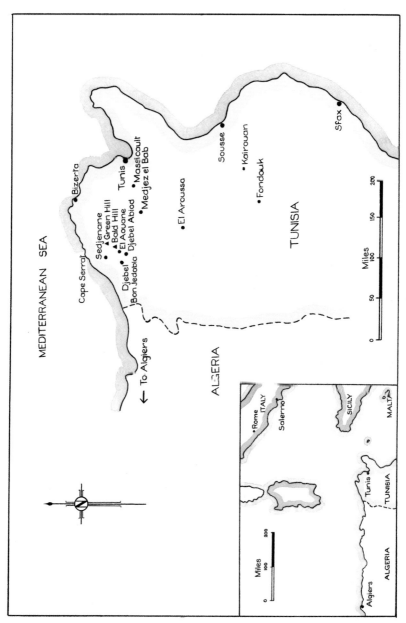

NORTHERN TUNISIA

ITALY – SALERNO AREA

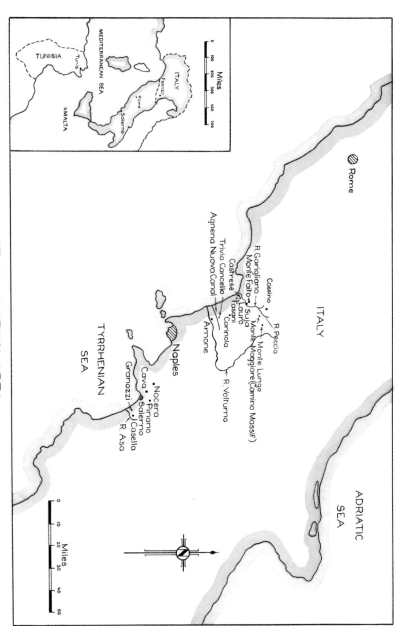

MEDITERRANEAN SEA

TUNISIA

Tunis

ITALY

Rome

Faenzo

Salerno

MALTA

Miles
0
100
200
300
400
500

Rome

ITALY

Cassino
R.Garigliano
Monte Lungo
Monte Faito
Sujo
Monte Maggiore(Camino Massif)
Castrese
Lauro
Fasani
Trivio Cancello
Coriniola
Agnena Nuova Canal
Arnone
R.Peccia
R.Volturno

Naples

TYRRHENIAN SEA

Nocera
Cava
Pinano
Granozzi
Salerno
Casella
R.Asa

ADRIATIC SEA

Miles
0
10
20
30
40
50

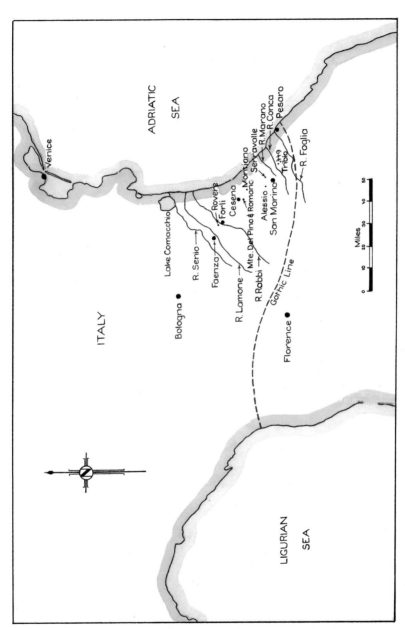

ITALY – GOTHIC LINE

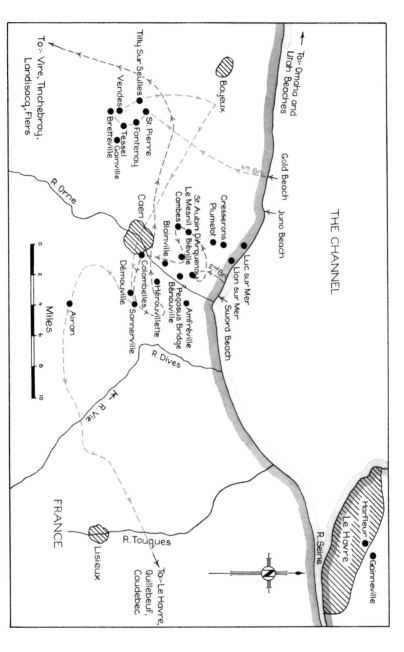

NORMANDY

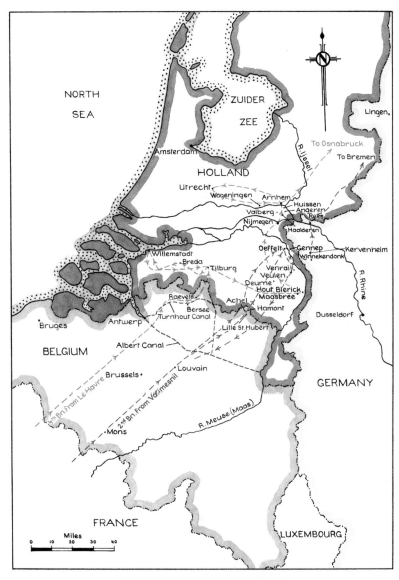

NORTH SEA

ZUIDER ZEE

Lingen.

To Osnabruck

To Bremen

R. Ijssel

Amsterdam

HOLLAND

Utrecht

Wageningen

Arnhem

Huissen

Angeren

Rees

Valberg

Nijmegen

Haalderen

Oeffelt

Gennep

Kervenheim

Willemstadt

Winnekendonk

Breda

Tilburg

Venraij

Veulen

R. Rhine

Deurne

Hout Blerick

Maasbree

Raevels

Achel

Bersee

Turnhout Canal

Hamont

Dusseldorf

Bruges

Antwerp

Lille St. Hubert

BELGIUM

Albert Canal

Brussels

Louvain

GERMANY

4th Bn from Le Havre

2nd Bn from Vaumesnil

Mons

R. Meuse (Maas)

FRANCE

LUXEMBOURG

Miles
0   10   20   30   40

THE LOW COUNTRIES

THAILAND

KEDAH

PERLIS

Kota Bharu

PROVINCE
Georgetown
PENANG
WELLESLEY

Kroh

Grik

Sungel Perak

PERAK   KELANTAN   TRENGGANU

Taiping   Salak
Kuala   Sungei Sipur
Kangsar   Sungei Kuang
         Tanah Hitam
         Ipoh   Tanjong Rambutan

Kuantan

Benta

Raub

MALAYA

Tekai
Kerdau
Bentong   Sungei   Pahang
Sabai   Temerloh

SOUTH CHINA SEA

STRAIT

OF

MALACCA

SELANGOR

Triang

Kuala Lumpur

Ayer Hitam
NEGRI
Bahau
Seremban
SEMBILAN

PAHANG

Ladang Geddes

MALACCA

Malacca

Cha'ah

Muar   Yong Peng

Batu Pahat

JOHORE

Kota Tinggi

Johore Bharu

Nee Soon
Singapore

Miles

0   25   50   75   100

LEGEND
......   State Boundaries
         States of Battalion Operations
- - - -   Railways
Sungei = River

MALAYA

Chapter 4
THE WAR IN SOUTH AFRICA.

While the 1st Battalion went to Cairo, Suez and thence to Secunderabad in India, the 2nd Battalion was ordered on the 16th December 1899 to proceed to South Africa, where war had broken out between the British and the Boer Republics of the Transvaal and the Orange Free State. The discovery of gold in the Transvaal in 1886 led to an influx of fortune hunters, many of them British. The Boers restricted the voting rights of these newcomers or Uitlanders, as they were called, and the situation was made worse by the abortive attempt to overthrow the Transvaal government by the Jameson Raiders. The Orange Free State supported the Transvaal. Later, there was a petition by over 20,000 Uitlanders for Queen Victoria to have full sovereignty over the Transvaal. The British government accepted the petition in May 1899 and negotiations between them and the Transvaal President, Paul Kruger, took place. However, no agreement was reached and the Boers declared war on the 11th October. The despatch of reinforcements to South Africa followed the disasters of 'Black Week' when the British were defeated at Stormberg, Magersfontein and Colenso. The 2nd Battalion of the Lincolns, who were to form part of the 14th Brigade of the 7th Division, left Southampton on the 4th January 1900. The strength of the Battalion was 25 Officers, 1 Warrant Officer and 959 N.C.O.s and men, who arrived at Cape Town on the 26th January and proceeded by train to Orange River which they reached the following day. On the 1st February, 'D' Company, under Captain Frederic Lloyd, was sent to join the 7th Mounted Infantry Brigade.

The 2 battalions of the Lincolnshire Rifle Volunteers, who had become part of the Regiment in 1881,were joined by a third battalion from Grimsby in 1900. Although not liable for service overseas, 3 companies – 1 from each battalion –fought in the Boer War.

The Lincolns marched towards the Orange Free State on the 3rd February, experiencing for the first time the heat and dust that would be theirs for the next four years. At Ramdam, they were the first infantry battalion to enter the enemy's country. The 7th Division, under Lieutenant-General Charles Tucker, left Ramdam on the 12th February on a journey that would eventually take them to Pretoria, capital of the Transvaal.

The Battalion formed part of the advance guard. They reached De Kiel's Drift at the Riet River exhausted, hot and thirsty. Having only recently arrived in South Africa, they had not had time to become accustomed to the climate. Although there was little water, the river had steep banks and confusion arose as no staff officer had been detailed to regulate the crossing of the transport of the various units. There was, also, a lack of information as to where water could be obtained. Accordingly, the

Commander-in-Chief, Field Marshal Lord Roberts, left the 7th Division at De Kiel's Drift to cover the passage of the transport, while the cavalry advanced to capture a drift over the Modder River.

Scarcity of water caused the 7th Division to be sent along the Riet River to Wegdraai instead of to the Modder. However, the movements of the various divisions led to the almost complete isolation of the Boer army, under General Piet Cronje, at Magersfontein and enabled Major General John French to relieve Kimberley. Cronje clung to his position although his communications with the Transvaal had been severed. Three courses were open to the Boer general: either to retreat north, move round the west of Kimberley and unite with General J. S. Ferreira on the Vaal at Warrenton, as some Burghers did; or to move east of Kimberley towards Boshof; or to go east towards Bloemfontein. Cronje thought the deep sandy roads and scarcity of water to the north made rapid movement impossible for his army with its great train of wagons and he hoped Ferreira would aid him to the east. Accordingly, he chose to go towards Bloemfontein and, on the 15th February, marched along the Modder River.

On that afternoon, the Lincolns, with the 2nd Norfolks, seven companies of the 2nd Hampshires and the 62nd Battery of Field Artillery were sent to reinforce the King's Own Scottish Borderers, who had gone to assist a convoy attacked by General Christiaan De Wet at Waterval Drift. Unfortunately, even with reinforcements, the British force was insufficient to repel the Boers and Tucker, who was in command, telegraphed for further troops. Lord Roberts preferred to lose the convoy rather than risk deranging his plans by sending back more men. Some of the convoy was saved but '170 wagons containing approximately 70,200 rations of preserved meat, 180,000 rations of bread stuff and groceries, 38,792 grain rations and eight wagon loads of medical comforts' together with the teams of ox wagons and some 500 slaughter cattle were abandoned.

Tucker brought his men back to Jacobsdal on the 17th February and Captain Herbert Harington with 'H' Company of the Lincolns was sent to escort a convoy to Klip Drift. On the 18th, the Battalion and the King's Own Scottish Borderers marched towards Paardeberg, where Cronje was located. The force marched in line and enemy action was constantly expected. Although the men were on half rations, few fell out in this, another magnificent march.

Captain Jasper Howley and a small party of 'A' Company reconnoitred Cronje's position on the evening of the 20th February and brought back accurate information on the Boer laager. Regrettably, the Lincolns and the King's Own Scottish Borderers were left too near the enemy position. At daybreak, the two battalions were spotted by the Boers who opened fire, forcing them to retreat. Their withdrawal was further harassed by cross-fire from a kopje about two miles south of the main Boer position. The Lincolns successfully stormed this kopje, capturing 48 prisoners as well as several carts and a large amount of arms and ammunition.

Major Thomas Day with 'A', 'C' and 'H' Companies of the Battalion took up an outpost line on the 22nd February. The main task of the Lincolns was to dig trenches with the remainder of the 14th Brigade in conjunction with the 9th Company of the Royal Engineers. Considerable hardship was involved in this work, which went on day and night, under enemy fire. There was little food and little sleep: it rained frequently, filling the trenches with water. Rations could only be brought up after dark, and the covering parties were often with no other food than a half or even a quarter ration of biscuit. These endeavours, however, succeeded: Cronje's laager was completely surrounded and bombarded by artillery on all sides. No Boer relief force broke through and Cronje's army was left either to break out on its own or surrender.

The 19th Brigade advanced on the Boers at 2.15 a.m. on the 27th February after heavy British artillery fire with Roberts' guns reinforced by four 6-inch howitzers and three 1-inch Vickers-Maxim quick-firers. At daybreak, Cronje surrendered with over 3,900 men, four field guns, a pom-pom and large amounts of rifles and ammunition. Later, nearly 11,000 tons of Mauser cartridges and a number of field gun shells were dug up. Paardeberg was the greatest battle of the South African War and the 2nd Battalion of the Lincolnshire Regiment played a notable part in it.

Lord Roberts moved his army to near Osfontein as the putrefying dead horses and debris of the Boer laager at Paardeberg endangered their health. He could not begin the march on Bloemfontein as his horses were exhausted and needed supplies. Roberts aimed to keep the Boers off the Bloemfontein roads and force them to get entangled in the difficult drifts of the Modder. While attacks were made by other parts of Roberts' forces, he instructed the 14th Brigade, having its left close to the Modder River, 'to threaten' the enemy. Accordingly, they advanced along the Modder to McKaw's Drift, a distance of about 5 miles, where 'A', 'C' and 'H' Companies of the Lincolns rejoined the Battalion on the 6th March. The next day, the Brigade moved forward and, coming under fire, shelled a feature known as the Table Mountain. The Boers retreated. The Lincolns served as an advance guard to their Brigade and, with some fighting on the way, reached Poplar Grove. Unfortunately, the Boers by skilful manoeuvres avoided being encircled.

Information reached Lord Roberts that De Wet, with some Boer commandos, was regrouping on kopjes near Abraham's Kraal. The Commander-in-Chief decided to advance in three columns, bypassing Abraham's Krall and turning Spitz Kop; then he would concentrate on one road to Bloemfontein. Lieutenant General Tucker commanded the Right Column, which consisted of the 7th Division, including the Lincolns, the 3rd Cavalry Brigade and Ridley's Mounted Infantry.

On the 10th March 1900, the Right Column advanced unhindered 18 miles to Petrusburg, while the other two columns encountered opposition. The next day, the Right Column moved forward another 13 miles to Driekop, again unopposed. However, the water there proved bad and insufficient so, on the 13th, the Division marched another 18 miles to Panfontein, while simultaneously Lord Roberts entered Bloemfontein and hoisted the Union Flag. The 7th Division was engaged in escorting supply convoys. The Lincolns formed the rear-guard of the 14th Brigade on the 15th March and the advance guard on the 16th. The Brigade bivouacked at Poundisford rather than venturing on to Bloemfontein owing to the limited water supplies.

The 'Digest of Services' for the 2nd Battalion stated that there was a shortage of food on this march. Three-quarter rations were issued on the 18th February but from then until the 22nd March, when the Battalion arrived at Bloemfontein, never more than half-rations with one-third grocery ration were available. Water was scarce and frequently bad. Heavy rainstorms added to the hardships of the troops. On the 14th March 1900, Lord Roberts issued an Order in which he said that the achievement of his army ' is a record of which any army may well be proud, a record which could only have been achieved by earnest, well-disciplined men, determined to do their duty, and to surmount whatever difficulties or dangers might be encountered.

Exposed to extreme heat by day, bivouacking under heavy rain, marching long distances (not infrequently with reduced rations), the endurance, cheerfulness, and gallantry displayed by all ranks are beyond praise, and Lord Roberts feels sure that neither Her Majesty the Queen nor the British nation will be unmindful of the efforts made by this force to uphold the honour of their country.' The 2nd Battalion of the Lincolnshire Regiment had played its part. The arrival in South Africa of the 6th and 7th Divisions plus Colonial contingents had given the Commander-in-Chief the increased numbers to make his strategy work.

Lord Roberts resolved to move on Pretoria, subject to his men and horses being rested. On the 27th March, the 14th Brigade advanced 18 miles to the Glen Railway Station, where the bridge over the Modder had been blown by the Boers. The enemy had to be driven off while repairs to the bridge were carried out. Accordingly, Tucker and his Division were instructed to dislodge the Boers from Karee Siding, while Lieutenant General French and his cavalry executed a wide turning movement to the west and Lieutenant Colonel Philip Le Gallais and his mounted infantry circled round to the east. The 14th Brigade led the 7th Division's attack. At 6.45 a.m. on the 29th March, the Lincolns, forming the advance guard, marched north for 7 miles. About 12.30 p.m., Tucker was notified that French had turned the enemy's right flank and the 7th Division advanced again. The Lincolns were held in reserve on the right rear and were reinforced by a section of field guns which were manhandled up a steep ridge. As soon as the Battalion reached the crest line, the Boers opened fire. The Lincolns replied and there was a fierce duel for about four hours. Then the Boers retreated towards Brandfort evacuating all their positions. The horses were too exhausted to pursue the enemy. The Lincolns lost 2 men killed and Captain Lancelot Edwards and 6 men wounded.

On the 1st April, the 14th Brigade marched about 8 miles to the south east and took up a line of outposts. The Lincolns were on the right at Klein-os-Spruit. From then until the 22nd April, the Battalion was engaged in outpost duty. There was also a change of Brigade Commander and Colonel Henry Roberts of the Lincolns was placed in temporary command of the Brigade. On the 23rd April, the Battalion was part of a force sent to Krantz Kraal, 11 miles away, to watch the fords. The only enemy activity encountered was sniping. Between the 24th and 29th April, the Lincolns were engaged in outpost duty and making defences, moving again, on the 30th, as advance guard, to Schanz Kraal. They stayed there until the 2nd May, and then proceeded 6 miles to a position about 8 miles east of Karee. The army then advanced on Brandfort. Stubborn fighting followed and the 14th Brigade, now under Major General J.G. Maxwell, drove the enemy back and bivouacked at Zuurfontein 7 miles east of Brandfort. The transport did not come up until the following day so the men were short of food.

The 14th Brigade marched again at 7.30 a.m. on the 5th May. There was some fighting along the route but, after a long day, the Brigade halted about 2 miles south of the Vet River at 9 o'clock that evening. Co-operation between the Brigade and the 11th Division opened the Vet to the main army. The next day the Lincolns crossed the river at the Taaibosch Spruit despite steep and difficult drifts. It was not until 8 p.m. that the Battalion bivouacked at Smaldeel, about two and a half miles south west of the junction of the Winburg railway line and the main line.

A reconnaissance on the 7th May revealed 6,000 Boers and 18 guns at the Zand River. On the 9th, the 7th Division joined with forces under Lieutenant General Ian Hamilton at Merriefontein and, the following day, advanced towards the river. The Lincolns were on baggage guard and did not take part in the action which drove the Boers from their position as it took until 9 p.m. to pass the baggage across the river.

While the Lincolns advanced on Kroonstad, the retreating enemy blew the railway bridge and destroyed the line to the north. Consequently, the Battalion assisted in repair work between the 13th and 21st May. This was arduous labour. The 'Digest of Services', while giving full credit to the Royal Engineers, stated that the reconstruction of the line 'was only rendered possible by the untiring energy and skilled labour of the infantry, many of whom were railway mechanics, platelayers, etc. These men, working six hours by day, and six hours by night, got through an amount of work which, when one remembers that they were on less than half rations, sometimes even on a quarter, can only be described as marvellous. The army advanced on Pretoria, sometimes in rain, always in intense heat during the day, with bitterly cold nights, on meagre rations and carrying 40 lbs of equipment.

Roberts' forces found the Vaal River, which flowed across their front, only lightly guarded and, on the 27th May, crossed it. The Lincolns bivouacked 2 miles north of the river and, on the 29th, as advance guard, crossed the Klip River and spent a cold night at Elandsfontein. The cavalry, under French, had seized the approaches to Johannesburg and, on the 30th May, the city surrendered. The Lincolns, with the remainder of the 7th Division, were ordered to support the mounted infantry in their pursuit of part of the Boers' rearguard. The Battalion did not take part in any fighting, and at night took up a position on the north east side of Johannesburg. On the 1st June, the 14th Brigade advanced 7 miles towards Pretoria and by the 3rd was at Leeuwkop, 18 miles from the Transvaal Capital. The Lincolns, as advance guard, marched at daybreak on the 4th June and, at mid-day, encountered the Boers on a range of kopjes, south west of Pretoria. In spite of heavy fire, the Lincolns held their position until 4 p.m. when the enemy's right flank was turned by the mounted infantry, under

Hamilton, which included the Lincolnshire Section*. There was a general advance by the British, despite Boer resistance, and on the 5th June 1900, Pretoria surrendered.

Yet again, the Lincolns had taken part in a gruelling march underpinning a successful campaign. Both Boer capitals had fallen but the efforts required had been enormous. An officer of the Battalion recorded in the 'Digest of Services':- 'There was no possibility of the infantry eking out their slender rations. All the produce had always been seized by the mounted troops a long while before the infantry came to places where purchase was possible.

The infantryman's lot on this march, compared with the other arms, was most trying. He had to endure the bitterly cold nights, the long, wearying marches commencing in the dark, stumbling over the rough ground through the mealie fields and the long grass, waist high, often not reaching camp before dark, hungry and tired with the long march on foot and the heavy load he had carried all day, only to find a night's outpost duty before him, and the prospect of a similar march on the morrow.'

The Official Record of the War states: - 'Averaging nearly seventeen miles a day, over apparently endless prairies, in blazing sun and bitter cold, swept now by hot and choking dust storms, now by rushes of icy hail, fording rivers and floundering through sand, with scanty food and shelterless bivouacs, their toil had been almost unlightened by anything but hope…The country itself but added to the heavy monotony which weighed upon their daily labour. On the vast levels there was nothing to be seen but their own long ranks, no sound to be heard but that of their own footsteps. Silence attended their marches, hunger, fatigue and discomfort their nightly sleeping places.'

Unfortunately, the Boers did not give up. Roberts sent his cavalry, under French, to encircle enemy forces north east of Pretoria but so much opposition was encountered that French struggled to hold his own. The Lincolns were ordered to advance in support and set out at 6.30a.m. on the 13th June. However, the fighting ended before the Battalion arrived and, on the 15th, they returned to Pretoria. The Lincolns remained constantly on the move; on the 16th June, they were sent 20 miles to Rietfontein, on the 17th, 14 miles to Commando Nek, where 'C' Company was left, then back to Pretoria on the 20th, where they remained until the 10th July. That day five Companies and the Headquarters of the Battalion were despatched to a pass on the Magaliesberg, about 18 miles north west of Pretoria, which was variously known as Nitral's, Zilikat's or Mosilikatze's Nek.

'A', 'B', 'F' and 'G' with the Volunteer Company and the Battalion Headquarters of the Lincolns were to relieve some cavalry, but each Company averaged only 40 to 50 men, with merely 11 officers. Colonel Roberts should have pressed for more men but the staff at the Army Headquarters, who should have known much more than the Colonel about the enemy's whereabouts and strength, were more culpable for the disaster that followed.

Although ordered to send on two Companies – 'F' and the Volunteer Company – to Commando Nek, Colonel Roberts decided, as it was late and the march had been long, to halt them for the night 900 yards to the rear of the other Companies at the southern end of the pass. It would have been better if he had not split his force. 'A', 'B' and 'G' Companies were to hold the Nek with two guns of 'O' Battery Royal Horse Artillery and a squadron of Scots Greys. Another squadron of the Scots Greys and the rest of 'O' Battery were about three miles away to the south-east. Sangars, with wire entanglements, had been made for the guns but the bush in front had only been cleared for a width of about 200 yards. There were steep heights on both sides of the pass, which commanded the position, but Roberts did not put his entire force on either of them. Instead, he sent for reinforcements, as he had only 240 men including the Scots Greys.

At 5.50 a.m. on the 11th July, the Lincolns' picket on the lower of the two heights was attacked by Boers who had advanced through a kloof to the east which had been reported as inaccessible. The picket surrendered after 4 men were killed. Worse followed, as the Boers surrounded the troops at the Nek. Some effort to assist was made by Major Edgar Herapath with 'F' and the Volunteer Companies, but they were compelled to retire to the remainder of the Scots Greys and artillery to the south-east. With Major Herapath wounded, no further help came from these troops. The fire from the Boers at the Nek was deadly and the gunners were unable to work their guns.

Colonel Roberts got a request through to Colonel Alexander of the Scots Greys to send up two guns to shell the kopje on the right of the Lincolns' position. This was carried out and proved effective until Alexander withdrew the guns as the approach of a further large enemy force threatened their capture. Seeing that Roberts could not extricate himself, Alexander presumably ordered the squadron at Commando Nek either to retire on him, or go back to Pretoria. Roberts, not receiving any response to his request for reinforcements, his ammunition exhausted and he himself severely wounded, surrendered. On the west side of the Nek, 2 officers and about 30 men resisted until dark when they withdrew to Rietfontein. Alexander, on his way to Pretoria, met a strong force of 150 mounted infantry, 500 infantry and 4 guns marching to the Nek. But they had set out too late.

The Battalion's losses at Zilikat's Nek were 1 officer and 21 N.C.O.s and men either killed or died of wounds and 4 officers and 27 N.C.O.s and men wounded. The Commanding Officer, the Adjutant and 86 N.C.O.s and men of the Lincolns with a squadron of the Scots Greys were taken prisoner. There was a lack of co-operation between the detachments in the engagement and a delay in the arrival of reinforcements, while the position taken up by the Battalion was far from ideal. It was unfortunate that the Boers were possibly 1,500 strong, and led by Jacobus De la Rey, an outstanding general who knew the area well. The officers and men captured were released on the 13th September. Colonels Roberts and Alexander were sacked. On the 6th October, Major Hugh Archdale of the Royal Welsh Fusiliers was appointed to command the Battalion though he did not arrive until the 2nd March 1901.

In October it was thought that Ex-President Steyn of the Orange Free State would try to break through the British forces and, on the 20th of that month, the Lincolns were formed into an outpost line of 7 to 8 miles, which involved every man being on duty nightly. Steyn did not appear. The Battalion remained in South Africa for the rest of the War, which became a counter-insurgency campaign against Boer guerrillas. Three drafts were sent to South Africa after the Lincolns originally went out. The first draft was not involved in action until it joined the Battalion. The second draft landed in South Africa on the 5th April 1900 and was attacked by a small Boer commando at Zuurfontein near Pretoria on the 19th December. The enemy was driven off. On the 12th January 1901, a heavier onslaught was made on Zuurfontein by General Beyers and 800 Boers. This too was repulsed after an engagement lasting three hours. On both occasions, Lord Kitchener, who had succeeded Lord Roberts as Commander-in-Chief, congratulated the garrison on its successful defence.

The third draft reached Cape Town on the 10th May 1900. News that De Wet and 3,000 Boers had attacked Vredefort Road Station was received on the 8th June. Subsequently, a force, including this draft, was sent there and succeeded in driving the enemy away. Nevertheless, the Boers returned with several guns and the British withdrew to Kromellenburg Spruit. Apart from six weeks at Rooderval, the draft remained there for a year and then joined the Battalion. Although peace came with the Treaty of Vereeniging on the 31st May 1902, the Lincolns were retained in South Africa until the 10th March 1904, arriving at Southampton on the 2nd April.

In common with other regiments which served in the South African War, the Lincolnshire Regiment supplied detachments for the Mounted Infantry Battalions. The 2nd Battalion Mounted Infantry, which arrived at Cape Town on the 15th November 1899, included 35 men under Lieutenant Roland Morant from the Lincolnshire Regiment. The Lincolns formed No. 1 Section of the Northern Company, commanded by Captain Hart of the East Surrey Regiment, and were in the force under Lieutenant General John French.

For the first six weeks after their landing, the 2nd Mounted Infantry was employed in the Colesberg area. The Boers were active in this district and the Lincoln Section took part in engagements at Arundel and Rensburg. On the 4th January 1900, Boer forces under General Schoeman attacked the left wing of French's troops. Although the Suffolk Regiment was at one stage hard pressed, the Boers were repulsed and Colesberg taken. The Lincoln Section formed the advance guard on a reconnaissance behind the enemy lines, covering 70 miles and obtained valuable information. French's Command was then broken up and, on the 3rd February, the Lincoln Section moved from Rensburg to the Orange River.

Having been sent with despatches from Lord Kitchener to Lieutenant General French at Klip Drift on the 14th February, the Lincolns were able to participate in the Relief of Kimberley. On the 18th, they served as escort to one of the batteries at the battle of Paardeberg. The Lincolns formed part of the advance guard of the 6th Division on the 7th March when the Boers retired from Poplar Grove and in the engagement at Driefontein they were the advance guard of Colonel Martyr's Mounted Infantry. The Regiment and another Company, dismounted, drove the Boers from a kopje west of Draaibosch pan and, later, the Section was part of the Mounted Infantry on outpost duty covering the 7th Division's bivouac at Yorkshire Kopje. The Lincolns were engaged in the defeat at Sannah's Post where De Wet took seven guns and a large number of prisoners: British casualties were 571. The 2nd Mounted Infantry, including the Lincolns, was then ordered to Thabanchu. Soon after its arrival, Sergeant A.C.Croydon and Private A. Cooper of the Section, with some other men, held a kopje although surrounded by the enemy. Both these soldiers received Distinguished Conduct Medals and were mentioned in the Commander-in-Chief's despatches.

The 2nd Mounted Infantry formed part of Lieutenant General Ian Hamilton's forces which advanced on Winberg on the 30th April. Half-way through that same morning, it formed the right flank guard and was attacked at Hout Nek, while Hamilton's main force was in action at Thoba Mountain. It took two days to defeat the Boers and the 2nd Mounted Infantry was in daily touch with the enemy, fighting nine engagements until it joined Lord Roberts' army on the 24th May. It then took part in the advances to Johannesburg and Pretoria followed by the action at Diamond Hill.

After this action, the 2nd Mounted Infantry pursued De Wet for thirty-eight days through Springe, Heidelberg, Villiersdorp, Frankfort, Reitz and Bethlehem, covering 440 miles and fighting 28 engagements, all on reduced rations. It took part in an action at Vredefort and relieved forces surrounded by Boers in the Maries district before returning to Pretoria. In September, Lieutenant Morant was invalided home while the strength of the Section was seriously diminished through sickness and deployment of details to garrison the lines of communications.

From September to December 1900, the 2nd Mounted Infantry was commanded by Major General Ralph Clements in the Magaliesberg district and a large detachment was sent to Machadodorp in the eastern Transvaal. There was frequent fighting in both the east and west Transvaal and, on the 13th December, a superior force of Boers, under General De la Rey, inflicted a defeat at Nooitgedacht on Clements, who retreated, leaving his camp in enemy hands. The 2nd Mounted Infantry as the rearguard on the retreat fought valiantly. On the 15th December, Lieutenant Frederick Spring and 30 men arrived from the 2nd Battalion at Pretoria. Following the reinforcement of British troops, the Boers were evicted from Nooitgedacht with the Lincoln Section part of a small force that defeated the enemy at Krugersdorp.

The Section was engaged in escorting columns to Rustenberg from the 4th to 19th January 1901 and, from the 24th to 27th, beat off an attack at Middelfontein. It was during these operations that Lance Corporal H. Wittington was promoted King's Sergeant and awarded the Distinguished Conduct Medal for gallantry when in charge of a picket. In March, the column to which the Lincoln Section was attached saw action on marches to Ventersdorp and Lichtenberg and captured a Boer convoy with two 15-pounder guns, one pom-pom and five maxims on the 24th. Throughout April, there were engagements in the Klerksdorp and Hartebeestfontein areas and a Boer force was surprised at Korannafontein on the 8th May. Large quantities of abandoned supplies and cattle were captured. Operations followed in the mountainous country north of Vlakfontein and a Boer convoy was taken near Parys on the 28th July. The 2nd

Mounted Infantry was in touch with the enemy for the rest of the year, fighting successfully in many small actions. A notable success took place near Ermelo in December when 400 prisoners and a large quantity of wagons and supplies were captured. The only transport with the troops in these campaigns was one wagon per battalion for blankets, a Cape cart per battalion for the officers and a few supply wagons containing three days' rations and groceries, with one day's forage carried on man and horse. The remainder of the baggage was left in camp under guard. In early 1902, the weather was bad making the long marches, with no tents, very trying for both men and horses.

Kitchener's strategy called for blockhouses connected by barbed wire with the Boers driven against these in an effort to sweep the guerrillas from the veldt. The Lincoln Section was involved in a big drive in February in the Orange River country which ended at Wolvehoek on the 18th with the capture of 300 Boers. The column to which the Section was attached then cleared the area around Vereeniging and Klip River, before sweeping south in another drive towards the Frankfort-Vrede blockhouse line and then on to the Harrismith blockhouse line.

On the 24th February, the column moved to the difficult, mountainous country of the Drakensberg on the left of the British line. A drive through this area from the 25th to 29th February proved tough: roads had to be made for two 15- pounder guns and the pom-pom which were with the column. The gradients were steep and the work exhausting. At one stage, the Lincolns formed part of the guard for over 600 Boers. A further drive from Harrismith to Koppies Station in early March proved abortive – the Boers escaped. On the 23rd March, the column was sent to the western Transvaal. Many prisoners were captured in a drive to the Schoon Spruit blockhouse line when in twenty-five and a half hours the troops covered nearly 90 miles. A further two drives took place in April and the remainder of the month was spent destroying crops west of Klerksdorp. On the 6th May, the Lincolns began their last drive, which was towards the Kimberley and Mafeking line, ending on the 11th at Devonshire Siding.

After the end of the War, the reservists went, on the 24th June, to the 2nd Battalion at Barberton, prior to returning to England. The Lincoln Section left, on the 9th August, to join the Lincoln Mounted Infantry Company, which was at Kimberley with the 7th Mounted Infantry Battalion. The latter had been formed at Orange River on the 1st February 1900 and consisted of four companies, each of about 120 N.C.O.s and men. The Lincolnshire Company was No. II. The horses were Argentine ponies with the majority of the men having no knowledge of horsemanship. On the 9th February, eight days after its formation, the Battalion joined the march to Bloemfontein and, two days later, skirmished with Boers near Ramah. The Battalion was ordered, on the 15th February, to assist the convoy at Waterval Drift. This was unsuccessful and 3 of the Lincoln Company were wounded, 2 of these becoming prisoners.

The Battalion was recalled to the main army at Paardeberg, where the Boers were laagered, and sent, dismounted, across the Modder River with men from many different corps. The troops advanced to within about 900 yards of the Boer position but were driven back by heavy fire. The Lincolns lost 1 man killed with several wounded or missing. After Cronje's surrender, the 7th M. I. were transferred to the 7th Division, of which the 2nd Battalion of the Regiment was also part, for the march to Bloemfontein. This began on the 6th March and, the next day, there was a successful skirmish between the Mounted Infantry and the Boers at Abraham's Kraal. The Lincoln and Hampshire Companies escorted a convoy to Petersburg on the 10th March and, after rejoining the main army, entered Bloemfontein on the 16th.

The Battalion remained there for five weeks carrying out occasional patrol duty and outpost work although badly affected by typhoid fever. They were reduced to Captain Frederic Lloyd and 30 men fit for duty. On the 22nd April 1900, the Battalion joined Lieutenant General Ian Hamilton's Column on its exhausting six-week march to Pretoria. All camp equipment was left behind at Bloemfontein so there was no shelter, the weather was bad, the marches continuous and the fighting hard. Winburg, Thabanchu and Mount Thoba saw the Mounted Infantry fully employed. However, Junction Drift on the Zand River was practically undefended and by nightfall on the 9th May, Hamilton held both banks. Further fighting took place after the Zand River was crossed during the nineteen days' march to Johannesburg.

After a sharp engagement, Lindley was taken and the Lincoln Battalion was engaged in a heavy rearguard action nearly all day on the 20th May. There was a baggage train, six miles in length, to cover and a Boer attack led to a running fight in which the enemy got between the column and the right flank guard, capturing nearly 40 men. However, the 19th Brigade launched an attack on the right flank of the Boers and drove them off. Hampered by lack of forage and difficulties at the drifts, Hamilton's force was faced with a hard action on the approaches to Johannesburg where, with the Boers extending their right flank westwards, a frontal attack was made. This was successful and Johannesburg was captured.

The Mounted Infantry played a conspicuous part in the fall of Pretoria, as did the 2nd Battalion of the Lincolns in the 14th Brigade. The M. I. executed an outflanking movement on the Boers' right, scrambling down a steep nek, leading their horses until the bottom was reached. The Boers, fearing to be cut off, fled and the 14th and 19th Brigades advanced to take the abandoned ground. In the course of the fighting, Private Newton of the Lincoln Company of the Mounted Infantry became separated from his unit. Knowing that Pretoria had been summoned to surrender, he thought the city was in British hands, and walked in, leading his horse, which was lame. He was taken into the house of a German doctor and cared for: Private Newton is believed to have been the first man of the British army to enter Pretoria other than as a prisoner.

Following the fall of Pretoria, the 7th M. I. took part in the Battle of Diamond Hill and here the Lincoln Company, occupying a hill to the north east of Tyger Poort, came under British artillery fire. Fortunately, the mistake was discovered before the results were serious. The Lincolns also took part in the occupation of Heidelberg on the 23rd June and the action at Reitz on the 7th July. It is recorded in the 'Digest of Services' that, 'after fighting all the morning, a cricket match was played in the afternoon against an eleven produced and captained by the Landrost of the town'.

Lieutenant General Sir Archibald Hunter, who took over from Lieutenant General Hamilton when the latter broke his collarbone, attempted to trap De Wet in the Brandwater Basin. He began operations on the 13th July. The enemy had set fire to the veldt and, with a high wind blowing, the charcoal dust from the burnt grass half-blinded the troops: De Wet escaped with 2,600 men, 4 guns and 460 wagons. The 7th Mounted Infantry, now under General Bruce Hamilton, was in action from the 29th to 31st July when 1,500 Boers surrendered.

After an abortive pursuit of the Boer General Olivier at the beginning of August, the Lincoln Company was detached from the headquarters of the Mounted Infantry Battalion. Its duties during the next weeks comprised patrolling, foraging and escorting convoys. On the 4th October, the Lincolns were involved in a sharp action at Wilkop when Captain Wiltshire was killed. The Company rejoined the 7th M. I. on the 6th December and was in one of the columns under Major General Charles Knox, who was driving De Wet and his men against the Thabanchu line. This was supposed to be well manned, though the Boers got through in broad daylight.

By the 12th January 1901, remounts were urgently needed by the Mounted Infantry and a halt was made at Winburg. The Mounted Infantry Battalions were now organised into Corps; the Lincolns being in the 7th Corps M. I., which fought a successful action with De Wet's rearguard on the 29th January. The Company made a charge on the Boer position and was complimented by its Commander. In that action 1 man was killed and 5 wounded.

The 7th Corps M. I. doggedly pursued the Boer forces over the next months, fighting severe actions on the 8th April at the Korannberg Mountains and on the 19th May at Lambrechtfontein. Here Corporal Shaw of the Lincoln Company rescued Lieutenant Coulson of the King's Own Scottish Borderers who had been wounded. Although Coulson was subsequently killed by a bullet that went through Shaw's body, the latter was recommended for the Victoria Cross. However, this award was not granted and Shaw received the Distinguished Conduct Medal.

Between the 29th May and the 7th June, the column containing the Lincoln Company carried out clearing operations towards Kimberley. The 7th Mounted Infantry helped beat off a Boer attack on the 19th June. For six weeks of wet weather during August and September, they were part of a column that swept the Stormberg area and other parts of Cape Colony. In October and November, General Joubert's commando was pursued leading to the capture of the Boer general and the breaking up of his force.

Vigorous pursuit of the enemy commandos in 1902 led to whole districts being cleared despite the 7th Mounted Infantry losing many horses. Notable actions included those at Aaronslaagte on the 2nd April, when the Boer leader, General Erasmus, was killed, and Griquatown on the 1st May, where the Boers were beaten at the cost of several casualties among the Lincolns, including 2 privates killed. This was the last action of the war in which the Lincoln Company was engaged.

The 'Digest of Services' stated 'In a campaign which lasted for two and a half years, perhaps the most remarkable feature was the incessant marching which fell to the lot of the 7th M. I.. The area covered was enormous, and a rough calculation of the marching in 1900 showed that the Battalion had averaged 10 miles a day throughout the year. In 1901 the average must have been higher, but it was a matter of impossibility to compute it, as so much work was done by patrols during the year...Only one pony, an Argentine, saw the campaign through, and the number which passed through the ranks was, like the marching, impossible to calculate.'

The 7th M. I. was broken up in February 1903 and the Lincoln Company was transferred to the 5th M. I. and then to the 8th M. I. before proceeding to England with the 2nd Battalion of the Regiment on the 10th March 1904.

During the South African War, the Lincolns lost 1 officer and 93 N.C.O.s and men killed in action or died of wounds, disease or other causes, while 9 officers and 68 other ranks were wounded. For their enormous efforts, the Regiment was awarded the Battle Honours 'Paardeberg' and 'South Africa 1900-02'.

In 1902 a new pattern uniform was issued with a khaki tunic and trousers. The legs were bound with puttees below the knees. The original headgear was a cap but this was replaced with a steel helmet during the First World War. A trenchcoat was worn in cold weather and equipment was carried on webbing straps.

As a result of the Territorial and Reserve Forces Act 1908 (the reorganisation carried out by the Right Honourable Richard Haldane, Secretary of State for War), the Territorial Force (later renamed the Territorial Army) was formed. Only two Infantry Battalions were required instead of the three Volunteer Battalions. The Regiment's Territorial battalions were numbered the 4th and 5th respectively, with the 3rd Militia Battalion becoming the 3rd (Special Reserve) Battalion.

Chapter 5
THE OUTBREAK OF THE FIRST WORLD WAR.

The 1st Battalion of the Regiment remained in India until it went to Aden in 1910 and returned to the United Kingdom two years later. The 2nd Battalion served in England up to 1911 when it went to Gibraltar, before moving to Nova Scotia and Bermuda in 1914. At the beginning of the First World War, the Lincolnshire Regiment consisted of five Battalions. The 1st Battalion (Regular) was stationed at Portsmouth while the 2nd Battalion (Regular) was in Bermuda. The 3rd (Special Reserve) Battalion, (formerly Militia), had its Headquarters at Lincoln and the 4th and 5th Battalions were the Territorial Battalions. The Headquarters of the 4th Battalion (South Lincs) was at the Drill Hall, Lincoln, and that of the 5th (North Lincs) at the Infantry Drill Hall, Grimsby.

The 4th and 5th Battalions, the Territorials, went to Bridlington on the 25th July 1914 for their annual training and, after being dismissed to hold themselves in readiness, were ordered to mobilize on the 4th August. At the outbreak of war, only five Territorial Battalions had signed the General Service obligation 'to serve overseas if required in time of national danger' but very soon afterwards most Territorial units volunteered for overseas service. For various reasons, not all ranks could undertake such service. Units in which not less than 60% volunteered were designated 'General Service' and were ordered to recruit up to 25% beyond establishment. As soon as units had reached a sufficiently high percentage of volunteers for service overseas, a second unit of similar strength was formed which was termed a 'Second Line' unit. Later, 'Third Line' units were established. The original Territorial battalions became the First Line units. Hence, the 4th and 5th Lincolns became the 1/4th and 1/5th Battalions. They were posted to the 138th Brigade, 46th Division, and went to France in February 1915.

The 2/4th and 2/5th Lincolns were formed at Luton in January 1915, and became part of the 177th Brigade of 59th Division. The men were taken from a Provisional Battalion at Dunstable in September 1914 and consisted of drafts from Lincoln, Grimsby and Leicester. After service in Ireland in 1916, the 2/4th and 2/5th went to France in February 1917. The 3/4th and 3/5th were set up in April 1915 and amalgamated in October 1916, but did not serve overseas. There was also, a Provisional Battalion, the 28th, later the 13th, which was classified as a Territorial Battalion.

The first New Army of six divisions was called to arms by Lord Kitchener, the Secretary of State for War, on the 7th August 1914. The New Army battalions were called Service Battalions and the 6th Lincolns was one of these. They were quartered in Belton Park, near Grantham, and, initially, had enthusiasm but no rifles or uniforms.

The second New Army of six divisions was ordered to be raised by the Government on the 11th September and the 7th (Service) Battalion of the Lincolnshire Regiment was formed. The 6th was in the 33rd Infantry Brigade, 11th Division, and the 7th was raised at Lincoln, and went to France on the 14th July as part of the 51st Infantry Brigade, 17th Division.

On the 13th September 1914, a third New Army was ordered to be raised and the 8th Lincolns came into being. This Battalion was in the 63rd Brigade, 21st Division, and concentrated in Halton Park, near Tring. They went to France in September 1915. The 10th (Service) Battalion grew from a nucleus of old boys of the Wintringham Secondary School, Grimsby, who styled themselves the 'Chums'. After forming themselves into an infantry company and carrying out training, they offered their services to the Officer Commanding the 5th Lincolns but that battalion was already at full strength. The Mayor of Grimsby, Alderman J. H. Tate, then approached the War Office for permission to form a battalion from Grimsby. This was granted and the former pupils of Wintringham were joined by those from Humberstone Grammar School, St. James' Choir School, Louth Grammar School and Worksop College as well as by a number of men from Grimsby. In a strangely appropriate echo of the days of the Earl of Bath, these soldiers were clad in blue uniforms, which had previously been worn by postmen. By the end of October, the Battalion had reached a strength of about 1,000, and became part of the 101st Infantry Brigade, 34th Division, moving to France in January 1916. Another contribution of Grimsby to the Western Front was the huge quantities of Tickler's jam supplied to the troops in France. Not only was this part of the rations, the soldiers considered the empty tins were ideal as hand grenades.

The 9th and 11th Service Battalions were retained in the United Kingdom for training and supplying drafts for the battalions overseas. The 12th (Labour) Battalion and the Labour Companies served in France and Flanders and suffered casualties. The 1st Garrison Battalion served in India for guard duties and the 2nd Garrison Battalion served in the United Kingdom. The Labour Battalion, Labour Companies and Garrison Battalions were largely made up of old soldiers. There was also a contingent of the Bermuda Volunteer Rifle Corps, which was attached to the 1st Battalion of the Regiment and served with it from June 1915 to May 1919. The two Bermuda contingents lost over 75% of their strength in killed and wounded and were, after the War, sanctioned by the King to appear as an 'Allied Regiment' in the Army List. In 2003 they are allied to the Lincolns' successor, The Royal Anglian Regiment.

The 1st Battalion received orders to mobilise at 6 p.m. on the 4th August 1914. Its strength was 24 officers and 673 other ranks. Most of the soldiers in the ranks were young men whose service ranged from a few weeks to two years. On the 8th, 543 mobilised reservists joined from the depot at Lincoln. Insufficiently trained men, those earmarked as reinforcements or as cadres of new battalions, were sent to the 3rd (Reserve) Battalion. The first reinforcements, consisting of 1 officer and 100 other ranks, were detailed to remain in Portsmouth until further orders. The 1st Battalion, 27 officers and 971 other ranks, left Portsmouth Town Station for Southampton on the

13th August, when they sailed for France on the *'Norman'* and the regimental transport embarked on the *'Italian Prince'*.*

The officers and men were not told where they were going, but landed at Le Havre the next day and marched past Harfleur to a camp on the plateau. It was a gruelling six-mile march over rough roads under a hot sun. On the 15th, the battalion left Harfleur by train for Landrecies, which was reached at about 8 p.m. on the 16th. The Lincolns formed part of the 9th Infantry Brigade, 3rd Division, British Expeditionary Force.

The B.E.F., before taking up its position on the left of the Fifth French Army, concentrated in an area between Le Cateau and Maubeuge, east of the Forêt de Mormal. On the 20th August, the 1st Lincolns moved to billets in Leval. That night, General Headquarters issued orders for a three-days' movement north, beginning on the 21st. The object of this advance was for the British Expeditionary Force and the Fifth French Army to hold in check the German armies coming from the Meuse, and gain time for an attack on the German centre by the French Third and Fourth Armies. The general situation on the 21st, however, was: the French First and Second Armies were retiring, their Third and Fourth had had a serious reverse, and their Fifth was in a salient about to be attacked.

There was a heavy ground mist that morning. The 3rd Division, on the right of II Corps, advanced to the line Bettignies – Feignies – La Longueville. Having arrived at their destination, the Lincolns were ordered to find outposts on the line of the Goegnies–Bray road from the Mons–Maubeuge railway to Riez de l'Erelle connecting with the outposts of the 8th and 13th Brigades on their flanks. The following day the 9th Brigade was ordered to march to Frameries, and cavalry contact with the enemy led to part of the Brigade taking up positions along the Mons-Condé Canal from Nimy to Mariette. The Lincolns were with the Brigade in reserve at Cuesmes. It was here that Captain Guy Ellison fired at a German aircraft that flew over the village. This was the first shot fired by the Lincolnshire Regiment in the War.

News now came in of large columns of enemy infantry advancing on Mons from the north. It was provided that if the 4th Royal Fusiliers were forced to retire from the Mons-Condé Canal, they were to do so to a position behind the Lincolns who, with two companies of the 1st Northumberland Fusiliers, were to leave Cuesmes and take up a position on the Cuesmes – Mons road. By 9 a.m. on the 23rd August, the massed German formations were being shot down in dozens by the 4th Royal Fusiliers. The Lincolns were sent three miles along the road to Mons. They erected four barricades, which were constructed of paving stones, sawn down trees, logs and iron piping found lying by the roadside, across a long, straight avenue, at intervals of 100 yards.

At 2 p.m., the Royal Fusiliers at Nimy had, as ordered, retired to Mons. Moving south towards Ciply, they passed through the Lincolns who prepared to meet the Germans. Shortly afterwards, enemy infantry swarmed round a corner into the avenue, across which the Lincolns had erected their barricades. Shots were fired by the Battalion and the Germans took cover in some houses and returned fire. The Lincolns sustained

* See Appendix 4 on page 154

casualties but the Germans, who had endured a hard day's fighting, turned away westwards.

Information from the French Commander-in-Chief and aerial reconnaissance convinced Field Marshal Sir John French, commanding the B.E.F., of the dangers from large German forces to his front and the retreat of the two French Reserve Divisions and the Fifth French Army on his right. Accordingly, he ordered the B.E.F. to retire at daybreak on the 24th August to the Maubeuge line. Meanwhile, the Lincolns had received orders at 6 p.m. on the 23rd to withdraw from the Cuesmes – Mons road and to act as rearguard to the 9th Brigade which was retiring on Frameries. The Battalion therefore marched in a south-easterly direction to Mesvin and Nouvelles, acting for a time in support of the 8th Infantry Brigade who beat off an enemy attack between 7 and 8 p.m. Marching on through Ciply, the Battalion arrived at Frameries.

On the 24th August, the 3rd Division was posted as follows:- 8th Infantry Brigade at Nouvelles, 7th at Ciply and 9th at Frameries. The 1st Lincolns were ordered to take over the northern edge of Frameries. Their position was in an orchard and, although dark, they entrenched and provided themselves with some overhead protection. Two sides of the orchard, at right angles facing north and west, were held, together with a ditch along a paved road, in front of a brick built factory. Being a mining district there were huge mounds of slag in front of the Battalion, and a platoon was in a detached post in front of the line. About 4 a.m. on the 24th the German artillery opened fire: shells burst on the paved road and set light to the factory. The heat from the flames made the ditch untenable and the men in it were withdrawn to the orchard.

'B' Company, holding the side of the orchard at right angles to the front, suffered many casualties but hung on with great determination. The night-long defensive preparations carried out by the Battalion proved their worth against the enemy shell-fire. Small groups of Germans tried to advance by working their way from stook to stook in a nearby cornfield but accurate fire from the Lincolns forced them to abandon the attempt. It is apparent from the History of the 24th (Brandenburg) Regiment that the enemy mistook the rapid rifle fire of the British infantry for machine gun fire. The South Lancashires, who were the rearguard for the 7th Brigade, and the 1st Lincolns, acting in a similar capacity for the 9th Brigade, held up the enemy advance and covered the withdrawal of the two Brigades to Genly. After about three or four hours' fighting, the enemy broke off the attack. The Lincolns, blackened by the smoke from bursting shells and their own rifle-fire, withdrew in a south-westerly direction. It subsequently transpired that a whole German division—the 6th of III Corps – had attacked the two rearguard Battalions. Regimental casualties on the 23rd and 24th August were 4 officers and 130 other ranks. Of the wounded, only those capable of walking escaped; the more severe cases and practically all the stretcher bearers were captured.

The Lincolns took the road to Eugies. The heat was fierce and the lanes dusty; the cook's cart with rations had gone on ahead. The troops therefore existed on iron rations which consisted of one tin of bully beef, eight biscuits, a piece of cheese and a tin containing a little tea and sugar. The men could not stop to make tea so water had to suffice. A message was received by the Battalion's Commanding Officer, Lieutenant Colonel W. E. B. Smith, from the Brigade Commander, expressing his appreciation of the splendid tenacity the Lincolns had displayed in maintaining their position, and his pride in having such a battalion in his brigade.

The Battalion marched roughly 14 miles on the 24th August and spent the night in a deserted harvest field at Bermeries. In order to 'march light', greatcoats and packs had been discarded. The threatened outflanking movements by the Germans meant that the B.E.F. had to continue withdrawing to the neighbourhood of Le Cateau. II Corps, including the Lincolns, were to fall back west of the Forêt de Mormal, while I Corps moved east of the forest.

The Lincolns set out at 4.30 a.m. on the 25th towards Inchy on the Le Cateau – Cambrai road. Even with a hot sun, no food and very little water, the troops had scant rest apart from the usual 10 minutes' halt at the end of every hour. Early in the day, the Lincolns opened fire on a German Taube aircraft, which was also attacked by a British aviator and brought down. The wings and fuselage of the plane were riddled with rifle bullets so the Lincolnshire Regiment shared with the British pilot the distinction of being amongst the first of the B.E.F. to bring down an enemy aircraft. The roads along which the Lincolns marched were congested with refugees, their accompanying farm carts, wagons, perambulators and other vehicles. Furthermore, there was a heavy thunderstorm between 4 and 5 p.m. Inchy was eventually sighted an hour later, but there was no food there, only washing and drinking water. The Battalion had covered nearly 20 miles in the day but the men were not permitted to undress and had to rest in their wet clothes.

At midnight, the Lincolns were ordered to stand to arms. Two platoons were sent to reinforce the outpost line. British mounted troops, passing through Inchy, had brought the news that the 3rd Division's rearguard had been engaged at Solesmes and I Corps had also been attacked. After many alarms, the night passed and, at 5 a.m. on the 26th, the Battalion was formed up in the main street and each man was given a piece of bread and a drink of tea. After this, the Battalion dug in to the south of the village about halfway down an open slope roughly 300 yards away.

The German artillery opened fire at around 6.30 a.m. and enemy infantry advanced down an open slope in extended lines. The British guns replied. The German troops entered the village and were also in large numbers along its edge. The British artillery fired frequently and set some buildings alight. German pressure on the right of II Corps led to a further withdrawal. The Royal Fusiliers were brought up from the reserve to the north western edge of Troisvilles and nearly all the wounded were evacuated. Following this, the Northumberland Fusiliers and the Lincolns were withdrawn with small loss. German skirmishers tried to hinder the movement but were silenced by the advanced sections of the 107 and 108 Batteries of the divisional artillery. As the last party of Lincolns came abreast of the advanced section of the 108 Battery, the gunners disabled and abandoned their guns, all ammunition having been fired.

The retreat continued: part of the way was across a beetroot field which was wet and slippery. Clods of clay soil stuck to the men's feet, making progress slow. Fortunately, the enemy did not press them closely. At a rallying point near Clary on the 26th August, the majority of 'A' and 'B' Companies and about half of 'D' were present. The majority of 'C' Company, who had retired through Troisvilles, rejoined on the 27th and another party of 'D' caught up with the rest of the Battalion later. This was the Lincolns' part in the Battle of Le Cateau where their losses were 1 officer wounded and left behind, 3 other ranks killed, 40 wounded and 50 missing, most of whom rejoined later.

The 9th Brigade, acting as rearguard to the 3rd Division, moved to Beaurevoir. It was very wet while the roads were bad and choked with troops and transport. The 5th and 3rd Divisions were intermixed and, at a crossroads two miles beyond Estrees, it was endeavoured to sort them out. Following this, the march continued to Hargicourt with the 9th Brigade still rearguard of the 3rd Division. Quartermaster Sergeant North of the Lincolns stated 'No one bothered about which villages were passed through. The only village that mattered was the one in which the battalion would billet wherever it might be, as there would then be a chance of getting some sleep and perhaps some rations.'

The Lincolns reached Villeret and went into billets but were ordered to turn out rapidly to cover the rear of the Brigade. A small party of German cavalry sent some shots into the village but retreated on fire being returned. The 9th Brigade then marched to Vermand. Without counting deployments, about 17 miles were covered on the 27th August. Halted temporarily at Estouilly, on the 28th, a party of Lincolns was sent to Ham for supplies but returned with only one tin of biscuits and a dozen small tins of bully beef. The Battalion set off for Noyon, again as rearguard to the 9th Brigade. It was very hot and straggling was noticeable. Stores and ammunition were off-loaded and dumped by the roadside to provide transport for those who, through exhaustion, could not march any further.

At about 6.30 p.m., the 9th Brigade, after marching 27 miles in the day, reached Crissoles and here the Lincolns found their transport with cooks and supplies. Tea was brewed, but in the dark, salt was added instead of sugar. The 29th August was to have been a rest day but, when it was nearly noon and they were anticipating their dinner, heavy gunfire from the direction of Ham caused the Battalion to fall in. They took the pots containing stew with them! The 9th Brigade was sent to a position 3 miles north of Noyon on the Ham-Guiscard road and, as the Lincolns marched back, the stew was consumed as they went!

The Lincolns formed the rearguard and, about 1 a.m. on the 30th, they were ordered to withdraw. The Battalion retired, accordingly, over the Oise Canal, where the bridge was demolished by the Royal Engineers one minute later. At 8 p.m., Ressons was reached. The day's march had been about 25 miles and when the roll was called, it was found that all the stragglers had rejoined. With less pressure from the Germans, the 15-mile march on the 31st was the most comfortable for a week. The Lincolns bivouacked by the roadside to the west of Vauciennes. The Battalion marched to Bouillancy on the 1st September, arriving there at 7 p.m., and on the 2nd, acting as rearguard to the Brigade, they set off at 4.30 a.m. and reached Penchard soon after noon. No doubt, the men were relieved that it had been a short march that day, as was the case on the 3rd September, when the Lincolns, leaving at 4.15 a.m., stopped at a farm between Vaucourtois and Maison Blanche shortly after 2 p.m. The weather was very hot.

The next day the Battalion did not move until 1 p.m. There was a halt after about a mile, as German cavalry had made contact with the 3rd Divisional Mounted Troops. After marching 10 miles on the 4th September and 16 during the night of the 4th/5th, the Battalion reached Liverdy and the great retreat ended. Between the 20th August and 5th September, the 3rd Division had marched 237 miles and fought two large battles. Even the fittest soldiers found the long marches on cobbled roads in heavy boots very trying.

Late on the 5th September, the Lincolns heard that the B.E.F. were to advance the following day with the French Sixth Army, attacking the right flank and lines of communication of the German forces, which were swinging round and moving in an easterly and south easterly direction. Accordingly, at 6 a.m. the Lincolns fell in and moved forward to the Chateau de Lumigny.

The advance continued on the 7th and 8th September and the Lincolns crossed the Petit Morin at Orly, where the 9th Brigade became advance guard to the Division. At Les Feucheres, the Lincolns formed outposts while patrols searched the woods that were at crossings over the River Marne. The 3rd Division crossed the Marne at Nanteuil and the 5th Division at Saacy. The 9th Brigade proceeded without difficulty to Bezu, where the Lincolns were detailed to capture a German battery that was seriously damaging the advancing British columns.

Lieutenant Colonel Smith with 'C' and 'D' Companies crept through the woods to within 150 yards of the guns and shot many of the Germans. However, when the party emerged from the woods they were hit by friendly fire from the 65th Battery who mistook the Lincolns for Germans returning to their abandoned guns. The Battalion's killed or wounded numbered 4 officers and 30 men, whilst the guns were removed by the 5th Divisional Ammunition Column the next day.

At nightfall on the 9th September, the Brigade was on the Chateau Thierry – Montreuil road and, on the 10th, crossed the River Clignon at Neuilly. The Brigade captured 600 prisoners and the Lincolns were engaged in searching the villages, fields and woods for stray Germans. The men were billeted at Dammard on the 10th September and moved on to Grand Rozoy on the 11th, the 9th Brigade was again at the front of the 3rd Division. On the 12th, the rain poured down, turning the roads into seas of mud. The aim of the British forces was to take the crossing places on the Aisne and hold the high ground north of the river. The Lincolns were the vanguard of the 9th Brigade which formed the advance guard of the 3rd Division.

At 10 a.m., the Battalion was ordered to capture a railway bridge half a mile to the east of Braisne and sweep north while the 1st Northumberland Fusiliers crossed the road bridge and moved west of the town. The Lincolns advanced but the enemy had retired and all that was captured were a few wounded Germans, a medical officer, a machine gun and a horsed ammunition limber. They then proceeded forward in extended order beyond Braisne, captured a few more prisoners, got soaked in the rain and were billeted at Brenelle. The tired men got little rest as they tried to dry their clothes. Supplies had not caught up with the Brigade and soldiers were permitted to consume their iron rations. No bridges over the Aisne were taken.

Orders from 3rd Divisional Headquarters reached the 9th Brigade at 5.15 a.m. on the 13th: they were to secure the high ground between Brenelle and Chassemy until the 8th Brigade had captured the latter, then they were to cover the 8th's crossing of the Aisne. The advance to Chassemy was difficult due to long range fire from German howitzers but the 9th Brigade eventually achieved its objective, and then had a wait of several hours. The road bridge over the Aisne at Vailly was destroyed with the gap spanned by a single plank so the 8th Brigade could only move slowly across. The 9th Brigade did not begin to cross until dark. The Lincolns commenced their hazardous crossing at nearly midnight. If a man fell from the single plank, certain death from drowning would follow. Fortunately, all got over safely inspite of enemy shellfire. Progress was slow and, once across, the men marched at the double for several hundred yards to where the Battalion reformed. When all were present, they proceeded to a high ridge south west of Rouge Maison Farm. On top of the ridge were the 4th Royal Fusiliers and the Lincolns extended the line to the right.

In the dark and rain, the Battalion entrenched and sent out patrols. The Germans then attacked and the Battalion was soon firing rapidly even though mud clogged many rifles. To make matters worse, enemy artillery shelled the Lincolns in enfilade from the right. At nightfall on the 13th, there was a gap of 5 miles between the right of the Battalion and the left of the 2nd Division. Throughout the morning of the 14th, the Germans repeatedly attacked the Lincolns and the troops on their left, but these assaults were broken up with heavy enemy losses. The British infantry also lacked proper artillery support as the guns were still on the southern side of the Aisne due to the road bridges having been destroyed.

The Royal Fusiliers requested support from the Lincolns and 'D' and 'B' Companies made a tremendous counter-attack, which pushed the Germans back to their starting point. The Lincolns' casualties were heavy and included Captain Herbert Dawson, the Officer Commanding 'B' Company. Further severe losses were suffered by the Battalion when the enemy succeeded in attacking from a wood on the right of the Lincolns. A message was sent to Brigade for support and two Companies of the Royal Scots Fusiliers were sent but driven back with heavy losses. The Lincolns were ordered to retire by platoons beginning from the right.

The Germans machine gunned the Battalion as they fell back and, as Vailly offered no defensive position, the Lincolns had to re-cross the Aisne. Three hours later, the Battalion crossed the river again, and took cover in a wood about 200 yards further on. After dark, the Lincolns advanced to Vailly where the men got what sleep they could. The Battalion's losses were nearly 200. Shortly before daybreak on the 15th, the Lincolns and the Royal Scots Fusiliers were sent in support of the 4th Royal Fusiliers and the 1st Northumberland Fusiliers, who were holding a ridge about a mile north of Vailly. The Battalion, in their supporting role, spent the last day of the Battle of the Aisne being shelled in a roadway cutting.

Following the destruction, by shellfire on the 16th September, of the cottage where the Battalion Headquarters were located, all ranks lived in primitive dugouts. There were no fires or lights allowed and the men were unable to do any cooking, rations being fetched at night by ration parties. The weather was wet and the nights extremely cold. The men were without overcoats and blankets; waterproof sheets were few. At night, the Battalion stood to arms once or twice, and always at daybreak. Enemy fire was suffered frequently both day and night. At this time, German artillery was superior to that of the British in number of guns and calibre. The enemy had howitzers of all calibres, notably the 8 inch one firing shells nicknamed 'Jack Johnsons', and a small high-velocity gun, firing what were termed 'whizz-bangs', the report of discharge and burst being practically simultaneous.

On the night of the 20th/21st September, under cover of continuous rifle-fire, the Germans began digging pits for field guns in front of their line, which was close to trenches held by the Lincolns. This suggested an attack would be launched. However, rapid fire from the Battalion frustrated the enemy. The Lincolns were relieved on the 21st, when reinforcements arrived. The survivors of the original Battalion that had left Portsmouth in August were now in disreputable uniforms from constant soakings and frequent contact with mud and with their boots full of holes.

On the 25th September, the Lincolns took over trenches about a mile to the left of their old ones. These were short lengths not continuous and only occupied at night, with pickets in gullies or amongst trees. There was some German shelling on the 26th and 28th and the next day, for the first time, the Battalion suffered aerial bombing. However, the bombs exploded harmlessly in no man's land. On the 2nd October, the Lincolns were relieved and re-crossed the Aisne for the last time. The Battalion was ordered to Servenay as part of the transfer of the B.E.F. to the Bethune - Ypres area so that the British were on the left of the Allied line.

The Battalion Diary stated 'The men were in a very exhausted condition. Seventeen days in the wet and mud of the trenches with no time to take off their clothing and only one day on which they could take their boots off had made their feet in a very bad state. Following this were three forced marches. These abnormal conditions accounted for their exhaustion. After a four hours' wait, during which the men were able to cook and make hot tea, the Battalion entrained and proceeded ... to Abbeville, where we detrained.'

Bully-beef, tinned vegetable stew with meat gravy and sometimes meat and vegetables were the main items in the soldier's diet. Usually for breakfast there were bacon, biscuits and plum and apple jam washed down with tea made with condensed milk and chlorinated water. The water was often carried in petrol cans and could have a tang of petrol about it. Food parcels from home were much appreciated. When resting, a soldier could visit a local estaminet for egg and chips with wine or watery French beer. The men also had a rum ration in the trenches, usually taken in cups of tea. The officers could afford to buy additions to their diet. Also while at rest, the soldiers could have a bath and change of shirts and underclothes, which helped to reduce lice.

The training and despatching of drafts to the battalions overseas devolved on the 3rd (Reserve) Battalion of the Regiment. They were stationed at Grimsby from August 1914 to November 1917 where they were also part of the forces guarding the coast on the south side of the Humber. The Battalion, in addition, furnished detachments at Killingholme Oil Tanks, Immingham Docks and Waltham Wireless Station. In November 1917, the 3rd Lincolns moved to Cork.

On account of Sinn Fein disturbances, the 3rd Battalion sent a detachment of 28 officers and 420 other ranks, in February 1918, to Tulla in County Clare. The detachment was recalled to Cork on the news of the German offensive of the 21st March and, shortly afterwards, the Battalion sent every available man to replace casualties. During the first months of the War, officers and men stayed long enough with the 3rd Battalion to be fairly well trained and gain some esprit de corps. However, as time went on, and the number of battalions at the front and casualties increased, training had to be intensified and shortened. When time allowed, home training was supplemented by that at base camps in France, such as Etaples.

In 1914, with less than five months fighting, the 3rd Battalion replaced 1,336 casualties. In 1915, with reinforcements needed for the 1st, 2nd, 6th, 7th and 8th Battalions, the numbers sent out were as follows:-

		To replace casualties
1st Battalion	1,430	at Ypres, first attack Bellewaarde
2nd Battalion	1,100	at Neuve Chapelle, Aubers and Bois Grenier
6th Battalion	1,082	at Gallipoli
7th Battalion	59	from early days in the trenches
8th Battalion	461	at Loos
Total	4,132	

Chapter 6
1914 TO 1915 ON THE WESTERN FRONT.

Meanwhile, in France, a further attempt was to be made to turn the right flank of the German armies. Accordingly, the 1st Lincolns, with other units from its Brigade, advanced to Sachin on the 10th October 1914, where the troops billeted. The 9th Brigade moved to billets at Busnes on the 11th and, the next day was in reserve when the 7th and 8th Brigades drove back the enemy. At dusk, the Lincolns were ordered to reinforce the 7th Brigade. The Battalion advanced in heavy rain during the night of the 12th/13th October. They had to cross a broad stream bridged only by a single plank at Richebourg - St. Waast, under shell and rifle fire. The Lincolns suffered their first casualties since the transfer of the B.E.F. from the Aisne, when 4 men were wounded. The Battalion lay down to await further orders after crossing the stream, as there was no room for them in the firing line. Several conflicting orders were then received culminating in a move to Lacouture to reinforce the 14th Infantry Brigade, 5th Division.

On the 14th, 'B' Company was sent to support the Manchesters of the 14th Brigade and, later, 'A' Company, with a machine gun, was despatched to reinforce the Duke of Cornwall's Light Infantry. The next day, the two Companies rejoined the Battalion and they marched back to the Brigade at Vieille Chapelle. The Lincolns relieved the 2nd Royal Irish Regiment (8th Brigade) near Rouge Croix on the 16th October, entrenching at a cross roads. The Battalion then advanced to the south of Aubers where they drove the enemy's rearguard from a ridge and took up a line beyond the road through Bas Wailly and L'Aventure. This was in advance of the general alignment of II Corps and so, leaving an outpost line of 'A' and 'B' Companies, the remainder of the Battalion withdrew to La Cliqueterie Farm for the night.

The village of Herlies was captured by the Lincolns on the 17th. For the last 1000 yards, the Battalion made short rushes, lying down between each advance and finally carried the enemy position with the bayonet. Unfortunately, the Divisional artillery, not knowing the village was captured, then shelled it, forcing the Lincolns to withdraw until firing ceased. By the time the Battalion advanced again, most of the Germans had escaped although 40 prisoners were taken. The Lincolns' losses were 3 killed and 83 wounded, 1 fatally. On the 19th, the Lincolns relieved the Royal Scots Fusiliers in the front line and were under attack each day until the 9th Brigade withdrew on the 23rd. During that time, the Battalion suffered 34 killed and wounded.

The 9th Brigade fell back to a line on the Richebourg - Armentieres road, with the Lincolns acting as rearguard. The Germans tried to advance on the 24th October but were driven back. Further enemy attacks on the 25th cost the Battalion 23 casualties. All ranks were exhausted and relief on the 26th was much appreciated. However, only a few hours' rest was possible as the Lincolns were required to support the 7th Brigade at Neuve

Chapelle at 3.30 p.m. the same day! 'C' Company, joined by 'B' Company shortly before dawn on the 27th, was ordered to reinforce the Wiltshires and 'A' and 'D', the West Kents. At 11 a.m., the Lincolns, with the Royal Fusiliers and the South Lancs., were detailed to recapture Neuve Chapelle.

The Regiments advanced at 3 p.m. with the Lincolns on the left. The right and centre were held up and, after going forward only 800 yards, the Lincolns were forced to shelter behind walls, tree trunks and other cover as available. When it became dark, primitive trenches were dug but the ground was so sodden that these trenches were only ditches of mud and water. The continual fighting and lack of sleep took their toll; if a man sat down he was instantly asleep. On that day, the Battalion lost 14 killed, 74 wounded and 7 missing; however the Lincolns held their trenches until the 30th, with relief by an Indian battalion on the 29th being delayed by heavy German fire. Eventually, they withdrew before dawn on the 30th but about 10 a.m., they were ordered to return to Neuve Chapelle. As they moved off, their destination was changed to Estaires. The Lincolns were moving from the area of the Battle of La Bassée to that of the Battle of Armentieres. However, the Regiment was only briefly at Estaires as at 6.45 a.m. on the 31st, it marched to Kemmel, 12 miles away, where, together with the 1st Northumberland Fusiliers, it reinforced the 2nd Cavalry Division. This was in the area of the Battle of Messines.

Confronting odds of about 12 to 1, the 415 men of the composite Household Cavalry Regiment were driven from Wytschaete and the Lincolns, the Northumberland Fusiliers and the 3rd Hussars were ordered to retake the village. The Lincolns went forward in two lines but, inspite of a gallant advance against strongly entrenched German forces and shellfire from their own gunners, they were forced to retreat. By now many losses had reduced the Lincolns to less than 100 all ranks and they withdrew towards Kemmel. However, at Lindhoek, they were joined by 3 Special Reserve Officers and about 100 stragglers. The Battalion was then 175 strong. At Kemmel, the Lincolns, encouraged by their Brigadier, bravely maintained their position, preventing the Germans seizing the tactically important Hill, but during the two days' fighting they sustained over 300 casualties. Lieutenant General Edmund Allenby, commanding the Cavalry Corps, wrote: 'the Lincolns, King's Own Scottish Borderers, King's Own Yorkshire Light Infantry and the Northumberland Fusiliers … arrived at a very critical time and their arrival saved the situation. I fear that they have suffered severe loss, but they fought brilliantly.'

After a short spell in billets, the Lincolns, with the rest of the 9th Brigade, marched from Bailleul to Hell Fire Corner on the Menin Road on the 6th November. The Battalion, with the Northumberland Fusiliers and the Bedfords, were ordered to counter-attack the Germans and retake some lost trenches, but not all the lost ground was recovered. Eventually, a line 100 yards short of the previous British position was entrenched. Tree roots and water-logged ground prevented deep trenches being dug and the Lincolns, subjected to heavy shell-fire and infantry attacks between the 8th and 10th, suffered casualties.

In the battle of Nonne Bosschen, between the 11th and 13th November, the Lincolns defeated tremendous German attacks, despite more losses. As the enemy gained ground on the left, the Lincolns were ordered to withdraw about 200 yards. After dark, on the 16th, the Battalion was relieved. On the 19th, 'A' Company was sent to reinforce the Northumberland Fusiliers, and 'B' and 'D' Companies to assist the cavalry. Later, the Regiment was sent to relieve the West Kents south east of Zillebeke. For more than a mile, the road, with mud knee-high, was impassable, so detours into fields were made. However, the relief was completed by midnight. The Lincolns spent a bitterly cold day on the 20th, close to the German trenches until relieved by French troops.

After a few days' rest, the 9th Brigade marched to Kemmel where the Battalion remained in trenches until the 30th. There followed another spell of rest before the Lincolns returned to the trenches at Kemmel on the 6th December. Men used fascines and wooden planks at the bottom of waterlogged trenches and wrapped straw round their boots and legs in a vain attempt to keep dry. An attack on German trenches on the 8th December was repulsed, despite brave crossing of no man's land. The men were stiff, wet and cold from being in the trenches and the advance was made over water-filled shell holes and slippery, muddy ground. On the 9th, the Battalion was relieved before one further tour in front line trenches between the 21st and 24th. New Year's Eve saw the Lincolns return to the front line.

The 2nd Battalion of the Regiment returned from Bermuda via Canada and joined the 25th Infantry Brigade of the 8th Division. They arrived in France, after re-equipping and training, on the 6th November 1914, taking over trenches at Laventie on the 14th. The frost and snow were especially trying having arrived from a warm, sunny climate. On the 23rd November, Lieutenant E.H. Impey and 8 men, covered in white sheets to merge with the snow-clad ground, successfully carried out the Battalion's first trench raid. They withdrew without loss after firing down the enemy trench. Trench raids were carried out with the object of capturing prisoners to obtain information. The Battalion moved on the 1st March 1915 to billets in La Gorgue, near Estaires, for intensive training. Between the 10th and 13th March 1915 the Battalion took part in the Battle of Neuve Chapelle. The original plan was to reach a position on the Illies – Aubers Ridge so as to threaten German communications between La Bassée and Lille. However, the French were heavily engaged in Champagne in February and March so no co-operation from them was possible. In view of this, the British High Command realized that it was only feasible to advance part of the way to the top of Aubers Ridge. Neuve Chapelle was to be captured first with the resulting gap in the German defences enlarged by simultaneous attacks to left and right.

The 8th and Meerut Divisions were detailed to take Neuve Chapelle. The 25th and 23rd Brigades of the 8th Division assaulted on the left. The 25th went forward on a front of 400 yards, with the 2nd Royal Berkshire Regiment on the right and the 2nd Lincolns on the left. Artillery fire began at 7.30 a.m. when 18–pounder guns, firing shrapnel, cut the enemy's wire entanglements, while other guns shelled selected German–held areas. Later, howitzers concentrated on the village while 18-pounders and 13-pounders put down a screen of fire east of Neuve Chapelle. The second bombardment lasted 30 minutes with about 350 guns taking part. Some tall poplar trees on their right gave a definite objective to the 2nd Lincolns.

Artillery fire destroyed most of the enemy wire except for a stretch of 400 yards on the left, and the German front-line trenches were practically obliterated. At 8.05 a.m., the barrage lifted off the front-line trenches and the 2nd Lincolns, who had suffered casualties from the British guns, advanced across no man's land. Germans emerged from cover and met the assaulting troops with rifle and machine gun fire. However, the 2nd Battalion captured the front-line trenches on their front with the loss of about 20 men.

Between the first and second German lines, the Battalion's Commanding Officer, Lieutenant Colonel George McAndrew, was mortally wounded. As he lay dying, he asked to see the 2nd Lincolns advancing. The Battalion Diary recorded that 'He died asking after his Regiment, without any complaint of the pain he was suffering'. The Battalion advanced, bridging a dyke with a plank. Unfortunately, British shells started to fall amongst the Lincolns on the far side of the dyke and they had to retreat 50 yards. As planned, the 1st Royal Irish Rifles passed through the Battalion, who then re-crossed the water and began to entrench their position. The results of the assault on the 10th March were the capture of Neuve Chapelle and a British advance of about 1,200 yards on a 4,000-yard front, but the Lincolns' losses were heavy.

The attack was resumed on the 11th March. The objective of the 7th and 8th Divisions was to be the line La Cliqueterie Farm – La Plouich – Rouges Bancs. The 23rd Infantry Brigade was ordered to take over the 25th Brigade line and support the 24th Brigade, which was to launch the attack by the 8th Division. The Lincolns remained in their trench, at one time under 'horribly exact' shell-fire, for two hours. At about 12.15 p.m., communication with Brigade Headquarters having failed, Major Samuel FitzGibbon Cox, commanding the Battalion, moved it into Neuve Chapelle in support of the Royal Irish Rifles. The Lincolns stayed in the village through the night of the 11th/12th March then returned to their trench. The British attack on the 11th failed to make any significant progress likewise a German counter-attack on the 12th. The Lincolns remained in their trenches through the 12th and the following night, while the opposing forces consolidated their lines. The Battalion carried out several reliefs and moved to a reserve position on the Tilleloy road on the 17th. At Neuve Chapelle the 2nd Lincolns lost over 300 killed and wounded.

Meanwhile, the 1st Battalion had spent January and some of February in a comparatively quiet part of the line east of Kemmel. With the rest of the 9th Brigade, the Battalion was ordered to Ypres on the 17th February and moved into the trenches on the 21st. 'B' Company found themselves up to their knees in water and mud with Germans actually in the same trench, 15 yards away, with only traverses in between. In places, the enemy were in the rear of the Battalion and sentries had to be posted back and front!

About the middle of March the 1st Lincolns were moved to the Hill 60 sector and, on the 2nd April, to near St. Eloi, in the most exposed part of the line. An officer called this period the most trying he experienced while serving with the Battalion. The Brigade, and the Battalion, were moved from one danger spot to another and retained in each until they gained mastery over the Germans, before being transferred elsewhere to repeat the process.

On the 22nd April, the 1st Battalion relieved the 1st Duke of Cornwall's Light Infantry in front-line trenches astride the Comines-Ypres Canal. The German front line was from 130 to 300 yards away. Enemy rifle-fire caused on average 2 casualties to each Company in every relief during the 5 weeks' tour in the trenches. This was in the First Battle of Ypres. On the 2nd May, mouth gags, soaked in soda and water, were issued to the Battalion to combat the German gas attacks. On the 5th, gas was spotted, and mouth gags and sprays containing carbonate of soda were used successfully.

The Lincolns held the Germans in check by rifle and machine gun fire, throwing bombs, harassing working parties, patrolling and blowing up enemy strong points. Nevertheless, the cost was great. The casualties were chiefly caused during reliefs and in the support and reserve lines. On the 26th May, the Battalion was relieved and between the 1st and 5th June the 1st Lincolns supported the 6th Cavalry Brigade around Hooge and Zouave Wood. The 2nd Lincolns, as part of the 25th Brigade of the 8th Division, took part in the Battle of Aubers Ridge on the 9th May 1915. After an artillery bombardment, the 2nd Rifle Brigade and Royal Irish Rifles advanced with the 2nd Lincolns following in the rear. In spite of heavy losses, the leading companies stormed the German lines and reached the first objective: the bend of the Fromelles road. 'A' and 'B' Companies of the Lincolns got to the enemy breastworks but further progress was impossible.

'C' and 'D' Companies were ordered forward as other troops withdrew from assaulting German trenches. The retreating troops were checked by Brigadier General Arthur Lowry Cole but were unable to advance again as heavy fire swept no man's land. However, 'C' and 'D' Companies got through the enemy lines to the west of the 13th Londons. 'C' Company took possession of part of the German trench and awaited further orders, but enemy machine gun fire meant that it was 4 p.m. before an order to retire was received and 8 p.m. before the retreat began. A party of 'A' Company, caught in no man's land, also returned under cover of darkness.

It was on that day that Acting Corporal Charles Richard Sharpe (1889-1963) won the first Victoria Cross gained by the Regiment since the Indian Mutiny, nearly 60 years before. Corporal Sharpe, who came from Pickworth near Sleaford, was the only Regimental V.C. to be born in Lincolnshire. He led a small blocking party sent to take part of a German trench at Rouges Bancs. His citation in the London Gazette of the 29th June stated: 'He was the first to reach the enemy's position and using bombs with great determination and effect, he himself cleared them out of a trench fifty yards long. By this time all his party had fallen and he was then joined by four other men, with whom he attacked the enemy again with bombs, and captured a further trench two hundred and fifty yards long.' As darkness fell on the 9th May, the 25th Brigade was relieved. The Battalion, having suffered nearly 300 casualties, got to their billets in Bac St. Maur at 2 a.m. on the 10th. The unexpected strength of the German positions meant that the battle was a failure despite the courage and resolution displayed by British soldiers.

Chapter 7

FROM BELLEWARDE TO THE BLUFF

The next operation involving the 1st Lincolns was the attack on the German-held Bellewaarde Ridge, which dominated the British defences. The assault was to be carried out by the 7th and 9th Brigades of the 3rd Division. The Battalion and the rest of the 9th Brigade practised the attack between the 6th and 15th June 1915, trying out a grey flannel helmet with a celluloid window as an anti-gas device. The material tucked into the neck of the soldier's tunic so that he could breathe only the air within the device but it had to be removed from time to time to avoid suffocation.

The bombardment began at 2.30 a.m. on the 16th June and continued with pauses until 4.15 a.m. when the artillery lifted and the first British line captured the German front line with little resistance. The 1st Lincolns were in the second line, with the 1/10th Liverpool Scottish, and advanced without any problems as the artillery fire had destroyed the enemy barbed-wire entanglements and made the trenches untenable. The second stage of the attack, which was to get to the Hooge - Bellewaarde Farm road, was also accomplished before difficulties arose.

The infantry had a timed artillery programme and were told that if the enemy resistance was light, they should send a message for the artillery to lift so that progress could continue. The final objective was the trench on the side of the Bellewaarde Lake but all telephone wires had been cut by shellfire. The early morning mist and smoke from the shells prevented the artillery observers seeing the flags carried by the infantry to indicate their arrival at various objectives. When the British guns lifted from the second objective, the Lincolns ' got ten minutes of the very best' plus German gunfire.

Further problems were caused by crowds of disorganised men in the trenches. Command and control became impossible. Heavy, accurate enemy artillery fire on the 3rd Division was followed by three German counter-attacks. At 9.30 a.m., with no bombs left, the British fell back to the first line of enemy trenches. About 12 hours later, the 1st Lincolns were relieved.

After the attack on Bellewaarde, the Battalion spent some time in the Ypres area, sometimes in the trenches at Sanctuary Wood, where they were relieved by the 1/4th and 1/5th Lincolns on the 30th June. The usual record in the Diary of the 1st Battalion was 'Conditions on our front normal' or 'All quiet' but each day there were casualties. On the 13th November, the Battalion was transferred to the 62nd Infantry Brigade of the 21st Division, in which it served to the end of the war. The Battalion moved to the Somme area on the 31st March 1916 but did not go into the trenches until the end of May, being engaged in preparations for attack.

The 1/4th and 1/5th (Territorial Force) Battalions of the Regiment had landed at Le Havre on the 1st March 1915, both Battalions being in the 138th Brigade, 46th

Division. After instruction in trench duties, they took over front - line trenches opposite Spanbrek Mollen on the 9th April. The 1/5th Battalion Diary recorded the wretched condition of the trenches including one where 'dead bodies are even half exposed in the parados'. Constant German artillery fire fell on farms held by the 1/4th Battalion whilst the 1/5th kept the enemy trenches under fire to assist operations at Hill 60. A great deal of work was carried out on the defences and a German attack was repulsed on the 13th May.

About mid-June, the 46th Division moved to the southern part of the Ypres Salient. The 1/4th Lincolns went into dugouts in Sanctuary Wood and Maple Copse on the 29th of that month, relieving the 1st Lincolns and the South Lancs. east of the Wood on the 30th. The 1/4th Lincolns were constantly under attack, even in support and reserve casualties were frequent. Tours in the front line from the 3rd to 8th and the 15th to 21st September saw the Battalion suffer further casualties. The 1/5th were relieved from the trenches east of Kemmel on the 21st June. They took over a trench east of Ypres from the 1st Lincolns and one from the 4th Fusiliers on the 30th. A strenuous time followed with a lot of damage from German 'whizz–bangs', but the Battalion snipers completely silenced those of the enemy. However, as with the 1/4th Battalion, there were constant losses during the 1/5th's tours in the front line and when in support and reserve. Much damage was caused by the German 'whizz-bangs' and 'crumps'. On hearing an officer from the Armentieres direction complain of 'nasty whizz-bangs' being 'quite dreadful', an officer of the Lincolns commented 'if only they could come here and learn that for every 'whizz-bang' that went over him we got about fifty 'crumps': one looks upon 'whizz-bangs' as gnats round here'. Terrific shell-fire was suffered on the 17th September and the British artillery did not respond to calls for retaliation. This led to the Battalion Diary grousing 'If some of the 'office' officers who arrange bombardments… would only spend a day in the trenches… while the enemy is bombarding them, then perhaps they would see the necessity for artillery support'. The 7th (Service) Battalion of the Regiment disembarked at Boulogne as part of the 51st Brigade, 17th Division, on the 14th July 1915 and 'B' Company went into the trenches on the 27th. Further front line tours followed in August and September.

Against his better judgement, Sir John French was forced to commit British forces to an attack at Loos by the general situation of the Allies and the local state of affairs in France. The Germans were making good progress against the Russians and the news from Gallipoli was depressing. Moreover, there were reports that the French government was concerned about lack of support from Britain. The main assault was to be made between Lens and La Bassée Canal by I and IV Corps of the First Army. Sir John French retained a general reserve in his own hands comprising XI Corps and two cavalry corps. The 8th Lincolns, a Service Battalion, were in the 63rd Brigade, 21st Division of XI Corps and took part in the main operations. The 1/4th and 1/5th Battalions were behind the lines in reserve and were later to be actively engaged at the Hohenzollern Redoubt on the 13th October. The 2nd Battalion took part in the subsidiary action of Bois Grenier.

The 8th Lincolns landed at Boulogne on the 11th September and, like all of the 21st Division, they had never been under fire. The Division made a difficult advance on the evening of the 25th September. It was dark, there were shell holes in which to stumble, dead bodies over which to fall, rifle and machine gun fire, shells screaming and loud explosions all around. After some fighting at Chalk Pit Wood, the remainder of the night was spent improving shallow trenches begun by other battalions in hard chalky soil. German artillery responded to the rifle fire of the 8th Lincolns at about 8.15 a.m. on the 26th September.

The attack by the Battalion on the 26th September resulted in an initial gain of 700 yards but this was reduced to 400 yards as the Lincolns were driven back owing to lack of support. A resolute counter-attack at the Bois Hugo by the enemy saw the loss of the trenches which had been occupied by 'A', 'B' and 'C' Companies and the three front line trenches of the West Yorks. Only the trench which held the two supporting companies of both battalions held out. Despite being practically surrounded, they did not retire until about 5.30 p.m. On the 27th, the remains of the Brigade finally concentrated about half a mile north west of Noyelles-les-Vermelles. The 8th Lincolns in their first battle lost almost 500 of all ranks, and they did not take over a portion of the front line until the 13th November, followed by periods in the trenches in the spring of 1916. The 1st Battalion relieved the 8th on the 22nd May in the line opposite Fricourt. At the end of June, the 8th was ordered to support the 8th Somersets in the attack on the German positions on the 1st July.

After the battle of Aubers Ridge, the 2nd Lincolns spent some time in the Laventie area, either in the trenches or in billets. The 8th Division was ordered to attack the Germans at Bois Grenier, with the 2nd taking part in the operations opposite Le Bridoux. This was a subsidiary action intended to divert the enemy's attention from the main attack at Loos. The Battalion was allotted a frontage of about 275 yards with the 2nd Royal Berkshires on their right. Artillery fire opened on enemy trenches at 4.25 a.m. on the 25th September. A sunken mine, running from the Lincolnshire trenches across to the German lines, exploded four minutes later. The excavation caused by the explosion was intended to form a communication trench. One minute afterwards, the Lincolns advanced across no man's land.

'D' Company, on the left, reached the German front line and, attacking along the enemy trench, linked up with the Berkshires. Violent counter-attacks were launched by the Germans and the supply of bombs ran out. Despite support by a platoon of 'A' Company of the Lincolns and part of two companies of the Royal Irish Rifles, pressure on both flanks and the front drove the British back. Unfortunately, the right of the Battalion had been forced to its left owing to a bombing attack on the Berkshires, while the left of the Lincolns was forced to the right. This led to the trenches becoming congested. A further supply of bombs came to hand and part of the trench to the right was retaken, only to be lost later. The Lincolns held their position until 5 p.m. when they were forced to give up their gains. The Battalion's left flank was exposed, and orchards, communication and other trenches afforded the enemy cover in rear, front and flank positions to discharge bombs and trench mortars. The Brigade narrative later drew attention to the need for lots of bombs of one pattern with a reliable mechanical lighting apparatus. Men could then be drilled, as with a rifle, so that movements became automatic. As it was, men forgot how to use the different bombs; fuses and matches got damp and many bombs were thrown unlighted. Casualties in the 2nd Battalion during this action were over 300.

After being relieved at 9 p.m., they did not return to front-line trenches until the 2nd October, at Bois Grenier. There followed a routine of service in the trenches and occasional periods behind the line until the 2nd Lincolns went from Merville to the Somme in March 1916, where they took over front-line trenches opposite La Boisselle. As one of the assaulting battalions of the 25th Brigade, 8th Division, they moved to their assembly position on the 30th June.

Before the 2nd Battalion left the Bois Grenier sector, the 10th Battalion (The Grimsby Chums) arrived there in the 101st Brigade, 34th Division. This Battalion had landed in France on the 9th January 1916. After an initiation in trench warfare, it was assigned to the Bois Grenier sector from February until the 8th April, when it marched to Eperleques. After resting, training and tours in the frontline, the Battalion went into the trenches on the Somme on the 28th June.

The 1st Lincolns did not, as a whole, take part in the attack at Bellewaarde on the 25th September 1915 but the Battalion bombers were engaged. At 8.15 p.m., the Battalion Headquarters took over the HQ dugouts and the Companies went into the trenches. The 1/4th and 1/5th Lincolns went into front-line trenches adjoining Hill 60 on the 26th September 1915. On the 30th, the enemy exploded a mine under Trench 47, held by the 1/5th, accompanied by a heavy bombardment. The following day both Battalions were relieved. An officer of the 1/5th said: 'We turned our backs on the Ypres Salient with great satisfaction.'

The 46th Division was attached to XI Corps and moved south to the Bethune area to take part in an attack on the Hohenzollern Redoubt. Accordingly, the 1/4th and 1/5th Lincolns marched to Hesdigneul on the 6th October for six days' practice of attack in open warfare. The 46th Division was ordered to capture the Hohenzollern Redoubt and Fosse No. 8 and the 12th Division to take the Quarries and establish communication with the 46th who advanced with the 137th Brigade on the right and the 138th on the left. In the 138th Brigade, the 1/4th Leicesters were on the right and the 1/5th Lincolns on the left, in the first line. The 1/4th Lincolns were in support and the 1/1st Monmouths in third-line trenches with the 1/5th Leicesters in reserve.

The Hohenzollern Redoubt was an oval-shaped work pushed forward from Fosse Trench which was the German main line. The Redoubt was situated on slightly rising ground and attached to Fosse Trench by several communication trenches. The attack of the two front-line battalions was to pass over the Redoubt without pause and go on to take Fosse Trench. There was to be a preliminary bombardment, then the guns would lift their fire and the infantry would advance covered by gas and smoke. The 1/4th Lincolns were to follow 100 yards behind the front-line battalions, clearing by bombing all trenches passed over by the 1/4th Leicesters and the 1/5th. The 1/1st Monmouths were to occupy the Hohenzollern Redoubt and connect it to the British front line. The 1/5th Leicesters were to take over the front-line British trenches after the attacking troops had left.

At 12 noon, on the 13th October 1915, the artillery opened fire. The Germans responded with increasingly heavy fire. At 1 p.m., with the wind favourable, gas was unleashed against the enemy lines, and smoke bombs were thrown. In addition to fierce enemy shelling, the ground over which the infantry was to advance was swept by German machine gun fire. The 1/4th Leicesters and 1/5th Lincolns, in four lines, went forward at 2 p.m. They crossed no man's land and entered the Redoubt but were cut down by machine gun and rifle fire when they attempted to reach Fosse Trench. The 1/5th went into battle with about 23 officers and 850 men, and only 1 officer and about 110 men survived. Captain R.E. Madge, who commanded the machine gun section, said 'Nothing could have been more admirable than the way the men behaved in this, their first battle'. On the night of the 13th/14th October, the 1/5th Battalion held the west face of the Hohenzollern Redoubt. The Diary of the 1/4th Lincolns stated: 'Redoubt taken, but at heavy cost. Incessant bombing, machine-gun and rifle-fire all the evening, also shelling. Gas and smoke were used to cover the advance but apparently with little damage to the enemy'. Many gallant deeds were performed by men of the Regiment at the Hohenzollern Redoubt. On being relieved, both battalions withdrew to the second-line trenches on the 14th October and were relieved again that evening. These were black days of the First World War for Lincolnshire. The 1/4th Battalion lost 172 men killed, the 1/5th 195 killed with about twice as many wounded.

November 1915 was spent by the 1/4th and 1/5th Lincolns in the front line near Neuve Chapelle. The ground was terrible and the only cover was breastworks of sandbags which were often levelled by rain and enemy shellfire. Trenches were impossible. Only two days were passed in the front line in December, then the 46th Division was posted to Egypt, where Lord Kitchener thought reinforcements were required. The 1/4th and 1/5th Battalions arrived at Alexandria on the 13th January 1916. At night, each battalion in turn provided an outpost line round their camp east of the Suez Canal. The evacuation of the Gallipoli Peninsula, discussed later, released many troops for service in Egypt and so the 46th Division moved back to France, arriving at Marseilles on the 9th February.

The 1/5th went into front-line trenches near Villers-au-Bois and the 1/4th moved to the support line in the Talus des Zouaves. The 1/5th engaged the enemy on the 12th March, while the 1/4th had a tour in the front line beginning on the 14th. Both Battalions were with the 51st Brigade north of Arras until the 9th May. They were then engaged in making fascines and similar work at Sus-St. Léger until the 21st. After this, the 1/4th Battalion went to Foncquevillers and the 1/5th to Bienvillers, both being employed digging communication trenches. On the 27th June, the 1/4th went into front-line trenches opposite Gommecourt. A raid on the enemy lines was made on the night of the 29th/30th. No prisoners were taken, although this and ascertaining the condition of the German trenches had been the objectives. A false trench was dug during the night of the 30th which was successful in drawing enemy artillery fire on the 1st July. The 1/5th Battalion was in Divisional Reserve at Warlincourt on the night of the 30th June.

The 7th Lincolns were near Ypres, an area of spasmodic, vigorous German action, from the 25th September to the end of 1915. The Battalion went to Maple Copse towards the end of October and to a new sector north of the Menin Road on the 10th November. Water was knee-deep, it rained incessantly and trench foot caused enormous problems. Trench foot was a common ailment caused by exposing the feet too long to cold water. The feet turned blue and red and became a mass of chilblains, and in extreme cases gangrene could set in. A soldier needed to keep an eye on his feet, have frequent changes of sock and apply grease or whale oil as necessary. Platoon commanders had to carry out frequent foot inspections. Another problem was trench fever due to lice and which had symptoms of typhoid and influenza, although it was not often fatal. On the 17th November, after intense suffering, the 7th were relieved. Conditions were so bad that, in December, tours in these trenches were reduced to forty-eight hours. There were constant casualties. In January 1916, the Battalion was relieved for rest and training at Hellebrouck near St. Omer. On the 7th February, the 7th returned to the trenches at the Bluff. This was a position of great importance for observation. However, the Germans held the eastern margin of the crest with support on the reverse slope.

On the 14th February, after hours of intense gun and mortar fire, followed by the explosion of three mines, the enemy attacked on the side of the Bluff near the Ypres-Comines Canal. The 52nd Brigade held the right of the British line, the 51st the left. The front of the latter brigade was held by the 10th Sherwood Foresters on the right and the 8th South Staffords on the left. The 7th Lincolns were in support and the 7th Borders in reserve. The enemy advanced and companies of the Lincolns were sent to reinforce the Sherwood Foresters. During the night of the 14th/15th, a British counter-attack, in which 'C' Company took part, was made on New Year trench but was driven back. On the 15th, the crest of the Bluff and the trenches north of it as far as the Ravine were held by the enemy but the support line remained in British hands. That day, the Lincolns, with the exception of 'D' Company, which was attached to the 8th South Staffords, were relieved.

A counter-attack took place on the same day by the 51st Brigade, reinforced by the 6th Dorsets and the East Yorkshires. The Lincolns and Sherwood bombers were to bomb towards Trench 32 and, on reaching the front line, the Sherwoods were to turn north and bomb towards the Borders and South Staffords; the Lincolns, assisted by other bombers, to turn south and work down Trenches 31 and 31A. Although the attack continued all night from 9 p.m., no progress was made. The 7th Lincolns held their position throughout the day until relieved at 1 a.m. on the 17th. Major General Pilcher, commanding the 17th Division, sent a message stating: 'He considers that the behaviour of every unit of this Brigade (51st) during the last few days has been magnificent and entirely worthy of the famous regiments to which they belong. He considers no troops could have done more than was done by this Brigade'. The Battalion lost over 100 men between the 14th and 17th February.

The 7th did not return to the front-line until the 1st March when it took part in an attempt to recover the Bluff. It was decided to alter the routine of two short bursts of artillery fire with a pause in between which preceded an assault. The enemy would remain under cover until after the second burst of fire. Thus, at 4 a.m. on the 2nd March, the 76th Brigade, with the 7th Lincolns and the 10th Sherwoods, crawled towards the German wire. At 4.30 a.m., there was one burst of fire, the British infantry attacked and took the Germans by surprise. The artillery reopened fire on the enemy's communications and the German front line was quickly captured with steady progress in the support trenches. The 7th were ordered to assist the 9th King's Own, who assaulted the Bean Salient, and the 1st Gordons, who attacked trenches in the north-west corner of the Bean. 'D' Company was sent to assist the second attack made by the 1st Gordons on their objective. Despite casualties, the Bluff was recaptured.

General Sir Herbert Plumer praised the Battalion during an inspection later that month. The 7th Lincolns were relieved on the 3rd March and did not return to front line duties near Armentieres until the 19th. In the middle of May, the Battalion, with other units of its brigade, went into training at Hellebrouck before leaving for the Somme on the 11th June. Then, on the 30th, they moved to Morlancourt.

Chapter 8
THE GALLIPOLI CAMPAIGN

The 6th (Service) Battalion of the Regiment was part of the 11th (Northern) Division, which reinforced General Sir Ian Hamilton's command in the Gallipoli operations. This campaign was a flanking movement intended to capture Constantinople, which might knock Turkey out of the War, and assist Britain's allies, the Russians, who were hard pressed in the Caucasus by the Turks. The Division consisted of the 32nd, 33rd and 34th Infantry Brigades; the 6th being in the 33rd. The Brigade, raised at Grantham in August 1914, had sailed from Liverpool on the 1st July 1915 and disembarked from lighters on 'V' Beach, Cape Helles, on the 18th. Other brigade units landed where they could due to shelling of the beaches. The Brigade was not collected until noon the next day, north-west of Sedd-el-Bahr, when they took over front-line positions, which extended about 1,000 yards across the Achi Baba Nullah with its left almost at Krithia. The 6th Lincolns went into the front line on the 21st July and at once began to strengthen the trenches despite enemy sniping. After six days, they went into reserve but remained under shellfire. A short tour in the forward trenches ended when the 6th Lincolns were relieved on the night of the 1st/2nd August. The period at Helles battle-hardened the Battalion but the filth, stench and flies, which caused dysentery, badly affected them. The 33rd Brigade joined the two other brigades of the 11th Division on Imbros.

With the object of cutting off the Turks opposing the British and French troops operating from the south, and in conjunction with an attack from Anzac, the 11th Division landed at Suvla Bay on the night of the 6th/7th August. The soldiers had practised embarking and disembarking from lighters for several days. However, only three destroyers and three lighters were allotted to the 33rd Brigade and the troops suffered much discomfort, being packed together. The Division was to secure the landings on beaches 'B', 'C' and 'A' and Suvla Bay, for the disembarkation of the 10th Division and stores. The 33rd Brigade (less two battalions) was to secure the right flank of the Division by taking up a position from the right of the landing place ('B' Beach) to the south-eastern corner of the Salt Lake.

In the dark, with lights out, the 33rd Brigade landed on 'B' Beach at 11.30 p.m., unopposed apart from Turkish snipers. The 7th South Staffords and 9th Sherwood Foresters were first ashore. The rest of the Brigade, including the Lincolns, followed in Divisional Reserve. The 34th Brigade's landing at 'A' Beach was opposed but, with help from the 32nd, they finally got ashore. The 32nd Brigade advanced to support the 34th along a narrow isthmus between Lala Baba and Hill 10. The 6th Lincolns and other troops in Divisional Reserve advanced behind the 32nd Brigade. After a halt at daybreak, the Lincolns moved at 2 p.m. in support of the 10th Division to seize Chocolate Hill (otherwise known as Hill 53).

'C' and 'D' Companies of the Battalion, supported by 'A' and 'B' Companies, set off immediately with the 6th Borders. The final advance, in extended order and parade-ground formation, was over the Salt Lake itself, which was dry but covered with caked mud making movement difficult. Enemy fire was heavy but, in short rushes, 'A' and 'B' Companies of the Lincolns with the Dublin Fusiliers advanced up the slope to some dead ground about 100 yards from the crest. Here they halted for half an hour while the divisional artillery and machine gun sections fired on the Turkish positions above. Then, with the order to charge, the Lincolns, inspite of losses nearing 100, captured Chocolate Hill. During the night, this position, which, with Karakol Dagh, was the most important ground seized on the 7th August, was occupied by the 31st Brigade. Captain Percy Hansen, temporarily in command of the Lincolns, with an officer of the Borders reconnoitred to Ismail Oglu Tepe (Hill W) without opposition. Hansen asked permission to take the hill, but was ordered in writing to withdraw to Lala Baba. The hill was never captured and its possession by the Turks cost thousands of lives.

The Lincolns with the Border Regiment and the South Staffords were ordered, on the 8th August, to attack the Anafarta Ridge on a frontage of about 1,800 yards. In view of the ground and extent of front, only a frontal attack was possible. The Brigade Commander, Brigadier General Robert Maxwell, was informed that the high ground from Scimitar Hill to the north, and the west of Anafarta, was held by British troops so that his left flank was secure. At 2 a.m., on the 9th, the Battalion left their bivouacs to attack. However, Scimitar Hill was held by Turks, who had been reinforced. British troops who had been in possession of Scimitar Hill, were withdrawn on the night of the 8th/9th August but the 33rd Brigade was not informed. Heavy fire, together with burning scrub, made an advance impossible and Lieutenant Colonel M. P. Phelps, commanding the 6th Lincolns, had to order a retreat. Battalion casualties were over 400 out of 578.

Captain Percy Howard Hansen (1890-1951), the Adjutant, called for volunteers and dashed through smoke and bullets into the burning scrub. Six times he went 300 yards into the inferno at Yilghin Burnu and rescued six men from certain death. For his courageous action, he was awarded the Victoria Cross. Hansen, who rose to the rank of Brigadier, was born in Dresden, Germany, and, during his career, also won the D.S.O. and the M.C. Many of the wounded were burned alive; none of the missing was ever seen again.

The 33rd Brigade dug in while, on the 10th August, the 53rd Division failed in a further attempt to take the Anafarta Ridge. Another attack in the afternoon was also unsuccessful but the 33rd Brigade, including the Lincolns, held on to the front occupied on the 9th. The Lincolns were relieved on the 12th and rested on the beach, where they remained until the 20th. The Battalion was so reduced in numbers, it was reorganised into two companies. The Turks entrenched all their positions, which commanded Suvla Bay, so that every part was exposed to fire from their guns. Reinforcements for the Turks could be brought up without being fired on or seen. The feature Ismail Oglu Tepe formed the south-western corner of the Anafarta Sagir Spur.

It was a hill, 350 feet high, with slopes covered with dense holly-oak scrub so attacking troops had to advance in single file along goat tracks between the bushes. West of Ismail Oglu Tepe was a strongly fortified Turkish redoubt at Hetman Chair.

An attack on these Turkish positions, known as the Battle of Scimitar Hill, was made on the 21st August. The 11th Division on the right and the 29th Division on the left were ordered to storm Ismail Oglu Tepe while the 53rd and 54th Divisions held the enemy from Sulajik to Kiretch Tepe. The 32nd and 34th Brigades of the 11th Division were to capture Hetman Chair and the 33rd Brigade was to drive home the attack over the highest point of the hill. The Brigade advanced from Lala Baba soon after 3 p.m. with the Sherwood Foresters leading followed by the Borders, South Staffords and then the Lincolns. Suddenly the 2nd Mounted Division, which was made up of dismounted Yeomanry regiments, appeared from the south-eastern corner of Lala Baba and broke through the line of march of the South Staffords. At that moment, heavy Turkish artillery fire opened, causing many casualties amongst the Yeomanry and others, and starting a bush fire which further disorganised the 33rd Brigade's advance. The South Staffords and the Lincolns moved to the right to avoid the artillery fire; however, the Battalion, less two platoons which followed the South Staffords, soon returned to their correct place in the fire zone.

The 32nd Brigade, instead of attacking Hetman Chair, lost direction and moved south of it. Consequently, the Sherwoods and Borders of the 33rd Brigade then attacked unsuccessfully. Lieutenant Colonel Phelps with about 80 men of the Lincolns remained in their fire trench, as ordered by Brigadier General Maxwell, it not being feasible to attack with them. Both their flanks were unsecured and there was no reserve behind them nearer than Lala Baba. The attack by the 29th Division also failed. At nightfall on the 22nd, the 33rd Brigade was relieved and marched back to Lala Baba. Their numbers were so reduced by casualties that they were temporarily organised into two battalions; the Lincolns and Borders forming No.1 Battalion. After a few days' rest at Lala Baba, the 33rd Brigade relieved the 161st Brigade on Kiretch Tepe Sirt. Here, as elsewhere on the battle-front, the digging of trench systems began. The ground was hard, with only two feet of soil above solid rock. The defences, therefore, often consisted of breastworks, insecure against rifle-fire. There were no dugouts. Life became a matter of sniping, bombing, night patrols and sickness. Dysentery was prevalent so that men struggled to carry stores from the beaches. Water was scarce and brackish. The bully beef went liquid in the heat. Fresh meat and bread were only issued twice a week. The flies were intolerable; it was an art to eat without taking in several flies with every mouthful at the same time. Ever present were unburied corpses and the stench of death although sea bathing was usually a safe relief. Nevertheless morale remained unbroken even though reinforcements also quickly succumbed to dysentery. On the 26th November, the hot, sultry weather dramatically ended in a blizzard. The trenches were flooded and several men drowned. Rain turned to snow, followed by nine degrees of frost with over 100 men of the Lincolns struck down with frostbite.

Suvla Bay was evacuated on the night of the 20th/ 21st December. On the last night, the Lincolns held the front line. Leaving behind a few lights, fires and various contrivances, which fired rifles at intervals to give the enemy the impression that the trenches were still held, the Battalion, covered by a rearguard, withdrew in parties to the second line. There, gaps were closed in the wire entanglements and a withdrawal was made to the third line and so on. The Lincolns embarked without a casualty and reached Alexandria on the 2nd February 1916.

Chapter 9
THE SOMME

The Somme offensive of 1916 had three objectives: to relieve German pressure on the French at Verdun; to assist Britain's allies in other theatres of war by stopping further transfer of German troops from the Western Front; and to wear down the strength of the enemy. Constant training and practice attacks were carried out as well as extensive preparations. Defences were maintained, communications and assembly trenches and dugouts were made ready. Huge stocks of ammunition and stores were collected into dumps and many miles of railways and trench tramways were constructed.

The German defences, on high ground, consisted of two main systems. Each had several lines of deep trenches, with bombproof shelters and dugouts, at depths which provided immunity from the heaviest shellfire. Among the German trenches, villages and woods were converted into fortresses while salients in their front-line trenches were self-contained forts, allowing no man's land to be swept by machine gun and rifle fire. Behind the enemy front line, strong redoubts and concrete emplacements had been built, from which his own trenches could be swept with fire. Barbed-wire entanglements, made of iron stakes interlaced with wire, often as thick as a man's finger, in places 40 yards wide, protected each system.

Seven battalions of the Lincolnshire Regiment were in the British front line on the 1st July. They were as follows:-

1st Battalion	62nd Brigade	21st Division
2nd Battalion	25th Brigade	8th Division
1/4th & 1/5th Battalions	138th Brigade	46th Division
7th Battalion	51st Brigade	17th Division
8th Battalion	63rd Brigade	21st Division
10th Battalion	101st Brigade	34th Division

The 1st, 2nd, 7th, 8th and 10th Battalions were to be engaged in the Albert area of operations. The 1/4th and 1/5th were in action at Gommecourt. The preliminary bombardment by 1513 guns opened on the 24th June with Zero Hour at 7.30 a.m. on the 1st July. Patrols reported that the German trenches had been badly damaged and it was believed that few men had survived the destruction wrought by the British artillery. It was anticipated that the enemy's first system of trenches, and possibly the second, would be rapidly taken.

Five minutes before Zero Hour, the 4th Middlesex and 8th Somersets with the foremost platoons of the 10th York and Lancaster on the right and the 8th Lincolns on the left advanced towards the German lines, but were met by violent machine gun fire. The British artillery fire lifted at 7.30 a.m. and the general advance began as machine gun and rifle fire tore gaps in the lines of advancing troops.

In minutes half of the 4th Middlesex and 8th Somersets were casualties in no man's land but the survivors passed over the enemy's front line and pressed on towards the second objective. The 8th Lincolns attacked with 'B' and 'C' Companies leading, supported by 'A' Company. 'D' Company followed behind as a carrying party with ammunition, bombs, picks and shovels and trench stores. The leading platoons lost half their number but the survivors crossed the German front line and entered the enemy communication trenches. Between 4 and 5 p.m., orders arrived from Divisional Headquarters for the 63rd Brigade to consolidate the positions held. When darkness fell, the 8th Lincolns were in line from Dart Alley to Lozenge Alley. The Battalion held its position that night, repulsing a German attack from the direction of Fricourt.

Long before darkness, the 1st Lincolns, in reserve with the 62nd Brigade, reached the German lines. They carried ammunition, Mills grenades and Stokes mortar bombs to a dump on a sunken road behind the enemy front line and then returned to consolidate a captured position while under machine gun and artillery fire. At 6 p.m., the 1st Lincolns were ordered to reinforce the 64th Brigade.

The 34th Division, on the left of the 21st Division, met similar costly resistance. The 101st Brigade attacked with the 15th Royal Scots on the right and the 10th Lincolns on the left. The 10th's objective was a German-held area known as the Bloater, between La Boisselle Salient and the Heligoland redoubt. A tremendous artillery barrage met the advance. The Divisional Commander, Major General E. C. Ingouville-Williams, said 'Never have I seen men go through such a barrage of artillery…They advanced as on parade and never flinched.' A few of the 10th managed to cross no man's land, which varied in depth from 100 to 800 yards, but could do no more. The 34th Division was relieved early on the 4th July.

The 8th Division was on the left of the 34th Division, with all its three brigades in the front line. The 25th Brigade was in the centre opposite Ovillers: the 2nd Royal Berkshires attacked on the right of the brigade and the 2nd Lincolns on the left, with the 1st Royal Irish Rifles in support and the 2nd Rifle Brigade in reserve. The troops advanced once the British barrage lifted and encountered severe rifle-fire and showers of bombs. After a hard fight, approximately 200 yards of German lines were captured by 7.50 a.m. with attempts made to consolidate in badly-damaged trenches but little cover was available. The Battalion remained in the enemy trenches for almost three hours but ammunition ran low and bombs were exhausted. The 2nd Lincolns first retired to shell holes in no man's land firing with ammunition collected from the wounded. Lieutenant Colonel Reginald Bastard, who commanded the Battalion, stated: 'As it was obvious we could do no good there, we retired to our own trench and reorganised to be ready for another attack if required. Orders were received from the 25th Brigade to withdraw to Ribble and Melling Streets and occupy the assembly dugouts, which was done.' He also said ' We went into the attack with 22 officers, all of whom were killed or wounded, except Leslie and myself, and we had bullet holes through our clothing. During the time I had the honour of commanding the 2nd

Battalion I never saw the men fight better; they were magnificent in the most trying and adverse conditions. The attack, though a failure, was a most glorious effort, and I was intensely proud of the Battalion.' At midnight, the 2nd Lincolns were relieved and went to Long Valley behind Albert. The 2nd Royal Berkshires, on the right of the 2nds, failed to take part of Ovillers and the 23rd Brigade, on the right of the 25th, suffered heavy losses. The 8th Division was relieved on the night of the 1st/2nd July.

The 138th Brigade in the 46th Division was in reserve when the Division's attack at the Gommecourt Salient ended in failure. Troops of the 46th and 56th (London) Divisions entered the German trenches but no support arrived due to the enemy barrage on no man's land and the British forces in the German trenches were wiped out or captured. The 1/4th Lincolns carried out a raid on the enemy lines on the 29th June and, during the night of the 30th June/1st July, they dug a false trench in front of the British lines to draw German fire. The Battalion was relieved at night on the 1st July.

The 1/5th Lincolns, at daybreak on the 1st July, were in reserve 1000 yards east of Souastre but at 8.30 a.m., they were sent to Midland Trench, west of Foncquevillers, where they spent the day under shell fire, losing 2 men. At 11 p.m., the Battalion was ordered to attack and consolidate the German front line. The orders were then changed and they were to contact the Sherwood Foresters and bring them back. At midnight on the 1st July, the front line platoons advanced but were halted by heavy enemy fire. The Divisional Commander cancelled another attack and the Battalion was withdrawn. On the night of the 3rd July, the 1/5th was relieved. The 7th Battalion was in reserve at Morlancourt throughout the daylight hours of the 1st July. At 8.55 p.m., they marched to the front line opposite Fricourt, where they relieved the 6th Dorsets of the 50th Brigade.

The Regiment's losses on the first day of the Somme were terrible. The 1st Battalion lost 9 officers wounded, 1 mortally, 3 other ranks killed, 105 wounded and 2 missing; the 2nd Battalion's casualties were 9 officers and 26 other ranks killed, 2 officers died of wounds, 9 officers and 303 other ranks wounded, 89 other ranks missing and 25 wounded and missing. The 1/4th Battalion lost 1 officer killed, 2 wounded and 1 evacuated with shell shock; the1/5th had 2 casualties on the 1st July but in the attack at midnight and subsequent retreat, they lost 1 officer killed, 2 officers wounded, 1 of whom later died, and 45 other ranks also became casualties. The 8th Battalion lost 5 officers and 30 other ranks killed, 8 officers and 171 other ranks wounded and 34 other ranks missing. The 10th Battalion's casualties were 5 officers and 66 other ranks killed, 10 officers wounded, 3 of whom subsequently died, 259 other ranks wounded and 162 men missing.

North of Fricourt, the 8th Lincolns made defensive preparations and were ordered to pass their ammunition reserve, rifle and hand grenades plus a squad of bombers to the 62nd Brigade. They were sent to Patch Alley where they continued works preparing the trench for defence until they were relieved about 2 a.m. on the 4th July. At Talmas, on the 7th, the Battalion was transferred to the 37th Division. The 1st Lincolns were heavily shelled on the 2nd July in the positions in Crucifix Trench and the Sunken

Road, which they had taken up on the 1st. An attack ordered during the evening was later cancelled and the night of the 2nd/3rd July passed quietly.

The 7th Battalion, as part of the 51st Brigade, was ordered to clear Fricourt of the enemy on the 2nd July with Fricourt Farm and Wood as secondary objectives. The 7th Lincolns on the right and the South Staffords on the left led the Brigade's advance. Clearing Fricourt's cellars and deep dugouts took time but, soon after noon, the Lincolns prepared to attack the Wood and the South Staffords sent patrols towards the Farm. Further orders were received to advance to the railway; the right was to link with the 7th Division, the left with the 21st. Between 2 and 3 p.m., the Lincolns advanced through the wood, which had been evacuated.

The next day, the 17th, 21st and 34th Divisions attacked the enemy. The Lincolns and the South Staffords were sent against Crucifix Trench. There was no bombardment so the enemy was surprised. All the objectives of the 17th Division were attained, nearly 1,000 prisoners, 11 machine guns and a large amount of stores were captured. The 7th Battalion's casualties were 3 officers and 30 other ranks killed, 6 officers and about 160 other ranks wounded or missing. The 7th and two other battalions of the 51st Brigade were relieved on the night of the 4th/5th July.

The 1st Battalion of the Regiment attacked Birch Tree and Shelter Woods after a heavy bombardment. The enemy fire was severe. 'A' Company suffered particularly and its supporting units and 'C' Company were rushed up. 'B' Company reached their objective without serious loss; they were reinforced by their supports and 'D' Company. Birch Tree and Shelter Woods were captured. The Battalion was relieved and withdrew to become a local reserve in the Sunken Road. During the day, the 1st Battalion's losses were nearly 250. The 62nd Brigade had captured 1,200 prisoners, 700 by the 1st Lincolns, who received congratulations from the Divisional and Brigade Commanders. On the 4th July, the Battalion withdrew to Dernancourt.

The bombers of the 51st Brigade, including those of the 7th Lincolns, reached the junction of Pearl Alley with Quadrangle Support on the 7th July but could not advance. Some progress was made on the 9th but at great cost. On the 11th, the 17th Division was relieved by the 21st. The 1st Lincolns were in support and provided carrying parties when the 62nd Brigade was ordered to clear the remainder of Mametz Wood, where, on the night of the 12th/13th, the Battalion endured a terrible bombardment. The following night, the 110th Brigade from the 37th Division also arrived in the Wood. On the 14th July, at the attack on Bazentin, the 1st Lincolns again provided carrying parties, returning with wounded and prisoners. The next day, the Battalion's bombers were in action in addition to support work. The enemy retreated more than a mile but British troops suffered from the effects of gas shells and lack of sleep.

On the 1st August, the 7th Lincolns took over Pommiers Trench. For several days, the Battalion was subjected to heavy shelling, machine gun and rifle fire. On the 9th, at dusk, the 7th managed to advance their line of posts about 50 yards out of Delville Wood and were relieved on the 10th August. During the Battle for Pozières Ridge, the 10th Lincolns took over a line of trenches north-east of Bazentin-le-Petit Wood on the

4th August where men of the Battalion unsuccessfully bombed the intermediary German trench. On the 6th, the 101st Brigade was relieved but the 10th were in the front line again on the 14th. Subsequently, on the 29th, they were at Bois Grenier.

'A' and 'B' Companies of the 1st Lincolns relieved the Coldstream Guards in the firing line about 1,300 yards south-east of Flers on the 17th September in the Battle of Flers-Courcelette. They did not have greatcoats, only waterproof sheets, and they suffered from heavy rain and continuous shellfire. The two companies were worn out when relieved on the night of the 19th/20th. On the 20th, the battalion bombers and company bombers of 'C' and 'D' Companies took part in a successful attack to clear Gas Alley. The 6th Lincolns, who had been on operational service in Egypt since February, took over front-line trenches opposite Beaurain on the 22nd July and remained there for a month. On the 15th/16th September, 'C' Company of the 6th captured Constance Trench, which was the 'jumping off ground' for the Sherwood Foresters and Borderers for their attack on Thiepval Ridge on the 26th. The 6th Battalion supplied carrying parties and established ammunition dumps near the front line in that Battle from the 26th to 28th September, performing gallantly under heavy shellfire.

On the 25th September, the 1st Lincolns took part in an unsuccessful attack on a track running south-east of Gueudecourt. The enemy fire was heavy and the 1st Contingent of the Bermuda Volunteer Rifle Corps, which was attached to the Battalion, lost half their men. The survivors were trained as Lewis gunners and amalgamated with the 2nd Contingent. The 6th Lincolns were under heavy shellfire during the Battle of Thiepval Ridge (the 26th to 28th September) but their gallantry contributed to the success of the operation. Between the 26th and 30th September, the Battalion lost 1 officer and 14 other ranks killed and 71 wounded. An attack on Zenith Trench on the 23rd October saw the 2nd Lincolns suffer grievous losses – 285 out of 486.

During the operations on the River Ancre, the 8th Lincolns took over part of a position captured by the Naval Division, which included some of Beaucourt village, on the 14th November and were not relieved until the 26th. The ground broken up by trenches, flattened by artillery fire and pitted with shell holes, compounded by rain and snow, was a mass of mud. Lieutenant Colonel Robert Johnston, the 8th's Commanding Officer, said: 'For twelve days...none of the Battalion had their clothes off, and on coming out of the trenches the men appeared covered from head to foot in mud'.

The Regiment suffered grievous losses, like many in the B.E.F., in the Battle of the Somme. However, the three main objects had been achieved: Verdun had been relieved; the main German forces had been held on the Western Front and the enemy's strength had been considerably worn down as shown by General Ludendorff's statement that by the end of 1916 the German Army 'had been fought to a standstill and was utterly worn out'.

Chapter 10
1917

The 1/4th and 1/5th Lincolns had the unpleasant experience of being in the front-line trenches at Bienvillers-Berles with 1244 gas cylinders awaiting a favourable wind. There was not only the constant annoyance of leakage but also the danger of a chance hit by an enemy shell discharging the poisonous fumes. Disaster struck on the 22nd August 1916 when hits on 6 cylinders badly gassed 1 officer and 14 other ranks of the 1/5th, one of whom later died. From January to March 1917, the eight battalions of the Lincolnshire Regiment in France moved frequently. Periods in training camps or duty as working parties, interspersed with tours in the trenches (accompanied by their dangers of shells and bullets and discomforts of water and mud) occupied them. At the end of February, the number of Lincolnshire battalions in France rose to 10 with the arrival of the 2/4th and 2/5th in the 177th Brigade, 59th Division.

Early in 1917, the German forces from opposite Arras to the Aisne valley withdrew to the powerful system of defences known as the Hindenburg Line. British divisions, some containing battalions of the Lincolnshire Regiment, followed the retreating enemy across a devastated area. Attacks were made by both sides. The 2nd, 2/4th and 2/5th Battalions were in action. The 2/5th Lincolns were driven back with heavy casualties at the Quarry and Cologne Farm on the 11th April. Trench warfare commenced all along the line, the British utilizing old German trenches where possible. Out of the line, training and route marches kept the 2/4th and 2/5th Battalions busy. At the end of August, they were moved, with the 59th Division, to the Ypres area. The 2nd Lincolns went into assembly trenches in preparation for the attack on Pilckem Ridge, in the Flanders Offensive, on the 31st July. The 1st, 1/4th and 1/5th Lincolns were also engaged in operations during the early months of 1917.

The 10th Lincolns spent May and June on the Arras front. The British positions facing the Hindenburg Line were still not complete when the Battalion went into forward defences on the night of the 25th/26th July. These works consisted chiefly of posts with a main line trench being constructed with strong points behind. On the 26th August, their Brigade was successful in gaining the high ground east of Cologne Farm, which gave observation of the Hindenburg Line, and on the 7th October, the 10th entrained for the Ypres Salient.

The First Battle of the Scarpe, which took place from the 9th to 14th April 1917, involved the 10th Lincolns, in the 101st Brigade, the 8th Lincolns, in the 63rd Brigade, and the 1st Lincolns, in the 62nd Brigade, which was in reserve. The 10th fought well inspite of losing direction during the advance. In addition to casualties from enemy action, the awful weather resulted in about 60 other ranks suffering from exposure and exhaustion. The 8th also fought valiantly encountering stiff German resistance north and north-west of Monchy.

The 62nd Brigade, including the 1st Lincolns, was sent to attack enemy trenches from a point about halfway between the Cojeul and Sensée rivers to the Henin-Heninel road, but there were few gaps in the German wire. As the leading waves reached the entanglements, enemy machine guns poured a murderous crossfire into the British troops. Great bravery and tenacity were shown by the Brigade, until their Commander ordered them to retire so that the artillery could re-bombard the wire. In the assault, on the 11th April, Lance Sergeant A. Walker fired his Lewis gun for six hours and seven times crossed open ground for more ammunition. He was killed about 12.30 p.m. His Commanding Officer, Acting Lieutenant Colonel Lewis Evans, wrote: 'To keep fighting a lost battle for six hours from an exposed position needs a determination that is given to few. I know of nothing finer in the war'. Next morning, the enemy evacuated his positions.

The 7th and 8th Lincolns fought in the Second Battle of the Scarpe on the 23rd/24th April, and the 10th was in reserve although bombarded almost continuously with gas shells. The 7th failed to take the village of Pelves, coming up against a barrier of intact wire. Losses amounted to nearly 200 all ranks. An officer who took part in the action stated: 'The Battalion, after determined attempts for one and a half hours, retired to the forming-up trench…and held this until relieved at night. The Battalion had been in the open for twenty days in frightful weather conditions—snow, rain and intense cold. In addition, biscuits and tinned beef alone were sent up as rations.'

The 8th Lincolns took part in the attack by the 37th Division, which reached the buildings west of Roeux Station and gained the slope of Greenland Hill. However, the Hill itself remained in German hands. At the Battle of Arleux on the 28th/29th April, the 10th Lincolns, in the 34th Division, attacked Roeux and the 8th Battalion, in the 37th Division, was engaged against the German positions along the Plouvain-Gavrelle road and Greenland Hill. In the attack on Roeux, staunch defence by the 20th Northumberland Fusiliers and the 10th Lincolns prevented a serious setback when the Germans counter-attacked. The Battalion's losses were over 400. The 37th Division failed to capture Greenland Hill, losing direction in the centre as it was dark and smoke from the barrage completely enveloped the troops. By the end of the day, the battalion was back in its original line. The 1st Battalion took part in the Third Battle of the Scarpe on the 3rd and 4th May. The 7th Lincolns moved to a line north of Roeux on the night of the 13th/14th May. They supported the counter-attacks of the 51st Division and 51st Brigade on the 16th May, which recaptured the Chemical Works, and Station buildings near Roeux and resulted in at least 2,000 German dead.

The 1/4th and 1/5th Battalions attacked towards Lens between the 8th June and 1st July 1917. The 1/4th's actions were a series of destructive raids and the 1/5th advanced successfully and helped repel three German counter-attacks. On the 1st July, both Battalions participated in a large-scale attack. The 1/4th, who were the assaulting battalion on the right, reached their objectives with few casualties and little opposition. On their left, the 1/5th encountered houses, which had been turned into machine gun posts, protected with wire. Despite gallant efforts, the Battalion was unable to capture the Cité de Moulin and, with their flanks open, were eventually forced to withdraw.

Pressure on the Arras front helped to prevent enemy interference with the preparations for the Flanders offensive. This began with the Battle of Messines and the explosion of 19 deep mines at the moment of assault on the 7th June. The 6th Lincolns helped capture a trench system 3 miles east of Wytschaete. Next was the Battle of Pilckem Ridge (the 31st July to 2nd August) whose objectives were the top of the high ground east of Ypres and the crossings of the Steenbeek. The 8th Division, including the 2nd Lincolns, attacked south of the Ypres-Roulers railway. Heavy machine gun fire eventually halted the Battalion and they consolidated on the reverse slope of Westhoek Ridge with Lewis gun posts pushed forward to the crest. Counter-attacks were beaten off, although the losses of the 2nd were severe, before they were relieved on the 1st August.

The 37th Division, including the 8th Lincolns, advanced south of the Ypres-Comines Canal on the 31st July. Heavy fighting resulted in severe casualties but the Battalion's 'B' and 'C' Companies reached the line July Farm - Wam Farm - Wambeke River. They were also relieved on the 1st August.

Bad weather forced a two-week interval: from the 31st July, it rained for four days and nights. The low-lying, clay soil was turned into vast muddy pools. The land became a bog, impassable except by a few tracks which were targetted by the German artillery. Off the tracks, there was the risk of drowning and both men and animals were lost in this way. Large-scale operations became impossible. However, the Battle of Langemarck, involving the 2nd and 6th Lincolns, began on the 16th August. For most of the operations, the 2nd Battalion was in support but even so suffered casualties. 'A' and 'C' Companies moved forward to the eastern slopes of Westhoek Ridge on the 16th where they were relieved at 11 p.m., although they were back on the Ridge on the 17th and 18th. 'B' and 'D' Companies of the 6th Lincolns acted as carrying parties for the 34th Brigade in the attack on the Pheasant Line, north of St. Julien. 'A' and 'C' Companies provided working parties for the Royal Engineers.

The 6th advanced with the 11th and other divisions on the 22nd August to gain and consolidate a forming-up line for an attack on the Pheasant Line. Ahead of the Battalion was Bulow Farm where the German defences were numerous strongly held concrete emplacements. The Lincolns went forward on a two-company front. The attack was successful, largely due to Captain T. D. Sutherland, Commanding 'B' Company, who gained his objective and took command of 'D' Company when the loss of officers and N.C.O.s made the situation critical. The 1st Battalion had several tours in the trenches before moving north and suffered casualties while digging trenches under shell fire at Clonmel Copse, Clapham Junction and Fitzclarence Farm at the time of the Battle of the Menin Road between the 20th and 25th September 1917. Having gained the Menin Ridge, the next objective was to advance the British line to where a direct attack could be launched on the ridge between Noordemdhoek and Broodseinde.

The ground had dried up on the night of the 25th/26th September when the 2/4th and 2/5th Lincolns formed up behind the Leicesters for this attack (known as the Battle of Polygon Wood), and neither regiment encountered much opposition except in the final stages. The captured ground was consolidated despite a terrific German barrage and a counter-attack.

Both the 1st and 8th Lincolns took part in the Battle of Broodseinde. The 1st Battalion attacked the Germans near the south-western corner of Polygon Wood near Zonnebeke on the 4th October. All objectives were taken and a tremendous part was played by the Battalion's Commanding Officer, Acting Lieutenant Colonel Lewis Pugh Evans, D.S.O. (1881-1962). He was born at Aberystwyth, Cardiganshire, and came from The Black Watch. He was awarded the V.C. and his Citation stated: 'Lieutenant-Colonel Evans took his Battalion in perfect order through a terrific enemy barrage, personally formed up all units, and led them to the assault. While a strong machine-gun emplacement was causing casualties, and the troops were working round the flank, Lieutenant-Colonel Evans rushed at it himself, and by firing his revolver through the loophole forced the garrison to capitulate. After capturing the first objective he was severely wounded in the shoulder, but refused to be bandaged, and re-formed the troops, pointed out all future objectives, and again led his Battalion forward. Again badly wounded, he nevertheless continued to command, until the second objective was won, and after consolidation collapsed from loss of blood. As there were numerous casualties, he refused assistance, and by his own efforts ultimately reached the Dressing Station.

His example of cool bravery stimulated in all ranks the highest valour and determination to win.'

The Battalion narrative stated: 'Throughout the operations very inclement weather was experienced, but the hardships were endured by all ranks with cheerfulness and as results show, it was plainly the determination of every officer and man in the Battalion to uphold the reputation of the 1st Battalion the Lincolnshire Regiment for consistent good work, and the staunchness and dogged courage displayed by all ranks in this battle has never been surpassed in the whole campaign.' Again casualties were heavy. It should be remembered that penicillin had not been discovered and so amputation of a limb was often the only way to prevent gangrene and save the soldier's life.

On the same day, the 8th Lincolns were held up south of the Menin Road by machine gun fire, which caused so many casualties that the attack was aborted. On the 5th, the Battalion advanced north of the Jute Cotts to within 50 yards of the German line, where they were relieved on the 6th October.

The 6th Battalion moved to support the 32nd Brigade at Poelcapelle on the 9th October and spent two days in shell holes under heavy fire until they were withdrawn on the night of the 10th/11th. The 7th and 10th Lincolns were also engaged in this battle. In spite of the unsettled weather and the ground becoming more boggy and thick with mud, further attacks were ordered. The 7th Battalion, in conjunction with the 10th Sherwood Foresters on their right and the 8th South Staffords on their left, successfully attacked the southern embankment of the Ypres-Staden railway (south of Houthulst Forest) as far as Turenne Crossing on the 12th October and consolidation took place despite enemy shellfire and snipers. This was in the First Battle of Passchendaele. Counter-attacks on the 13th were repulsed and the 7th were relieved on the night of the 13th/14th after considerable losses. The 10th Battalion arrived at Langemarck from the Somme on the 9th October. From the 6th October to 10th November, the 1st Lincolns suffered casualties during the Second Battle of Passchendaele either in the front line in the Polygon Wood area or when providing working parties. The 7th Lincolns were in the line at Brombeek from the night of the 27th/28th October, moving back to Proven on the 29th/30th.

The 2/4th and 2/5th Battalions were involved in the German counter-attacks at the Battle of Cambrai, where, initially, with the first use of tanks in large numbers, British troops over-ran the main system of the Hindenburg Line and attacked the Reserve Line. Bourlon Hill and Wood had been reached but the gains were not secure. Subsequently severe fighting took place between the 30th November and 7th December. The 59th Division, including both the 2/4th and 2/5th Lincolns, in the 177th Brigade, was at Cantaing, north-east of Flesquières, having moved south after the Battle of Polygon Wood. The 2/5th went into front-line posts running from the south-eastern corner of Bourlon Wood on the 2nd December, there being no continuous trench. The 2/4th came up on their left, in the Wood, on the 3rd. There was heavy gas shelling. As this section of the British Line formed a dangerous salient, it was decided to retire to near Flesquières. Pack ponies and limbers took ammunition and stores and then the battalions withdrew by platoons virtually unscathed.

The 2nd Lincolns endured a short but costly tour in the front line near Passchendaele between the 17th and 19th November 1917. More casualties were incurred in an attack on the 2nd December, which stopped, and the men dug in, about 30 yards from the main German trench, where they were relieved. It took one company 5 hours to reach the head of the duckboard track, which was the only way to the front line across the clinging mud.

The 1/4th and 1/5th Battalions spent from August to December in the trenches south-east of Bethune, between Loos and La Bassée Canal, relieving each other. The routine was 6 days in and 6 days out of the trenches. The Diary of the 1/4th, relieved on the night of the 3rd/4th August in the Hulluch-Loos sector, stated that as the troops 'had been working and fighting six days and nights in water nearly up to one's knees, ambulances were in readiness at Mazingarbe to convey anyone unable to walk.' The 2/4th and 2/5th Lincolns organised and consolidated new defences in the front line around Flesquières in December amidst shell and machine gun fire.

The 6th Lincolns gradually improved poorly maintained front-line trenches east of Loos for two months from the 22nd October. The 7th were in the front line from Turenne Crossing to Gravel Farm between the 22nd and 26th November. After being in the former British front positions near Trescault, they were in the old Hindenburg Support Line, from the 25th to 30th December. Although the 8th Battalion had tours at the front, they also formed working parties when out of the line and the 10th spent some time in the front line in the Somme area up to the end of 1917.

Chapter 11
THE LAST YEAR OF THE WAR
ON THE WESTERN FRONT

From the beginning of January to the third week of March 1918, the weather on the Western Front was miserable. The losses during the fighting of the previous year had caused a manpower crisis. Therefore, in January, the Army Council decided to reduce divisions from 13 to 10 battalions, each infantry brigade consisting of 3 battalions, the 10th becoming divisional pioneers. Some battalions were disbanded or reduced to training cadres and several divisions disappeared from the active list. The 62nd Brigade, 21st Division, was re-formed on the 3rd February and included the 1st and 2nd Battalions of the Lincolnshire Regiment. The changes introduced new methods in the tactical handling of troops, which were made difficult by the vast works required on the defences. The expectation of a large-scale German attack, as the collapse of Russia released numerous enemy divisions for transfer to the Western Front, made the construction of new lines of defence behind the front-line system vital, although men could not be spared to undergo the necessary training when not at the front. The 1st Lincolns spent at least half of the time when they were not in the line in February carrying out work on the defences. The 2nd Battalion successfully raided the enemy in Beet Trench on the 18th/19th March.

In accordance with the reorganisation of the B.E.F., the 1/4th Lincolns was divided up. Battalion Headquarters, 12 officers and 200 other ranks went to the 2/4th Battalion (becoming the 4th Battalion) and 12 officers and 250 other ranks went to the 2/5th, who were in Divisional Reserve in Mory on the eve of the German offensive. On the 20th February, there were reports that the enemy was using a new kind of insidious gas and, in some parts of the line, gas casualties greatly affected the fighting strength of British divisions. It was said that: 'No immediate effects [were] observed, but after forty-eight hours men developed lachrymation of the eyes and slight bronchitis.' In one company, there were 61 casualties. The 6th Battalion was in billets on the 20th March and the 7th was defending Hermies, having held front-line trenches on the northern flank of Flesquières salient from the start of the year to the third week in March.

The 8th Lincolns carried out three tours at the front in the Tower Hamlets - Dumbarton Lakes sector between the 15th February and the 13th March 1918 and, on the 20th, was in Canada Tunnels in support. The 10th Battalion spent the 17th and 18th March improving defences in the front line north-east of Croisilles, and was relieved on the 19th. Two days later, shortly before 5 a.m., the Germans opened a tremendous bombardment from the Oise to the Scarpe rivers; pounding roads and communications behind the front. The bombardment continued for about four hours, then around 9.45 a.m., under cover of a thick fog, the German infantry advanced. At least 64 enemy divisions took part in the attacks on a front of about 54 miles. The German offensive spread northwards on the 28th March, until 73 German divisions were engaged against the British Third and Fifth Armies and the right of the First Army, on a front of about 63 miles.

The four sectors in which the Lincolnshire Regiment was involved were:- east of Epéhy and at the southern point of the Flesquières salient, held by the 21st Division (the 1st and 2nd Battalions), between Flesquières and the Canal du Nord, held by the 17th Division (the 7th Battalion), Bullecourt, held by the 59th Division (the 4th and 2/5th Battalions), and Croisilles, held by the 34th Division (the 10th Battalion).

Thanks to a very efficient lookout man, the Battalion Headquarters 1st Lincolns evaded capture by the advancing Germans and moved, fighting, up Chapel Hill. They formed a defensive flank along the southern edge of Genin Well Copse No. 2 with some of the 2nd Lincolns. In the thick fog, a large number of the 1st Battalion's machine guns, firing on fixed lines, expended nearly all their ammunition so that when the fog lifted and the enemy became clearly visible, these guns had little or nothing with which to fire. The Battalion stood firm and most of their trenches, which ran from Birchwood Copse to Chapel Street, were practically intact. That night, the Brigade Commander sent a message that the Battalion 'had done magnificently, and had saved the situation.' The 2nd Battalion maintained their positions throughout the day. 'C' Company was under the orders of the Commanding Officer of the 1st Lincolns, Lieutenant Colonel Bertie Fisher, left sector front line. 'A', 'B' and 'D' were about 1,000 yards west of Vaucellette Farm and, at noon, some Germans got round the left flank of the Battalion but they were killed or captured.

The 7th Lincolns were not in the front line on the 21st March but manned battle positions of trenches round the eastern, northern and north-western exits of Hermies. They were bombarded all day, suffering casualties, but they had no contact with the enemy infantry. The 177th Brigade of the 59th Division was in reserve, the 4th and 2/5th Lincolns being in Mory Camp. The violent bombardment of the front at 5 a.m. meant both Battalions were ordered to stand to and then to move immediately, with other units of the Brigade, to their allotted positions in the third system support line running just east of the Vraucourt – St. Léger road. At noon, the 2/5th Lincolns and 4th Leicesters were ordered to occupy the second system trenches, the 4th Lincolns remained in the third system. However, it was discovered that the Germans had occupied the second system and before the 2/5th Lincolns could extend, three companies were cut off. The remaining company took up position in the front line of the third system with the 4th Lincolns and 4th Leicesters. The third system was merely a line of incomplete trenches, affording little cover, but the men dug in and held their position.

The 10th Lincolns, in the 103rd Brigade, were 300 yards southeast of Boiry - Becquerelle on the morning of the 21st March. At 2.50 p.m., as the Germans had broken through and advanced on Croisilles, 'C' Company moved to Henin Hill and the rest of the Battalion to positions south and west of Croisilles. Battalion Headquarters was in a sunken road between St. Léger and Croisilles.

The comparatively quiet night of the 21st/22nd March ended with fog. At noon, the 2nd Battalion was attacked. The 1st was then at Pioneer Camp at Heudicourt having been relieved at 8 a.m. that day. Epéhy had fallen and so the 2nd's right flank was threatened. Major Edward Lloyd of the Battalion said: 'The characteristics of our men can seldom have been more clearly shown than in this situation. Although being driven back by vastly superior numbers, with flanks and rear threatened, and with no prospect of immediate help, there was no semblance of panic, the men withdrawing in good order, fighting stubbornly and taking every opportunity of inflicting casualties on the advancing enemy.' At night, the German attacks ceased and there were only 80 men of the 2nd Lincolns who marched back to Gurlu Wood. The 1st Battalion also fell back contesting every foot of ground to a line west of Aziecourt-le-Bas.

The 7th Lincolns did not retreat on the 22nd March but slaughtered hundreds of the enemy who were attacking the 51st Division on their left. The 4th and 2/5th Lincolns with the 2/4th Leicesters were forced back to positions south-west and west of Mory owing to progress made by the enemy on their left and right flanks. The 10th Battalion was also compelled to retreat to a line north-west of St. Léger, before they were relieved shortly before dawn on the 23rd March.

Further German attacks in large numbers, on the 23rd, led to the 1st and 2nd Battalions retiring. Captain D. F. Neilson of the 1st Lincolns, with about 40 men, held a line east of Bouchavesnes and other small numbers of the Battalion were around Maricourt. The 2nd Lincolns were on a line about midway between Cléry and Bois Marrieres, being down to 6 officers and about 70 other ranks. The 7th Battalion retreated under fire to a position 1 mile south-west of Villers-au-Flos and the 4th and 2/5th withdrew to high ground east of the Ervillers – Béhagnies road. For two days, the two battalions fought almost continuously, with practically no sleep or rest. This was the Battle of St. Quentin. The 10th Lincolns were not engaged on the 23rd and so continued their march westwards. In spite of the loss of ground, stores, ammunition and many prisoners, there had been no real breakthrough in the British front. The valiant fighting of the Lincolnshire Regiment had played a notable part in preventing this.

The 1st Battalion did not take part in any fighting on the 24th. However, the 2nd was involved in a series of delaying actions as far as Hem. The next day, part of the Battalion joined a composite one formed from units of the 62nd Infantry Brigade. The remainder of the Battalion marched to Chipilly with part of the 1st . The 7th Battalion was involved in heavy fighting and, by nightfall on the 25th, was on the eastern side of Fricourt Wood. These actions were part of the First Battle of Bapaume. The 4th and 2/5th Lincolns retired to Bienvillers that day and the 10th Battalion reached Berlincourt. However, by the 27th, the German offensive had practically ended in the Somme area and the enemy had not captured Amiens.

The Germans attacked again on the 4th and 5th of April, latterly north of the Somme in the Battle of the Ancre. At Rossignol Wood an attack by the 8th Lincolns and 8th Somersets, with the 4th Middlesex in reserve, disorganised the German advance but they launched another offensive in the Lys Valley on the 9th. The 10th Battalion held front-line trenches south-east of Armentieres and was involved in heavy fighting at Gris Pot (Battle of Estaires). Although the Germans were held in check here, the flank on the right of the 34th Division had been driven back, so a general retirement was ordered by Brigade Headquarters. This was protected by covering parties, including 'B' Company of the 10th Lincolns who had received a draft of 97 19 year olds, who behaved splendidly. Few losses were incurred due to tremendous fighting by defensive flanks. The three days from the 9th to 11th April saw the 10th Battalion display great courage and tenacity.

The 2nd Lincolns had been in action further north. As a result of attacks on the 9th and 19th Divisions, the 2nd Battalion and the 12th/13th Northumberland Fusiliers were ordered to retake Wytschaete and re-establish themselves on the Messines – Wytschaete road before dawn. This they successfully achieved on the night of the 10th/11th April, contributing to the re-establishment of the line and delaying the German advance (Battle of Messines). The Battalion held its position, despite heavy shelling, until the night of the 15th/16th when it was relieved by the 1st Lincolns.

Four Battalions of the Regiment were involved in the Battle of Bailleul from the 13th to 15th April. The 1st Battalion was in front-line trenches in the Wytschaete sector. The 10th, after heavy fighting, was relieved on the 15th and retired to Haegedoorne where they again became front-line troops when the 59th Division, including the 2/5th and 4th Lincolns, was driven from its positions the same day. Both these Battalions were heavily engaged with the enemy and sustained many casualties. They were holding a line of advanced posts on the forward slope of the Ravetsberg Ridge and late on the 15th April were ordered to withdraw to Locre.

The 1st Lincolns broke the enemy's attack on the 16th April at the line Bogaert Farm – Stanyzer Cabaret crossroads and enabled a defensive flank to be formed and reserves to be brought up in order to prevent a break-through. Hard fighting left the enemy disorganised and unable to consolidate. This helped the counter-attack in the evening, in which the 2nd Lincolns vigorously participated.

The 4th Lincolns was reorganised on a two-company basis on the same day and, on the 17th, the 2/5th, owing to weakness of numbers, was placed under the orders of Major R.N. Holmes, the Commanding Officer of the 4th Battalion. The Composite Battalion fought in and behind a wood about 750 yards south of Locre and the 10th Battalion inflicted great losses on the enemy at Haegedoorne during the First Battle of Kemmel.

On the 25th and 26th April, the 1st and 2nd Lincolns came under heavy shellfire incurring further casualties. The 1st was made up of new drafts, mainly boys aged about 20, who remained under fire for several hours in very inadequate shelter - a magnificent feat of endurance. Both Battalions held up the advance of the numerically superior German forces, and the great losses during the Battles of the Lys were again made up with young reinforcements. On the 5th May, the 4th and 2/5th Battalions were reduced to Training Cadres, as was the 10th on the 11th.

The 1st and 2nd Battalions came under shellfire in the Second Battle of Kemmel on the 25th-26th April but were not heavily engaged again until the 27th May 1918: the Battle of the Aisne. The enemy broke through the line of posts held by the 2nd Lincolns, who became surrounded, only 2 officers and 30 other ranks getting away. For three days, the 1st Lincolns' gallant rearguard actions against greatly superior numbers of the enemy helped the retirement of their own and neighbouring divisions. Retreats had to be carried out to avoid having flanks unprotected when neighbouring units withdrew. The narrative of the 62nd Brigade Headquarters referred to a rearguard action to positions behind the River Vesle: 'The last to leave the position on the hill were the 1st Lincolnshire Regiment, under Lieutenant Colonel Gush, M.C., who were the right flank of the brigade. They did not arrive south of the Vesle until 11 p.m. Their tenacious fighting had completely deceived the enemy, who imagined the line still held intact along the whole spur, and this fact enabled the remnants of the other units to withdraw, reorganise and take up position preparatory to the fresh German advance.' By 7 p.m. on the 29th May, the 1st Battalion numbered a mere 8 officers and 42 other ranks.

On the 11th July 1918, the Padre of the 8th Battalion, the Reverend Theodore Bayley Hardy, D.S.O., M.C. (1863-1918) was awarded the Victoria Cross 'for most conspicuous bravery and devotion to duty on many occasions.' Four dates were specially brought to notice: the 5th, 25th, 26th and 27th April 1918 near Bucquoy and east of Gommecourt. Padre Hardy was born at Southernay, Exeter, and died of wounds on the 18th October 1918. Completely regardless of his own safety, he frequently tended the wounded under fire. He visited the trenches at night distributing cigarettes and sweets, greeting the troops with 'It's only me, boys'. In addition to his bravery, the Chaplain's energy and endurance for a man over fifty years of age in that era were amazing. On one occasion, after a shell exploded in the middle of one of the Battalion's posts, the Reverend Theodore Hardy went to the spot despite trench-mortar and shell fire. He extricated a man who had been buried alive and another who was found to be dead. All the while he was digging, the Padre was in great danger both from enemy fire and the condition of a wall hit by the shell which entombed the men.

After the 29th May, the Lincolnshire Regiment was not involved in major operations until the 21st August 1918, the Battle of Albert. The 7th Battalion was in reserve at the Battle of Amiens on the 8th August. This Battalion with the 1st, 2nd and 8th was engaged between Miraumont and Moyenneville on the 21st. The 8th Battalion did not take part in any attack on the 21st but was under heavy shellfire the whole day. The 2nd Lincolns captured Beaucourt and, since the movements of the remainder of the 21st Division depended on this success, they sent the news to Divisional Headquarters by carrier pigeon. Visual communication was impossible in the early morning mist and to use a runner was unreliable owing to shelling and gas. The 1st Lincolns, who were ordered to extend the right flank of the 42nd Division on their left, advanced successfully. Later, two companies of the 2nd Battalion were sent through the 1st Battalion to reach a sunken road running north-west from Baillescourt Farm. The 7th Lincolns, in the 17th Division, were at Hedauville from the 21st to the 23rd August.

The 111th Brigade was supported by the 8th Battalion in an advance on the 23rd and then all four Lincolnshire battalions went forward on the 24th. The 1st, 2nd, 7th and 8th Lincolns were in the area of the Second Battle of Bapaume between the 31st August and 3rd September without taking part in the fighting. The British divisions drove the enemy back to the Hindenburg Line. Losses were heavy but, by early September, the 1st Lincolns had reached Le Sars, the 2nd, Warlencourt, the 7th, Martinpuich Valley and the 8th were north-east of Achiet-le-Petit. To advance across old trenches, discarded wire entanglements, shell holes, ruined villages and destroyed roads and fight at the same time was difficult. 'C' Company of the 1st Battalion reached the Revelon Ridge and Railton on the 7th September and the 2nd Battalion got to the high ground south of Heudicourt. The 7th Battalion lost heavily in an attack, on the 5th September, towards a sunken road north of Equancourt, but held their position until the 7th Border Regiment arrived to carry on the attack southwards. The 8th Battalion established a post west of the Canal du Nord and 'C' Company advanced to Yorkshire Bank.

The 6th Battalion spent most of the spring and summer of 1918 in the line near Loos. They successfully raided the German trench line about 600 yards north of Bois Hugo, north-east of Loos, on the 2nd April. This earned them congratulations from the Corps Commander, Lieutenant General Sir Arthur Holland, who wrote: 'Great credit is also due to the Officer Commanding (Lieutenant Colonel G.T. Bruce) and all ranks of the 6th Battalion, Lincolnshire Regiment, for the way in which the plans of the higher commanders were carried out: fearless and cool leading among the junior officers and dash and enterprise among the men were exemplified in the highest degree, and it was these characteristics which ensured the success which was obtained.'

The Battalion's next major operation was the Battle of Drocourt-Quéant on the 2nd-3rd September. The 6th was the right-hand battalion of the 33rd Brigade, which was on the right of the 11th Division, who covered the left flank of the 4th Division, which attacked towards Étaing on the 2nd September. A patrol of the 6th Battalion, reconnoitring on the west bank of the River Cojeul, saw a German machine gun post on the east bank. Lance Sergeant Walter Simpson (1891-1936) volunteered to swim the river. Successfully getting across, he shot two of the enemy and took four more prisoner. An officer and another man joined Simpson, but they came under machine gun and rifle fire. Despite the officer being wounded Simpson was able to cover the withdrawal of the party and prisoners. He was awarded the Victoria Cross and, later on, also won the Distinguished Conduct Medal. A native of Everton, Liverpool, Simpson's original name was Arthur Evans. It is said he deserted from The 1st King's Liverpool Regiment and joined the 6th Battalion of the Lincolns. He was always a mystery man who appears to have served in the Merchant Navy and adopted the name Walter Simpson before 1914. After the War, he joined the Australian army and rose to the rank of Sergeant in three years.

On the 18th September, the 1st, 2nd and 7th Lincolns were in an attack by the Third and Fourth Armies on a seventeen-mile front between Holnon and Gouzeaucourt in the Battle of Epéhy. The 1st Battalion reached trenches west and east of Vaucellette Farm, the latter having been the British front line on the 21st March 1918. The 2nd Battalion occupied Plane Trench, their third objective, and the 7th reached as far as Quentin Redoubt north of Gauche Wood. Later, the 1st and 2nd Lincolns were engaged at Gouzeaucourt and Gonnelieu during the Battle of the Canal du Nord (the 27th September – 1st October) and the 6th Battalion was in support.

The 1/5th Battalion had been in the Bethune area engaged in defensive warfare since March 1918. With the remainder of the 46th Division, it took part in the relief of elements of the 1st and 4th Australian Divisions in September. Although it was involved in the attack on the St Quentin Canal, on the 29th September, it was not in the initial assault, which was made by the 137th Brigade. The 138th Brigade, including the 1/5th Lincolns, leap-frogged the 137th and captured Magny-la-Fosse and the high ground beyond. The Battalion, at comparatively small cost, took 400 prisoners, 7 field guns and 20 machine guns. On the 3rd October, the 138th Brigade was in reserve during the Battle of the Beaurevoir Line, but, at one period, the 1/5th were detached to assist the 139th Brigade. On the 9th October, the 1/5th advanced again, in the 138th Brigade, and reached the Bois de Riquerval the next day.

Six Battalions of the Regiment were engaged in the 1918 Battle of Cambrai. The 1st and 2nd Lincolns, in the 62nd Brigade, captured Walincourt and the high ground west of Selvigny on the 8th/9th October. The 1/5th in the 138th Brigade advanced to Fresnoy. The 7th Lincolns, in the 51st Brigade of the 17th Division, proceeded through Tronquoy and across the Cambrai railway. The 8th Lincolns going forward with the 8th Somersets, in the 63rd Brigade, reached a position south of Haucourt Mill on the 9th October. By the 11th, one and a half platoons of the 8th were on the eastern bank of the Selle. The 6th Battalion, with the 7th Staffords, captured Hem Lenglet. The Lincolns killed 50 enemy and captured 1 officer, 11 other ranks and 4 machine guns.

By the middle of October, it was necessary to halt the rapid pursuit of the Germans, to keep the front line troops supplied with food and ammunition, bring the guns forward and establish communications. In addition, the progress of the 46th Division was checked for a week by hard fighting of the German rearguards. Frontal assaults on Riquerval Wood and the Forest of Andigny were beaten back and the attack was switched towards the Bohain - Wassigny road. The Battle of the Selle raged from the 17th to 25th October. The 1/5th Lincolns advanced in a fog on the 17th October and, despite some loss of direction, captured Regnicourt and, after the enemy had withdrawn, occupied Andigny-les-Fermes. The Fourth Army was very successful and the Germans were forced back across the Sambre et Oise Canal everywhere south of Catillon.

The Third Army followed this up with an attack on the 20th October. After the 50th Brigade of the 17th Division had taken its objectives, the 51st Brigade, including the 7th Lincolns, passed through and captured Amerval. 'B' Company of the Lincolns and a company of the Sherwood Foresters then extended the line northwards. The 2nd Lincolns, despite vigorous opposition, took Vendegies and reached a line on the high ground between it and Poix du Nord on the 23rd October. The 1st Lincolns assisted in clearing the line of the River Harpies and the south-western part of Vendegies-au-Bois and then pushed on beside the 2nd Battalion. On the 24th, the 1st Battalion captured Poix and the road beyond, taking over 100 prisoners.

The surviving six battalions of the Regiment took part in the Battle of the Sambre in November 1918. The 8th Lincolns were in action at Ghissignies on the 2nd. The 1/5th relieved the Black Watch on the 4th and, on the 5th, captured four 77mm. and three 10.5cm. guns with several machine guns. The 1/5th had great difficulty crossing the Petit Helpe River as the current had washed away the footbridge. Resourcefully, they tipped carts into the water and put planks and ladders across which allowed 'A' Company to proceed. 'B' and 'C' Companies, having no carts, planks or ladders, used trees held in place by their officers until a footbridge was constructed. It was a severe test of the supply organisations of the British armies to keep supplies and ammunition up with the troops. However, the enemy continued retiring and the 1/5th were at Sains du Nord when the Armistice came into force.

The 7th Battalion advanced with the 51st Brigade to Beaufort on the 8th November. The Battalion was relieved the next day and returned to billets in Aulnoye until hostilities ended. The 1st and 2nd Lincolns attacked with the 62nd Brigade towards Berlaimont on the 4th, 5th and 6th November. The 1st Battalion established posts along the Berlaimont-Aulnoye road and, on the 7th, marched to billets in Aymeries, where they remained until the 11th. The 2nd Battalion followed the 1st to the western edge of Berlaimont under heavy shell fire. The 110th Brigade passed through the 62nd, leaving the latter in support although still under attack. From the 6th to 7th November, the Battalion was attached to the 110th Brigade and then also moved into billets in Aymeries.

The 8th Lincolns, as a whole, were not engaged with the enemy on the 4th November. Two platoons of 'D' Company and two of 'D' Company were engaged in mopping up operations. The 63rd Brigade marched back to Ghissignies and, on the 5th November, went to billets in Neuville, where it stayed until the 12th. The 6th Battalion supported the 9th Sherwood Foresters in crossing the Aunelle at Sebourg. The Lincolns then passed through the Foresters, crossed the Grande Honelle River and proceeded to Aulnois: a difficult march along bad roads blocked with traffic. On the 10th, the Battalion moved to l'Ermitage and, on the 11th, to Quevy-le-Grand. Thus, the 6th (Service) Battalion was nearest to Mons (where the senior battalion of the Regiment began operations in the War) when the Armistice was declared. All six battalions of the Lincolnshire Regiment on the Western front were actively engaged in completing the defeat of the Germans in France right up to the last week of the War.

General Sir Julian Byng, Commanding the Third Army, issued a Special Order of the Day to his troops, which included the 1st, 2nd, 7th and 8th Battalions of the Lincolnshire Regiment, but it applies equally to the 1/5th Battalion in the Fourth Army and the 6th Battalion in the First Army. He said: 'Since August the 21st you have won eighteen decisive battles, you have driven the enemy back over sixty miles of country…That is your record, gained by your ceaseless enterprise, your indomitable courage, and your loyal support to your leaders.'

The Lincolnshire Regiment gained 69 Battle Honours in the First World War. In addition to the 5 Victoria Crosses, members of the Regiment won many other awards including 62 Distinguished Service Orders, 176 Distinguished Conduct Medals, 206 Military Crosses and 765 Military Medals. Numerous Mentions in Despatches were earned. The Lincolns' losses, including the attached contingent of the Bermuda Volunteer Rifle Corps, were nearly 9,000 of all ranks killed in action.

Chapter 12

THE INTER-WAR YEARS AND THE EARLY PART OF THE SECOND WORLD WAR

After the end of the First World War, the 2nd Battalion was the first to return to England, but in the autumn of 1919 they sailed to India where they remained until 1928; then they were at Khartoum up to 1930. The 1st Battalion was sent to Ireland, where they had two arduous years during the struggles that culminated in the truce of 1921 and the subsequent formation of the Irish Free State. The Battalion moved to Aldershot in 1924 and remained in England for six years. They then went to Gibraltar and met the 2nd Battalion, who called at the Rock on the 6th April 1930 on their way to England. This was the first occasion on which the two regular battalions had come together in peacetime since they met at Malta on the 19th April 1895.

Meanwhile, the 4th and 5th Territorial Battalions had reformed in Lincolnshire as units of the 138th Infantry Brigade of the 46th (North Midland) Division. The Service Battalions raised for the duration of the war were disbanded and the King's Colours of the 6th, 7th, 8th, 2/4th, 2/5th and 1st Garrison Battalions were laid up in Lincoln Cathedral on the 9th October 1926. The 3rd (Special Reserve) Battalion became just a name in the Army List.

The 1st Battalion was at Gibraltar until 1931 before going to Shanghai to protect foreign lives and property within the International Settlement from internal disorder and external aggression. The Lincolns patrolled and manned sandbag defences. Fortunately, no casualties were suffered. In September 1932, the Battalion (752 all ranks) sailed to Hong Kong and, early in January 1936, moved to Nasirabad, Rajputana, India.

The Italian-Abyssinian War of 1935 saw the 2nd Battalion sent to Malta, where practice air raids were common and defence schemes put in force and rehearsed. The Lincolns led a peaceful existence during an unusually fine winter. The war ended in May 1936 and, on the 10th July, the Battalion with the 2nd South Wales Borderers was ordered to Palestine, where a civil war had developed. The situation deteriorated after the Arab Higher Committee declared a General Strike in objection to Jewish immigration. The Battalion was based at the Arab town of Tulkarm, midway between Haifa and Tel Aviv. Duties included keeping the railway open, escorting road convoys and aiding the Civil Police when called on for assistance. A successful action was fought against a large force of Syrian and Transjordanian bandits near Bala on the 3rd September; on the 12th October, the General Strike was called off and life returned to near normality. The Lincolns sailed for England on the 11th December, having won six decorations and fourteen Mentions in Despatches whilst in Palestine.

During 1936 and 1937, the threat of future German air attacks led to increases in the air defence units, at the expense of the infantry of the Territorial Army. One of the divisions which suffered temporary eclipse was the 46th (North Midland), to which the 4th and 5th Battalions of the Regiment belonged. The 4th Lincolns became part of the 148th (North Midland) Brigade of the 49th (West Riding) Division; the 5th Battalion became the 46th Searchlight Battalion, Royal Engineers, Territorial Army, although the link with the County was retained by the addition of (The Lincolnshire Regiment) to their title. Only the 5th Battalion mobilized during the Munich crisis of 1938.

More mechanical vehicles were allotted to infantry battalions as first-line transport. New equipment began to appear: the Lewis gun was superseded by the Bren light machine-gun and anti-tank weapons were issued. The Lee Enfield .303 rifle remained the main British infantry weapon during the Second World War, but it underwent several changes after its introduction. Adjustments were made to improve accuracy, it was shortened and the bayonet was changed. In November 1939 manufacture of the altered weapon, known as 'No. 4 Rifle Mark 1', started. To assist quick movement in the Far Eastern jungles, a lighter No. 5 Rifle, also called the 'Jungle Carbine', was made. This rifle incorporated a device to prevent the flash from the muzzle giving away the firer's position.

In 1938, the tunic was replaced by battledress, which reached to the waist and was buttoned to the trousers at the waistband. At the foot of each trouser leg was a small flap, which allowed the trousers to be buttoned round the ankles. A khaki forage cap, or service cap, was the headgear until it was superseded by a beret in 1943 but a steel helmet was worn in battle.

On the 22nd June 1938, due to the efforts of the 2nd Battalion's Commanding Officer, Lieutenant Colonel Percy Hansen, V.C., D.S.O., M.C., the Battalion received the King's Drums. These are the only drums presented by a reigning monarch to an infantry battalion of the British Army.

The private soldier received 2 shillings (10p) a day in 1939, which was increased in 1940 to 2 shillings and 9 old pence (about 13p). Soldiers lived in more comfortable dormitory barracks with heating and showers. Married men lived in married quarters with their families. Soldiers had free uniform and equipment and free medical and dental treatment. Food was greatly improved and there was 28 days' leave a year with free rail travel. In addition to military training, the men were given schooling and physical education.

The Prime Minister, Mr. Neville Chamberlain, announced, on the 29th March 1939, that the Government had decided to double the establishment of the Territorial Army. Thus, it was hoped, to provide an immediate addition of over 200,000 volunteers for the Army. Four weeks later, a form of conscription was introduced: all 20-year olds were called up for six months' service with the Regular Army, followed by three and a half years in the new Territorial divisions. By the middle of May Lincolnshire had all its Territorial units up to their new establishments and, together with Westmorland, was the first English County to report completion. The immediate effects on the 4th Lincolns were the reorganisation of existing companies, the formation of new detachments and a series of recruiting drives. The Battalion was first organised as an Original Battalion and a Duplicate Battalion and, in August, as the 4th and 6th Battalions. The 4th Battalion remained in the 148th Infantry Brigade; the 6th was transferred to the reconstituted 46th (North Midland) Division. On the 31st August, the Army Reserve and the Supplementary Reserve were mobilized and, the following day, orders were issued for the Territorial Army to be embodied. Two days later, in view of Germany having ignored the ultimatum to withdraw from Poland, war was declared.

The 2nd Battalion, as part of the 9th Infantry Brigade of the 3rd Division, landed at Cherbourg on the 3rd October. Coincidentally in 1914, the 1st Battalion of the Regiment had embarked as part of the 9th Infantry Brigade. The 2nd Lincolns moved to Ronchin near Lille to dig a complete trench system to form the divisional reserve line. Despite the prolonged winter frost and as much training as could be fitted in, the whole line was almost completely dug, revetted and duck-boarded by the spring of 1940. On the 1st May, the 6th Battalion, as part of the 46th (North Midland) Division, arrived near Rennes to be employed as a Labour Unit to assist in building a railway to a large arsenal. However, the Battalion spent the whole time training, but as the Division was short of equipment and transport, little collective training could be attempted. The Divisional artillery had been left behind in England, and the battalions, on arrival in France, had only 4 2-inch mortars without ammunition, 18 Bren guns, 10 anti-tank rifles, 1 motor-cycle, 1 car and 12 other vehicles.

It was decided by the Allies that if Germany invaded Belgium, the French and British forces would advance to the River Dyle. This was Plan 'D' and offered a shorter line of defence than a position further west, with greater depth; the northern end of the line rested on inundations and it represented a smaller enemy penetration into Belgian territory. On the 10th May, Germany invaded Belgium: the 3rd Division, part of II Corps, was on the left of the British sector of the front and was allotted roads running through Brussels and to the north of it. The 2nd Battalion advanced by motor transport to Villevorde, north-east of Brussels, the next day and was part of a force occupying Louvain from the 12th to the 16th. The Battalion frontage was about 3,500 yards, and, as the sluices had not been blown, they found no flooding to the south of the town as they expected. There was also a gap of at least a mile between the right flank of the Battalion and the nearest unit of I Corps on the right.

Early on the 14th, contact was made with the enemy all along the front. Although the Germans suffered severe losses and the Battalion few, it soon became obvious that the general situation had deteriorated so much that Plan 'D' could not be continued. In the north, Holland was held by the enemy; in the south, the French Ninth Army appeared to be in danger of disintegrating, which meant that Arras and the Allied right flank were threatened. Accordingly, the Lincolns were withdrawn, without incident, to the River Dendre, and it was learned afterwards that the Germans, ignorant of events, shelled Louvain for twelve hours after it had been evacuated.

On the 18th May, orders were received for another retirement, this time to Denderhauten, south of Oudenarde, where the 10th Foot had been with the Duke of

Marlborough. As it was too far to march and no troop-carrying transport was available, orders were given by Brigade Headquarters for everything non-essential to be dumped and unit transport used to capacity. Owing to bad organisation, traffic congestion at Heldergem, on the 19th, was appalling. Vehicles were lined up head to tail, three and four abreast; British and Belgian troops and refugees were hopelessly mixed together. Nevertheless, the Battalion was eventually embussed in its own transport for an uneventful journey. The Lincolns took up a defensive position behind the River Escaut. Orders were received on the 22nd for another withdrawal, to Tourcoing, where they arrived the following day and stayed until the 27th.

The situation further south steadily worsened, and by the 20th May, the Germans occupied Abbeville and were pushing a column to Boulogne. The communications of the British Expeditionary Force had been cut, laying open their rear and right flank which were only protected by a series of improvised forces mainly drawn from three incomplete Territorial divisions. The supply situation presented increasing difficulty. By the 22nd, Boulogne and Calais were out of action and Dunkirk under heavy air bombardment. The next day, the B.E.F. were put on half-rations. The 2nd Battalion was obliged to live partially off the country and, in the Tourcoing area, the civilian population needed feeding too.

Meanwhile, the 6th Lincolns, moving by road and rail, detrained at Lille on the 19th and marched to Pont Marc, where they stayed two nights. On the 24th, the Battalion was ordered, as part of the B.E.F. defensive flank, to occupy the line of the Canal du Nord at Douai and took up position soon after dark. The Battalion was then directed back to the Forêt de Nieppe via Raches. Despite continuous Stuka raids, no casualties were suffered and they arrived on the 27th.

The Germans reached the Channel coast on the 24th May. The British Commander-in-Chief, General Viscount Gort, decided on a further withdrawal towards the sea. On the 29th, the Secretary of State for War advised Lord Gort that, owing to the inability of the French to mount a counter-offensive in sufficient strength in the Somme area, the safety of the B.E.F. had become most important. Lord Gort was informed on the 27th May that the King of the Belgians had asked for an armistice to take effect that night which set the stage for the evacuation of the B.E.F.

The 6th Battalion withdrew to Dunkirk via Berthen, where the Commanding Officer, Lieutenant Colonel S. B. Harrison, made the correct decision to bivouac in the fields rather than the village, inspite of the weather. While breakfast was being prepared, several squadrons of dive-bombers wrought terrible destruction in the village, where an ammunition dump exploded. The Battalion proceeded along a road between abandoned vehicles and ahead lay a pall of black oil smoke from burning installations in Dunkirk. On the beaches men queued, waiting to be taken off. The Lincolns hung on during the evening of the 1st June until they were evacuated after midnight, the lights of the ships lying offshore being visible all the while.

The 2nd Battalion was also ordered to withdraw and left the Tourcoing area on the 27th May and, after a tedious journey, took up positions behind the Yser Canal. Enemy shelling increased, particularly to the south, moving perceptibly farther round the right flank. Accordingly, the Brigade including the Lincolns was ordered to face south. On the 29th, the Battalion fought an action at Zuydschoote in conjunction with the 4th Royal Berkshires but was ordered to withdraw. It was very difficult to disengage the forward companies, who were in really close contact with the Germans. Artillery support was impossible as the gunners had gone in order to leave the roads clear, and the only remaining 3-inch mortar was without ammunition. The Lincolns withdrew fighting but incurred considerable casualties. Later, the Commanding Officer was told by General Sir Alan Brooke that, on the 29th May, the 8th and 9th Infantry Brigades held up the advance of two German Army Corps for a whole day, thereby aiding the evacuation of thousands of the B.E.F. from Dunkirk. The 2nd Battalion got away on the 31st May and 1st June. The 3rd Division was under orders to return to France within ten days but the imminent collapse of French resistance altered this to four years.

Brigadier W. Robb, Commander of the 9th Brigade, wrote to Lieutenant Colonel A. G. Lawe, who was then commanding the Battalion: 'The discipline, endurance and magnificent fighting quality of your Battalion, shown during our advance to Louvain and withdrawal to the beaches of Dunkirk, have been beyond all praise. No task has been too difficult, dangerous or bad, and every call made on the Battalion was cheerfully and willingly answered.

The action of the Battalion at Zuydschoote on the Ypres Canal, when the Battalion covered the withdrawal of both 8th and 9th Infantry Brigades in daylight, perhaps stands out...The final withdrawal of the Battalion to the beaches was carried out with splendid discipline and in excellent order. The magnificent fighting qualities of your Regimental Officers, N.C.O.s and men were maintained in face of every difficulty and danger, and so long as we have this spirit we cannot be defeated.'

The winter of 1939-40 saw the 4th Battalion of the Regiment at Ripon but long spells of frost, heavy falls of snow and an epidemic of measles meant there was little but individual training. On the 12th April 1940, they embarked for Norway as part of a force under Major General Adrian Carton de Wiart, consisting of the 146th Infantry Brigade (British) and the 5th Demi-Brigade of Chasseurs Alpins (French).

The idea of sending an Allied Expeditionary Force to Norway had arisen because German vessels laden with iron ore from Narvik were using Norwegian inshore waters to avoid detection by the Royal Navy. To stop this, minefields were laid by British destroyers and it was decided to send an Expeditionary Force to forestall German reprisals and occupy Narvik so cutting off the supplies of iron ore. However, without a formal declaration of war, Germany attacked Norway and, by the 11th April, Oslo, Narvik, Trondheim, Kristiansund, Stavanger and Bergen had been taken.

The 4th Lincolns took part in a pincer movement to retake Trondheim as part of a force landed at Namsos, 100 miles to the north of this objective, while another body of troops went to Andalsnes, 150 miles to the south-west. From these two bridgeheads, an attack could be made on Trondheim. Unfortunately, the Luftwaffe had almost complete freedom over Norway and the British a dearth of maps.

By the 17th April, the Battalion had arrived at Namsos and advanced to Steinkjer at the head of Trondheim fjord on the 19th. 'B' Company and a section of 'D' fought the Germans near Vist but had to retreat after the hay-loft of the farm they were occupying was set on fire by incendiary bullets. Two sections, and 3 men who were tending the wounded, were captured by the enemy. Meanwhile, the remainder of the Lincolns were under heavy air attacks at Steinkjer. Part of H.Q. Company was sent to Korsen cross-roads, one and a half miles south-west of Vist, and 'C' Company was ordered to fill the gap between the H.Q. troops and 'B' Company. 'B' and 'D' Companies experienced heavy machine-gun, mortar and light artillery fire, to which no effective reply could be made.

As enemy pressure increased, a general withdrawal was ordered. Snow lay two or three feet deep so Bren gun tripods and boxes of reserve ammunition were abandoned as being too heavy to carry. Over 200 men of H.Q. and 'C' Companies reached Namdalseid and Rodhammer on the 25th April after covering 45 miles in 49 hours in low temperatures. Despite most of the journey being through deep snow, not a man fell out. Although the Battalion was no longer in contact with the enemy's ground troops, German aircraft were always in evidence forcing the British to keep under cover. The nights were bitterly cold and, as all the Lincolns' stores had been left in Steinkjer and destroyed in air raids, there were no blankets and few greatcoats. No mail from England had been received since landing in Norway and there had been only one pay parade. Rations, however, were plentiful and the men remained in good heart.

By the 27th April, owing to pressure of events elsewhere, the War Cabinet decided to evacuate central Norway. Accordingly, on the 2nd May, the 4th Battalion moved to Namsos for re-embarkation. The Lincolns sailed on the French Auxiliary Cruiser *El Kantara*. Despite German air attacks, they reached Scapa Flow on the 5th May and Glasgow on the 8th.

On the 24th June, the 4th Battalion went to Iceland, which the British Government had decided to occupy to prevent its use by the Germans as a base for submarines and aircraft. The local inhabitants at first resented the arrival of British soldiers, but the good behaviour and tact of the troops gradually established friendly relations. Companies took it in turns to provide garrisons for observation posts on the coast and other detached duties, which demanded initiative and self-reliance from the young officers and N.C.O.s who were in command. They were often many miles from other troops and had to organise and dig their own defences, do their own cooking, and soldier on under hard climatic conditions. In 1942, American forces began taking over the defences of Iceland and, by the 9th September that year, the Lincolns had arrived back in England. The next two years saw the Battalion in constant training in readiness for the invasion of Europe.

Other County Units

Also in England were 46 Searchlight Regiment, R.A., which could be called the lineal descendant of the 5th Lincolnshires (T.A.). They were converted to an A.A. Searchlight unit in 1936 and kept watch on such places as the Humber Estuary, Rosyth

Dockyards and, later, large reservoirs. In November 1944, they moved to north-west Europe as No. 606 Garrison Regiment R.A. They saw service at Dunkirk and Antwerp as infantry-trained garrison troops. When disbanded in 1946, they were guarding war criminals and political suspects in Germany. The Regiment later became 581 (Mixed) H.A.A. Regiment, R.A. (Royal Lincolnshire).

The 7th Lincolns, who were raised at Tollerton Park, near Nottingham, in July 1940, were converted to 102 Light Anti-Aircraft Regiment, R. A. on the 1st December 1941. The Battalion served in England until they landed in Normandy on the 13th June 1944. Over the years, Royal Artillery personnel had filled vacancies as both officers and other ranks but a strong Lincolnshire element remained and the Regiment carried a red 'X' on a blue ground as a special insignia throughout its existence. During the North-West Europe Campaign they carried out anti-tank and ground shoots in addition to their anti-aircraft role, at times fighting as infantry. In November 1944, they were one of the first regiments to be equipped with rocket projectors, which they used at Venlo, Gilbrath and Arnhem. The end of the War found them at the Ems-Zaole Canal, and occupation duties followed until the Battalion was disbanded in February 1946.

The 8th Lincolns, who were disbanded in July 1943 shortly after becoming the 101st Anti-Tank Regiment, R. A. (Lincolnshires), were only in existence for three and a half years, having spent their time coast -watching and draft finding, interspersed with constant changes and reorganizations. At one time, they became the 50th Battalion The Lincolnshire Regiment.

The Home Guard was raised all over the County in the summer of 1940. All ranks wore the cap badge of the Lincolnshire Regiment, in which many had previously served; a green 'Lincoln Imp' was the distinctive shoulder flash. The units were organized into 23 battalions: 13 in Lindsey, 3 in Lincoln, 4 in Kesteven and 3 in Holland; each having its own operational role, and they were grouped into zones and sectors in accordance with their tactical employment. When the order to 'stand down' was issued in December 1944, the total strength of the Home Guard throughout the County was around 25,000 all ranks.

Chapter 13

THE 1ST BATTALION IN INDIA, BURMA AND SUMATRA

When War broke out on the 3rd September 1939, the 1st Battalion was at Nasirabad in Rajputana with one company on detachment at Ahmedabad in the Bombay Presidency. Early in 1940, the Battalion moved to Dinapore in Bihar for internal security, and a company was detached to Muzzafapur.

About the middle of that year, the Battalion was ordered to stand by for a move to England but this was cancelled. Shortly afterwards, they moved to Nowshera in the North West Frontier Province. In 1942, the Battalion was sent to Bengal as the Japanese threatened invasion. They were part of the 71st Brigade in the 26th Indian Division, commanded by General Haywood, and formed a defensive area or 'harbour' at Deula, from where they could send out columns to deal with any attempted Japanese incursions. The whole Brigade area was wired and platoon and company posts were constructed in depth. Most of the ground was paddy with patches of slightly higher ground on which were clusters of trees, usually palms, and native huts of mud and thatch. All the villagers were evacuated and the Battalion took over their houses, although some soldiers lived in tents.

The monsoon was new to the Lincolns. They spent many hours baling out and re-revetting positions. Intensive training was carried out, particularly in jungle warfare. The Brigade consisted of the 1st Lincolns, the 7th/15th Punjab and the 9th/15th Punjab. The heat and humidity took their toll and the number of sick assumed alarming proportions. Much of this was due to skin diseases such as boils, impetigo, jungle sores and ringworm. Malaria at this time was not such a common disease as later. A large draft of East Surreys was absorbed into the Lincolns and served with them until those that remained were repatriated towards the end of the War. The Battalion was at Deula for the cyclone in 1942 and sent two companies to help restore order in the Midnapore district where there was looting and rioting.

Early in February 1943 the 71st Brigade was sent to reinforce the 14th Division in the Arakan. The Brigade moved via Calcutta and Chittagong to Maungdaw. The Arakan was densely wooded with thick jungle and less paddy than Deula. It was hilly country, rising in places to over a thousand feet; very hot, extremely dusty, had swarms of flies and mosquitoes and was one of the worst malarial areas in the world. At Indin, the Battalion suffered its first casualty in the Arakan when Private King was bitten by a snake. He eventually recovered.

On February 22nd the Battalion took over a part of the line, which ran from the foothills of the Mayu Range to the sea, a distance of about 1 mile, and was held by two battalions. The Lincolns were on the right with their flank on the beach, and the

7th/15th Punjabis were on the left. The Lincolns left the 71st Brigade for a short time and came under the command of the 6th Independent Brigade when a combined attack with five battalions was planned.

The Lincolns attacked at Donbaik on the 18th March 1943 but were ordered to withdraw as the Brigade attack had been halted elsewhere. The single file withdrawal through thick jungle, guided by compass and the North Star, lasted six hours. They were then sent a few miles west of Buthidaung on the Letwedhet chaung below Point 551 as the Japanese had broken through at Htizwe. The Lincolns again came under the command of the 71st Brigade, which was now joined by the 4th Brigade, in Mayforce under the command of Brigadier Curtis.

The Lincolns moved to the Aungtha chaung, carrying a fantastic amount of kit, including twenty tons of ammunition, which, with the stores, had to be unloaded when crossing two rivers by ferries and loaded again onto lorries the other side. In addition, 52 Battalion mules and well over 100 attached mules had to be ferried across the rivers.

The Battalion successfully attacked on Hill 201, south–west of Taungmaw, and was then withdrawn. This type of 'tip and run' operation became a regular feature of the Lincolns' fighting, but, as Major A.W. Innes of the Regiment said, they 'ached to be part of a larger force and throw the Japs out of the Arakan for good and all'. The Battalion was ordered back to Buthidaung to come under the command of the 4th Brigade. This entailed moving all the stores and mules back over the two rivers and a very exhausted unit finally arrived!

Casualty evacuations through sickness, mostly malaria, were now very high and over 100 a week were quite normal. Reinforcements arrived but were insufficient to keep pace with the evacuations. New officers and men quickly settled down and became 'Lincolns' and many who joined remained with the Battalion till the end of the war. There were two companies at Kindaung under Major Charles Hoey, which became known as 'Hoey Force' and carried out strenuous patrolling.

The Japanese attacked on the 3rd May and the Lincolns were ordered to withdraw first to a supporting position north of the Letwedet chaung and then north and west across the Mayu Range. The Battalion was next sent south to the area of the western tunnel on the Maungdaw – Buthidaung road: a most difficult area to hold. During their time at the tunnel, only desultory shellfire bothered the Lincolns who were very under strength and deficient in all stores and equipment. The 71st Brigade, to which the Battalion had returned, was ordered to spend the monsoon at Nhila on the Teknaf peninsula about 15 miles north and slightly west of Maungdaw. On arrival at Nhila, the Battalion numbered about 350 out of an establishment of 830 and those who were left were very tired. Battle casualties had not been heavy and when the Lincolns had met the enemy, they had more than held their own. Three months living in the open with no mosquito nets and anti-malarial mepacrine not always available, constant moves combined with long marches, moving tons of stores and preparing new positions, took a very heavy toll in sickness. During the three months they spent in the Arakan in 1943, the Lincolns averaged three days between moves.

The first four weeks at Nhila were spent preparing defences, reorganising and refitting. Reinforcements arrived, sick and wounded returned and the Battalion was soon over strength. Shortly after their arrival, the Lincolns started patrolling, as they were responsible for the whole of the Teknaf peninsula. Not once while the Regiment was in Nhila did the Japanese set foot in this area. The Battalion was also kept busy training and the incidence of fever decreased.

'B' Company, under Major Hoey, took part in a successful large-scale raid on Maungdaw from the 10th to 13th July 1943 and held it for a day. The Japanese had 22 killed and a quantity of stores captured. The Lincolns lost 1 killed and 2 wounded and received congratulations from the Commander-in-Chief, India, the Air Officer Commanding-in-Chief Eastern Command, the Corps and Divisional Commanders.

Early in 1944, the Battalion moved to a camp in the jungle at Barabakund about 20 miles north-west of Chittagong. Here they worked hard at training, particularly night operations and then it was back to the Arakan. At Goppe, the Lincolns had their first experience of being supplied by air. Signal fires were lit and Dakotas came over by night and unloaded tons of supplies. They were the leading troops in the advance south which moved just east of the Mayu Range. At Badana West, the Lincolns raided the Japanese lines to attack positions on Point 315 overlooking the 'Sinzweya Box'. Casualties were heavy on both sides but the Japanese thrust was weakened and their remnants started to straggle back.

In the fighting near the Ngakyedauk Pass on the 16th February 1944, Temporary Major Charles Ferguson Hoey, M.C. (1914-1944) won the Victoria Cross. His company came under heavy fire but, although wounded in the head and leg, Major Hoey went forward alone and destroyed a troublesome enemy strongpoint, killing all the occupants. Unfortunately, he was mortally wounded and died the following day. Hoey was a Canadian, born at Duncan, Vancouver Island, British Columbia, and the grandson of Major General Charles Simpson, the Colonel of the Lincolnshire Regiment.

The Battalion was one of the few units, and the only British one, to be sent back to fight a second campaign in the Arakan. The Lincolns had a short rest at Goppe Bazaar from the 18th to 23rd February 1944. Then they moved south again to Badana East to round up small parties of the enemy by active patrolling and prevent them rejoining the Japanese main forces further south. The Division gradually moved forward to the Maungdaw – Buthidaung road.

As the main battle was being fought at Kohima and Imphal in the north, it was not until the end of March that the Lincolns met the Japanese in force in a series of skirmishes in the Wet Valley that lasted for about three days. The Battalion worked well with the tanks of the 25th Dragoons who kept up a barrage of fire literally within a foot or so of the heads of the leading troops. The Lincolns had very few casualties from their own tanks and were saved heavy losses from the enemy. The Japanese kept well down in their bunkers during the initial bombardment and, as soon as the guns stopped firing, would emerge to meet the advancing British troops. With tank assistance, the latter practically reached the enemy positions before the supporting fire was lifted and so the Japanese had to keep under cover.

The Lincolns' next task was to capture two hill features known as 'Spit' and 'Polish', near the village of Dongyaung, in the area where the Battalion had had their headquarters in 1943. With the help of maps, air photographs and knowledge of the ground from the previous year's operations, a complete sand model of the hills was made. Thorough preparation, added to surprise, brought success to the Battalion, although casualties were fairly heavy. However, the enemy suffered far greater losses and the Lincolns' communications were excellent. Major General Cyril Lomax said that this action was probably the biggest killing of Japanese in any single operation in the Arakan. The attack was assisted by dive-bombing aircraft.

After this, the Lincolns were based to the south of Ngakyedauk chaung with a large area to patrol. The 71st Brigade then moved to relieve the 36th Brigade in the Buthidaung district. The Battalion was well spread out. It was hotter and dustier than ever and the country showed evidence of fighting. The Lincolns were constantly patrolling, having many minor clashes with the enemy, frequently in the 'Maze', where the Japanese had the advantage of sitting in wait. The Battalion was ordered not to advance further than the Buthidaung road and to withdraw for the monsoon to a more northerly line, which was easier to hold and supply. Before moving back to their monsoon quarters on the 2nd June 1944, the Battalion beat off an enemy attack on the 5th May.

The Lincolns' monsoon quarters were a few miles south of Bawli Bazaar, a depressing area consisting of very poor and only partly finished bashas built into the sides of small hills, separated from each other by patches of paddy. A contrast to the previous year's quarters at Nhila! The monsoon started in earnest and everyone was weary and very wet. The Battalion was sometimes referred to as 'The 10th Foot (Web Mark III)' as this was its third wet season in Bengal or Burma. The first task for the Lincolns was to dig a system of drains at the same time building up and revetting bunds or footpaths about two or three feet high wherever it was necessary to cross over the low lying paddy ground. In addition, defences had to be dug, revetted and roofed where necessary and a patrol area covered. However, they were able to dispense with the dawn to dusk stand-to and have hurricane lamps at night. The Lincolns were separated from the Japanese by the Mayu Range but it was never safe to be too sure of this. Patrols became arduous. The going was extremely difficult, the country was waterlogged: all the chaungs were swollen and often impassable. It was the season for leeches, which frequently caused slow healing septic sores.

At the beginning of September, the Lincolns were ordered over the Mayu Range to form the garrison at Taung Bazaar. Early in October, they engaged some Japanese forces who were withdrawing close to the Battalion's position and only a few of the enemy escaped. The Lincolns were relieved on the 12th October and went to Taungbro and then moved further back for rest and recreation. Following this, the Battalion was sent to the Combined Operations Training School at Coconada, north of Madras, where the course included practising landings from the sea and marching with heavy kit to harden their feet after the monsoon.

The Battalion took part in the daylight assault on Ramree Island, on the 21st January 1945, which had strong naval and air support. The Lincolns and the 5th/1st Punjab were the leading battalions: the Lincolns landed on the right on White Beach, a few miles west of Kyaukpyu. There was very little opposition initially and the first objective was gained without loss. The enemy's resistance then stiffened but, although suffering casualties, the Battalion took its further objectives. The inhabitants were pleased to see the attacking troops and helped as far as they could by giving information of the whereabouts of the Japanese.

Oil bombs were a great success and set fire to much of the undergrowth. Ramree, the capital of the island, was entered on the 9th February, less than three weeks after the Lincolns landed near Kyaukpyu. Despite the ground conditions, tanks kept up with the Battalion, who spent the next few weeks rounding up enemy stragglers. The Commanding Officer of the Lincolns, Lieutenant Colonel C. A. C. Sinker, had the honour of hoisting the Union Flag over Ramree.

On the 27th March, the Battalion sailed for Madras but returned to Ramree Island on the 5th April for the Rangoon operation. This was a race against time as, apart from the Japanese, the South West Monsoon was expected, when seaborne assaults in small craft might be impossible. The Fourteenth Army was advancing from Mandalay, and was outstripping its supply lines owing to the difficult country and lack of roads for heavy vehicles. Furthermore, there were insufficient aircraft available to maintain so large a force by air during the monsoon season. A determined stand by the Japanese north of Rangoon would cause problems as it was the only port in the south of Burma that could be used to supply the Fourteenth Army by sea. The Japanese were withdrawing speedily towards Malaya and so, if Rangoon was taken, there would be a chance of cutting the enemy line of retirement.

The convoy containing the 26th Indian Division, including the 1st Lincolns, sailed from Ramree Island on the 30th April in pre-monsoon weather of showers, heavy squalls and a choppy sea. The Battalion was to form the initial beachhead on the east bank of the Rangoon River. It was necessary to anchor 25 miles off the mouth of the river on account of shallow water and unswept minefields. D-day was the 2nd May 1945. The weather was poor - heavy rain and a big swell with squalls at sea. The 25-mile run-in to the beaches was one of the longest for any operation of the war. The Lincolns landed at the mouth of the Hwawnun chaung, 15 miles south-east of Rangoon. The 'beach' was a bank of deep mud with flooded paddy fields beyond. They encountered no opposition during the landing and the initial objectives were quickly overrun. The advance was uneventful. On D-Day +3, the 71st Brigade entered Rangoon. The Lincolns moved to Mingala Don, 14 miles to the north. Patrols were sent out and the few small parties of Japanese located hastily withdrew. Contact was established with the Fourteenth Army and, by the 16th May, the Battalion was at Taikky, 50 miles north of Rangoon. Having accomplished their task, the Lincolns were ordered back there and the Japanese flag, which had been flying over Government House, was given to the Battalion. They reached Rangoon on the 18th May and Bangalore on the 25th.

The Repatriation and Release Schemes came into effect resulting in most of the senior officers, over half the N.C.O.s and 250 men leaving. The majority of those remaining were reinforcements with little training. This together with the low numbers of the unit resulted in the Lincolns being withdrawn from the 26th Indian Division and being posted to the 109 Lines of Communication Area in Bangalore, part of General Headquarters (India) Reserve.

Preparations to attack Malaya were being made when Japan surrendered on the 15th August. The 26th Indian Division was allotted Sumatra as its occupation area and, on the 10th September, the Battalion was reposted to that Division's 71st Indian Infantry Brigade. For the first time since the South African War, the Lincolns crossed the Equator on their uneventful voyage to Sumatra.

The reception by the Indonesians was cordial but cool and no trouble was encountered in the initial occupation of Padang by the Lincolns. Owing to the size of Sumatra and the small Allied force, certain oilfields, food and Japanese army store dumps were left to the Japanese to safeguard until the Allies could take them over. It was evident that there was very bad feeling against the Dutch by the local population and the Indonesians, fostered and armed by the Japanese during the previous three years, demanded 'freedom' and independence from Dutch rule. Later, it became clear that a number of Japanese had deserted their forces and led and trained the Indonesians. Some better educated Sumatrans realised they would have to rely on Dutch or Allied technical help and advice, whereas the uneducated masses demanded complete independence and resented any interference by the Allied forces.

The Lincolns carried out guard duties and, apart from a few small incidents, such as attempts to break into internee areas where Dutch individuals were protected, there were no major crimes or disturbances in Padang while the Battalion was there. On the 13th March 1946, they moved by air for the first time and were concentrated at Palembang by the 15th. In Padang, the Battalion lost 1 killed and 1 wounded, whereas in Palembang, the casualties were 3 killed and 11 wounded. However, after some incidents in March, the Battalion's duties consisted mainly of anti-looting guards. The 1st Battalion left Palembang in November and moved to Taiping, Malaya, under command of 49th Indian Infantry Brigade in the 23rd Indian Division.

With the exception of four months in Bangalore in 1945, the Lincolns had been in operational areas, most of the time on active operations, for nearly four years. In his Foreword to 'The History of the First Battalion The Lincolnshire Regiment in India, Arakan, Burma & Sumatra September 1939 – October 1946' by Major L.C. Gates, Field Marshal Viscount Slim wrote: 'The First Battalion The Royal Lincolnshire Regiment, in an army where there were many fine battalions, held a reputation second to none for those cardinal virtues of the British Infantryman – cheerfulness, steadiness, stubborn valour and a morale that never faltered.'

Chapter 14
THE 6TH BATTALION IN TUNISIA AND ITALY.

On their return from Dunkirk, the 6th Battalion re-formed at Manchester with the rest of the 46th Division. Within a month it was better equipped than it had ever been in France. Training was carried out at Hawick, Dumfries, and in Cambridgeshire, Kent and Sussex. For a month in May 1941, the 46th Division took over the Norfolk coast defences and in November was posted to defend Romney Marsh, where it remained for the next year.

About midnight on the 8th January 1943, the 46th Division, including the 6th Lincolns, sailed for North Africa, and arrived at Algiers on the 17th. They reinforced the hard-pressed First Army, which was grimly holding on after the failure of its ambitious dash to capture Tunis. The enemy was estimated to have 35,000 troops in Tunisia, apart from those facing the Eighth Army, which was advancing from the east. The Axis tank strength was about 300. The Lincolns started for the front on the 18th January, going to Munchar and then Medjez-el-Bab, the main pass into Tunisia in the centre of the line, and it was here that 'C' Company killed the first German and the Lincolns had their earliest casualty of the Campaign. On the 21st February, orders came for a move to the Northern Sector. The Battalion was placed in hills nestling under enemy-held positions of Green Hill and Bald Hill. The Lincolns' area had previously been held by two battalions, so that company positions were a considerable distance apart, necessitating constant aggressive patrolling by night. By day, mortaring and shelling were continuous and it was a relief when orders were received after four days to move back to El Aouana and then Sedjenane, which the Lincolns had to hold at all costs, as there were no troops in position in the rear.

The area was difficult to defend with so few troops but the Battalion adopted an all-round defence, with three companies in a basin surrounded on two sides by hills and high ground rising to the east and south. The field of fire in every direction was limited and the country was ideal for infiltration by the enemy. Communication was established with the 139th Brigade Headquarters and a Forward Observation Officer from a Field Artillery Regiment and a Battery Commander from a Medium Artillery Regiment were installed with Battalion Headquarters. The Germans were reported to be advancing on the 3rd March and a heavy concentration of field and medium artillery was brought down on them. However, all through the day, the 6th Lincolns were constantly mortared and shelled, gun positions were dive-bombed and machine-gunned. By 5 a.m. the next day, the enemy possessed the village and the station but a threat of encirclement was staved off. After the Brigade Commander had unsuccessfully tried to visit the Battalion, Major K. G. Barrell was sent to report the situation to Brigade Headquarters. He returned with written instructions for the

Lincolns to withdraw, which they did under tank and artillery cover. During the fighting at Sedjenane, the Lincolns had 21 killed, 46 wounded, including the Commanding Officer, and 98 missing. The next day, another 2 men were killed and 6 captured in a patrol encounter.

During the night of the 7th/8th March, the 6th Lincolns moved south to take over the positions of a regiment of the Corps Franc d'Afrique. Almost immediately, two German attacks were beaten off. The rain and constant local attacks made life generally unpleasant, but in all cases the onslaughts were driven back, with only slight losses to the Lincolns after the first morning. On the 13th March, the Battalion moved back to Djebel Abiod for four days' much needed rest. After being posted to the north and then to Djebel Bou Lahia, they were detailed to take part in the operation to recapture Sedjenane.

The 1st Parachute Brigade was to attack on the left, starting just before midnight, 27th/28th March, with heavy artillery support, whilst the 36th Brigade marched off an hour later. A special force from the 138th Brigade, including 'A' Company and the Carrier Platoon of the Lincolns, was to make a wide outflanking movement to the right, through thick scrub, over wooded hills and to come into Sedjenane via the mine, thus completing a pincer attack. Supplies, mortars and other heavy equipment were to be carried by mules. The Lincolns moved off at 6 p.m. on the 27th March. In the dark, two mules, each carrying a No. 11 wireless set, rolled down a steep hill, but both mules and wireless sets were found to be in comparatively good order when recovered.

The parachute troops captured their objectives before dawn and the 36th Brigade also advanced according to schedule against light opposition. The 138th Brigade went forward with the special force in the lead. However, the tanks and carriers of the latter found the going difficult owing to the steep, rocky ground and the absence of tracks other than for goats. Accordingly, the 6th Lincolns were ordered to take the lead and press on to Sedjenane mine. After hard fighting, 'A' Company, who had rejoined the Battalion, advanced with fixed bayonets (as at Sobraon), and occupied the ridge overlooking the mine on the 29th March. Next day, with little opposition, the Lincolns took the area of the mine and, on the 31st March, the Reconnaissance Regiment entered Sedjenane. On the night of the 2nd/3rd April, the Lincolns moved to Djebel Bou Jedabia and, on the 6th, set off for a concentration area near El Aroussa.

The enemy had withdrawn into the mountains covering Tunis and Bizerta. The Axis forces were pressed from the south by the Eighth Army, whilst the First Army in the west built up and comprised two Corps. The 46th Division was moved south under IX Corps to deliver the final punch. The 138th Brigade attacked Argoub Sellah on the left on the 22nd April. Despite tough opposition, particularly from the Hermann Goering Division, the Battalion's 'A', 'B' and 'D' Companies took their objectives. Sadly, the Lincolns' Commanding Officer, Lieutenant Colonel J.Y.E. Myrtle was killed. Hundreds of armoured fighting vehicles of the 6th and 1st Armoured Divisions moved through close to the Lincolns' left. Soon after midday, the battle died down in the Battalion's sector and casualties were evacuated through mined cornfields.

The Lincolns moved forward and, on the 26th April, reached an eminence with two crests known as the 'Twin Tits' in some hills two miles from Djebel Kournine. Here, the enemy had repulsed several attempts to dislodge them and the Lincolns' attack also failed but with few casualties.

The Battalion then moved, via Medjez-el-Bab and Chassart Teffaha, to a gully at the base of Longstop Hill, and the 46th Division took no active part in the final operations. On the 12th May, when the Axis forces in Tunisia surrendered, the 6th Lincolns were in cornfields near Massicault, on the main Medjez-Tunis road.

For four months after the capitulation of the German and Italian armies in Africa, the 6th Lincolns trained and prepared in Algeria and Tunisia for their next assignment - the invasion of Italy. Sicily was occupied by British and American forces by the end of August 1943 and, by the 3rd September, the Eighth Army had landed on the 'toe' of Italy.

The Battalion was to act as advance guard to the 138th Infantry Brigade, whose task was to seize Salerno and its port, and then go forward as rapidly as possible to the Nocera- Pagani area, preparatory to proceeding to Naples. The Lincolns embarked on the 4th September, in infantry landing craft belonging to the United States Navy and in nearly every case, British rations were heavily supplemented by American ones. This was much appreciated by all ranks. The crossing, via Palermo, was uneventful until the 8th September when one landing craft hit a mine and sank off the Italian coast. It was then that the Battalion heard from the BBC that Italy had surrendered, and her troops in the Salerno area were disarmed by the Germans who manned the coastal defences during the night.

The planned programme for disembarkation vanished as, although the 128th Infantry Brigade cleared Red Beach on the right, Green Beach on the left was held by the enemy, preventing any landing there. On the 9th September, the Battalion put ashore at Red Beach or on the beaches farther to the south, which had originally been allotted to the 56th Division. 'C' Company came under heavy shellfire immediately on grounding, their ship being hit sixteen times in a few minutes. 'D' Company landed and advanced without difficulty. The situation was most confused while companies were assembling. The narrow roads near the beaches, with deep ditches on both sides and abandoned vehicles blocking the access for long periods, caused considerable difficulty. Control was almost entirely lacking, and what progress there was was due to the initiative of those on the spot. On landing, the Lincolns' Commanding Officer, Lieutenant Colonel D. Peel Yates, was told that the Battalion had been placed under the 128th Infantry Brigade.

The Lincolns moved south-east, established a strong-point in the Casella area and mopped up southwards to Green Beach, 2 to 3 miles away. 'A' Company went to the Granozzi area and, with a troop of tanks, mopped up south-east to the River Asa. The Battalion completed its tasks in spite of casualties. Although the Lincolns did not inflict many losses on the enemy, their rapid, determined moves were largely instrumental in clearing Green Beach and its exits so that the landing places could be used.

The Battalion came under 138th Infantry Brigade, 46th Division, and was ordered to move as quickly as possible to Salerno to assist the Special Service Brigade in making the Vietri defile secure and to defend Salerno from penetration from the north-west. Local civilians showered grapes and pears on the men as they moved off. The fighting that followed was not completely in the Lincolns' favour - 'B' Company failed in an attempt to occupy Alessia - but the Battalion remained covering the Vietri defile and Salerno until relieved on the night of the 19th/20th September, before which patrols had operated actively day and night in spite of being shelled and mortared.

After three days' rest in Salerno, 'D' Company advanced on the night of the 22nd/23rd September to capture the Costa Pinano ridge overlooking Cava. Heavy enemy fire was encountered and, in the dark, control was extremely difficult, the Company becoming very scattered in the dense undergrowth. However, Captain D.B. Tyler and 9 others succeeded in occupying, in daylight, the eastern end of Costa Pinano although it had been intended that this operation would be carried out by a full company at night with heavy artillery support. Sadly, Tyler was killed while consolidating his position but his inspired leadership led to the early capture of a feature on which the success of the whole divisional attack depended. 'C' Company were sent to take a 'pimple' 600 yards south of Costa Pinano, and achieved their objective, after heavy fighting. 'A' and 'B' Companies were despatched to reinforce Tyler's men at Costa Pinano. Late on the 23rd September, the Battalion was ordered to hold the ground that had been gained. Yeoman service had been done throughout this time by Major J.E. Fletcher and his assistants who organised daily carrying parties to keep the front-line troops supplied with ammunition, water and rations. This involved climbs of up to 12,000 feet over distances of 1 to 2 miles, often under fire, several times a day.

The Battalion moved to Nocera, through torrential rain, thunder and lightning, on the 27th September and stayed there until the 6th October, mainly occupied with training. The Lincolns, with the remainder of the 138th Infantry Brigade, were in reserve when the 46th Division crossed the River Volturno on the 15th October, and then moved forward to a very wet bivouac area at Arnone. The Battalion was then sent to occupy about 1,500 yards of the Agnena Nova Canal about 2 miles north of the river. Confronted by the dominating Massico – Mondragone ridge, the main axis of advance from Salerno was switched to Capua – Francolise. However, perhaps to convey the impression that an advance in strength on the original axis was to proceed, the Lincolns and the York and Lancasters were ordered to advance on the 23rd October and secure the line of the main road running north-east and south-west through Trivio Cancello between 1 and 2 miles north of the Canal. The advancing troops were to push forward fighting patrols to locate and, if possible, deal with enemy opposition. Failing this, leading companies were to attack on the information supplied by the patrols.

The Battalion secured its preliminary objectives but was then held up by well-constructed defences and machine gun fire. The York and Lancasters, finding enemy resistance less strong on their front, made progress throughout the day and, with heavy artillery support, captured the position round Trivio Cancello by nightfall. The Lincolns were ordered to exploit this success and it was found that the enemy had withdrawn in front of the Battalion, who carried out deep and active patrolling until relieved on the 27th October. On the 2nd November, they moved forward to high ground east and west of Jiusti on the northern slopes of the Cascano pass, and, on the 6th, advanced towards the River Garigliano. The pioneer platoon dealt with a very large minefield in the Fusani area. One assault section lifted 54 mines in three hours, and the other disarmed over 100 in the same time. Having been ordered to reconnoitre the Garigliano for crossing-places and destroy any enemy found south of the river, the Lincolns carried out intense patrol activity. With fine weather, the carrier platoon watched the whole Battalion front, allowing the forward companies to rest more men during the day. The leading section of the carriers survived an ambush on the 14th November, inflicting heavy casualties on the enemy. The Battalion was relieved the same night. Three days later they occupied a position covering the villages of Castrese and Lauro, as the enemy had withdrawn, and were then relieved again and billeted in Carinola.

On the 1st December, the 46th and 56th (London) Divisions launched an attack on the Camino massif, which was an important bastion of the German Winter Line. Coincidentally, these divisions had fought side by side 27 years earlier in the diversionary attack on Gommecourt, on the first day of the Battle of the Somme. The Lincolns assaulted Le Croce, a spur between the massif and the Garigliano on the 7th and found that the enemy had evacuated the position. 'D' Company and two dismounted scout sections of the carrier platoon were ordered next day to exploit and hold the road junction in St. Nicola. By midnight, 'D' Company had secured its objective without loss. The Scots Guards advanced through the Lincolns to cut the road leading north from Rocca D'Evandro. During the night of the 9th/10th December, the Battalion was relieved and, the following night, themselves relieved the Scots Guards in the Rocca valley.

Administration was a big problem. No vehicle could get past San Clemente, and Rocca was three to four hours further on over or round the mountains. Mules were not available, so ammunition, rations and other necessities were carried by such porters as the Lincolns could produce. After early problems, it was thanks to their efforts that the Lincolns never ran out of ammunition or food; even a blanket and greatcoat per man were brought up and a proper line of communication was eventually organised. Up to the 12th December, torrential rains fell incessantly, turning the low-lying ground into a sea of mud and soaking the soldiers to the skin.

The Lincolns remained covering the Rocca valley until Boxing Day. Lieutenant John Brunt led a fighting patrol in a successful attack on an exposed enemy post at the main road junction 200 yards north of the River Peccia on the 14th/15th December, winning the Military Cross. Unfortunately, a forward platoon of 'A' Company lost 1 killed and 14 prisoners on the 21st. The weather broke again and continued patrolling demanded the greatest determination and fortitude. Nightly patrols went out in pitch darkness and heavy rain, wading through flooded fields and swimming the River Peccia. On several occasions, the Divisional Commander commended the Battalion's efforts. The Lincolns were relieved on the 26th/27th December and returned to the line between Montes Maggiore and Lunga on the Peccia at the end of the month. The weather was bitterly cold; snow and rain fell frequently, and there was no cover from the elements.

In the attack across the River Peccia on the night of the 4th/5th January 1944, the 138th Brigade was to protect the left flank of the 6th United States Armoured Infantry, who were to capture Monte Porchia, an isolated hill covering the approaches to Cassino. The York and Lancasters were on the right and the 6th Lincolns on the left. Not more than two companies of the Battalion were to be employed. 'B' Company crossed the river, which was swollen by rain and snow, by a ford, greatly helped by a concentrated artillery bombardment on the previous four or five evenings. Unfortunately, in their very rapid move from the river line 'B' Company's wireless set was lost and it was a considerable time before definite news of their success reached Battalion Headquarters. The fighting patrol was unable to get over the river by another ford and was caught in a heavy concentration from a Nebelwerfer.

As soon as information was received of 'B' Company's success, 'A' Company was ordered to cross the river and pass through. However, by this time the moon had gone down and progress was very slow. The Company was caught in a heavy artillery concentration with negligible cover, and soon suffered fifty per cent casualties and had to be withdrawn to reorganise. The American attack on Monte Porchia made little progress and the 138th Brigade was left in a very exposed position. Accordingly, the York and Lancasters, with 'B' Company of the Lincolns, were ordered to withdraw under cover of darkness. Unfortunately, heavy casualties ensued, and it was another two nights before the Battalion was relieved.

After a short, uneventful stint in the Rocca D'Evandro sector, the Battalion was in Corps reserve with the remainder of the 138th Infantry Brigade on the 19th January. This was at the start of a major offensive which had the primary object of holding the maximum enemy forces in the south away from the forthcoming landing near Rome. On the 20th, the 138th Brigade was sent to join the 56th Division in the Suja area. Unfortunately, the Battalion was not allowed to bring machine guns and mortars owing to traffic congestion on very indifferent roads. This severely handicapped 'C' Company in its subsequent engagement with the enemy at Castello where 36 casualties were incurred. 'A' and 'C' Companies were amalgamated and the Battle Patrol swelled the numbers of 'B' Company. By the 27th, preparations to resume the offensive were complete and the Battalion, with machine guns and mortars, successfully recaptured Castello and cleared the whole of the Suja valley.

After a short rest and receipt of reinforcements, on the 7th February, the Lincolns attempted to capture Monte Faito, a long knife-like ridge, 2,600 feet high, very steep, rocky and almost devoid of cover. Faito was under enemy observation from San Ambrogio to the north-east and Castelforte to the west. These disadvantages, added to strong German resistance supported by artillery and mortar fire, led to the operation being abandoned on the 10th after heavy fighting in which the Battalion lost 110 all ranks. On the 14th February, the Lincolns crossed the Garigliano again and took over a comparatively easy sector on the extreme right of the bridgehead. There was a proper road running through the position which eased the supply problem. By day, the Battalion's gunners and mortars harried any suspicion of enemy movement. At night, aggressive patrolling was carried out and, after about a week, the Germans withdrew their forward troops about 500 to 600 yards. The Battalion was relieved on the 1st March and moved to Le Vaglie and, later, Taranto. On the 16th they left for rest, refitting and training in Palestine and Syria. When the Lincolns returned to Italy on the 3rd July, Rome had fallen and Normandy had been invaded. The enemy had been forced back to the Gothic Line, guarding the North Italian plain.

After further training, the 6th Lincolns concentrated at Sasso Farrato on the 23rd August. The 46th Division, to which they belonged, had become part of the 5th Corps, which, with the 1st Canadian Corps, was taking post behind Lieutenant General W. Anders' Polish Corps on the Adriatic front with the aim of breaking through the Gothic Line. After the Lincolns' pioneer platoon had crossed the Foglia and improved the track northwards, a successful assault was made on a ridge 1,000 yards north of the river on the 1st September. Despite the enemy's deep, well-constructed defences with armoured turrets and concrete emplacements, the Battalion's losses were only 8. The British forces crossed the rivers Ventina and Conca and, on the 10th/11th September, the Lincolns took Hill 449 and the Tribio ridge. The fighting was extremely bitter and the artillery fire was the fiercest and most concentrated that the Battalion had experienced in the campaign. Their casualties for the action were 150 and 'B' Company had to be disbanded. In spite of reinforcements, the 6th Lincolns operated with only three rifle companies.

The Battalion continued to advance to Vallecchio and crossed the River Marano to Monte Lupo, where 'A' Company was held up. Considerable fire from a large yellow farmhouse was a major problem; however, after several attacks by the Lincolns, the building was eventually occupied by an assault troop of the Reconnaissance Regiment, who had proceeded by a circuitous route. Many prisoners and much booty were captured but the Battalion lost 95 men.

On the 20th, the Lincolns advanced to Serravalle but the counter-attack that was feared failed to materialize and they were able to rest. The Battalion moved, on the 6th October, to an area south-west of San Angelo. The weather was still unsettled and order and counter-order followed in quick succession. The Lincolns were eventually detailed to hold the Monte Albano ridge whilst an attack by the 128th Brigade went in, and then to relieve the 3rd Royal Garhwal Rifles on Monte Gattona. On the 11th October, the Battalion cleared the ridge where the village of Montiano stood. One enemy sentry was found asleep behind his machine gun! The advance was continued and 'C' Company took Almerici while the carrier platoon cleared houses to the west. Further fighting saw a dominating bare hill and Monte del Pine taken and the road-bends round

Romano secured. The Battalion moved to Serravalle on the 17th and, a week later, to Urbino for rest and training.

After ten days, the Lincolns went forward again. 'A' and 'D' Companies crossed the River Rabbi on the 7th/8th November, struggling through three feet of rapidly flowing water. The advance progressed along the general axis Rovere – La Carrozze – Il Palazzo – Casa Betti. Enemy resistance varied from isolated machine guns hidden in the vines and fruit trees to cunningly-sited positions such as that which temporarily held up 'D' Company on the 14th.

The Battalion was ordered to hold fast in the area won and to form a firm base for an advance by the 139th Brigade on Castiglione. Much detailed information about enemy dispositions was obtained. After the mortar platoon had taken part in an attack on the 21st/22nd November, the Lincolns were transported back to Forli. They remained there, resting, until the 5th December. On their return, the weather was atrocious and the roads in the low ground narrow, muddy and unmetalled. However, the 138th Brigade was ordered to capture the high ground south of Faenza and establish a bridgehead over the River Senio south of Castel Bolognese. The other two battalions of the Brigade were to take the high ground, and the Lincolns were to form the bridgehead.

The Lincolns crossed the River Lamone on the night of the 6th/7th December and were ordered to enlarge the bridgehead by pushing on to Celle. The advance met with considerable opposition and orders were issued to hold firm all positions, and defence tasks for artillery and mortars were developed. Despite the full force of the German 90th Light Division being launched against them on the 9th December, the defences of the 6th Lincolns were never pierced and the enemy's attack was brought to a complete standstill.

The mainstay of the defence had been the heroic actions of Temporary Captain John Henry Cound Brunt (1922-44). A native of Priest Weston, Chirbury, Shropshire; he rallied his men when the house around which his platoon was dug in, was destroyed by mortar fire. Moving to another position, Captain Brunt and his men held back the enemy although heavily outnumbered. This aggressive defence enabled Brunt to reoccupy his previous position and get his wounded away. Similar aggressive and inspiring leadership by this young officer caused the final withdrawal of the enemy. The next day, Captain Brunt was killed by mortar fire. He was posthumously awarded the Victoria Cross.

The Battalion suffered 102 casualties during those few days' fighting but a prisoner of the 90th Light Division stated that of his company only 5 were left after the attack. This was virtually the end of the enemy's attempt to drive in the Lamone bridgehead and the last serious action in which the 6th Lincolns were engaged. They were relieved on the night of the 10th/11th December and, after a rest, served in Greece from February to April 1945. The Battalion then returned to Italy and moved northwards as the campaign ended. After occupation service in Austria, it was disbanded in February 1946.

Chapter 15
THE 2ND BATTALION IN NORTH WEST EUROPE.

The 2nd Battalion of the Regiment, who had been in Great Britain since Dunkirk, undertook special training for the invasion of France and campaigning in north-west Europe in June 1942 and April and July 1943. On the last occasion, training on Eigg and Rhum included their first experience of an assault beach landing. Owing to the greater variety of weapons, the time needed to obtain them and the increased individual skill and knowledge required, it took longer to train an infantry battalion for active service than it had done in the First World War. In September 1943 further rehearsals were carried out in Kilbride Bay and the Battalion went to a tented camp, A.12, in Creech Walk Wood, 4 miles north east of Portsmouth, in April 1944.

After a false start the previous day, the Lincolns sailed from Southsea pier on the 5th June. Maps for the expedition were first produced on the Channel crossing and anti-seasickness tablets issued. The latter were thankfully effective. Despite the odd mortar bomb, the Battalion cleared the beach without any casualties. Contact was made with elements of the enemy who all surrendered. The plan was for the Lincolns to advance as part of the 9th British Infantry Brigade Group on the right of the 3rd Divisional axis through Cresserons and Plumetot to Cambes and Galmanche. However, the seaside hamlets of Lion-sur-Mer and Luc-sur-Mer, which should have been cleared by the 41st Royal Marine Commando, proved strongly held. Accordingly, Battalion Headquarters dug in in an orchard. 'A' and 'B' Companies moved out to the west and dug in. 'D' Company guarded a crossroads between Battalion Headquarters and the sea and 'C' Company watched the rear. The Battalion suffered its first casualties, 1 man killed and 12 wounded. During the night 6th/7th June and the following morning, the Lincolns came under sporadic mortar and shell fire and suffered further losses.

The Battalion came temporarily under the command of the 8th British Infantry Brigade and was ordered to clear the enemy from the chateau and village of Lion-sur-Mer. 'B' Company attacked with 'C' Company in support. When 'B' Company reached a sunken road, they were confronted by heavy mortar and machine gun fire which temporarily checked their advance. 'C' Company moved behind 'B' and got into the chateau grounds, which they cleared of Germans. 'B' Company advanced on the village driving the enemy back into a strongpoint. The Battalion then proceeded, without incident, to take up a defensive position in the St. Aubin D'Arquenay area, with one company guarding the bridge over the River Orne at Bénouville. By dusk, three companies and Battalion Headquarters were in the village and 'D' Company was in position around Pegasus Bridge. On D-Day +3, the Lincolns consolidated in the area of Le Mesnil and came back under the command of the 9th British Infantry Brigade.

It was clear that the advance was going to be slow. The 185th Brigade was

2. *The 10th Foot at the battle of Steenkirk, the 3rd August 1692.*

3. *A Grenadier of Granville's Regiment of Foot in 1685.*

4. *A Grenadier of the 10th Foot in 1751.*

6. An Officer of the 10th (North Lincolnshire)
Foot - Indian Service Dress 1859.

5. An Ensign of the 10th (North Lincolnshire)
Regiment of Foot in 1826.

7. A Private of the Lincolnshire Regiment 1903.

8. The Regimental Colours.

9. *Major Pitcairn entering Lexington 1775.*

10. Victoria Cross Winners.

Private John Kirk

Lieutenant Henry Marsham Havelock

Private Denis Dempsey

Acting Corporal Richard Sharpe

Captain Percy Hansen

11. Victoria Cross Winners.

Acting Lieutenant Colonel Lewis Pugh Evans

The Reverend Theodore Bayley Hardy

Lance Sergeant Walter Simpson (Arthur Evans)

Temporary Major Charles Ferguson Hoey

Temporary Captain John Henry Cound Brunt

12. *Major General Sir Thomas Harte Franks, K.C.B.*

13. *The 10th (North Lincolnshire) Foot at Yokohama circa 1870.*

14. The 1st Battalion The Lincolnshire Regiment with Dervish trophies after the battle of the Atbara, the 8th April 1898.

15. The 1st Battalion The Lincolnshire Regiment building a zariba before the battle of Omdurman, the 2nd September 1898.

16. *The 2nd Battalion The Lincolnshire Regiment crossing Modder River on chains circa 1900 during the South African War.*

17. Breakfast at Riet River, South Africa circa 1900.

18. Some of the Grimsby Chums 1914.

19. The death of Lieutenant Colonel George Burbury McAndrew at the battle of Neuve Chapelle, the 10th March 1915.

20. The battle of Epéhy. The Lincolnshire Regiment holding a captured reserve trench beyond Epéhy, the 18th September 1918..

21. The 1st Battalion The Lincolnshire Regiment on Ramree Island, Burma, February 1945.

22. A 3-inch mortar of the 6th Battalion The Lincolnshire Regiment going into action at Faenza, Italy, December 1944.

23. A party of the 4th Battalion The Lincolnshire Regiment who went out on a patrol across the islands seen on their return, Holland 1945.

24. Members of the Mortar Platoon The Royal Lincolnshire Regiment on a jungle landing zone near Chemore, Perak, January 1958. Left to right Lance Corporal Rogers, Lieutenant John Wooddisse, Guyang (Eban tracker), Corporal Alan Bond, MM, Corporal Gooch and Blauan (Eban tracker).

compelled to withdraw from Le Bisey Wood; there were few supplies and reinforcements for three days due to poor conditions in the Channel; the Germans put up a stubborn defence. The Battalion improved trenches by day and laid minefields at night. At intervals, the Lincolns moved to Cambes to relieve troops there or back to Le Mesnil for comparative rest. However, in this phase, the Battalion gained invaluable battle experience, undertaking many patrols. On the night of the 17th/18th June, 'C' Company occupied Cambes Wood and planned to move out to midway between their own and the enemy positions, with one patrol descending on the enemy from the east and another from the west. Fierce hand to hand fighting ensued and there were many casualties on both sides.

A three divisional front attack on Caen took place with the 3rd Canadian Division on the right, the 59th British Division in the centre and the 3rd British Division on the left. The Lincolns concentrated at Blainville on the 6th July, under the command of the 185th Brigade. They were to move up in line with the leading battalions, their left flank on the river, to capture the village of Hérouville (or Hérouvillette). The plan was for 'B' Company to clear the village and 'A' and 'C' to pass through and exploit along the river bank to the junction of the Canal de Caen and the River Orne. Caen fell on the 7th/8th July, after a terrific air bombardment and a determined assault by the 2nd Royal Warwicks and the 2nd King's Shropshire Light Infantry; but it was on the left flank, in the narrow strip of land between the river and some rising ground, that the bloodiest fighting took place. Here, the Battalion, practically unsupported, met stiff opposition with fierce fighting at close quarters. The enemy occupied the high ground east of the river and the extensive factory area at Colombelles where the tall chimneys were used as observation posts. When the Germans finally gave up the village, they continued to subject the British to heavy mortar and artillery fire from the other side of the river. The Battalion pushed the enemy back slowly and by the morning of the 9th July, 'A' Company reached the river beyond Hérouville. During the afternoon, the Battalion consolidated in that area, commanding the Colombelles bridge with patrols forward to the outskirts of Caen, and between the river and the canal. The Lincolns' casualties were 2 officers and 30 other ranks killed and 6 officers and 132 other ranks wounded, with another officer dying of wounds. The action of the 2nd Lincolns on the 8th and 9th July ranked highly among the contributory factors in the fall of Caen. On the 10th July, the Battalion was relieved by the 3rd Reconnaissance Regiment and went back to the Lion-sur-Mer area for a rest.

On the 16th July, after five days rest and reorganisation, the Lincolns moved east of the River Orne and were in reserve near Amfréville. As the enemy fell back to a strongly prepared line amidst fierce fighting, the Lincolns moved into the devastated area of Sannerville, encountering heavy shellfire, and dug in for the night. The Battalion was sent to create a diversion, on the 19th, by proceeding south towards the Caen – Troarn road, east of Sannerville, where they were involved in two days' heavy fighting in Black Orchard. At the end of the first day, the Lincolns were ordered to withdraw but, when the expected counter attack failed to materialize the next day, they were sent to occupy the ground from which they been instructed to retire. Lacking sleep, soaked by thunderstorms and plastered with clay, the men managed to edge forward despite heavy fire and dug in. In the two days' fighting, the Battalion's losses were 10 officers and 200 other ranks. On the 22nd July, the Battalion was relieved and moved to Escoville to reorganise. During the two and a half days there, about 60 reinforcements were received.

The 2nd Battalion returned to the line in the area north east of Troarn on the 25th and was relieved on the 1st August by the 4th Lincolns: the first time that the two Battalions had been in contact in France since the First World War. The 2nd Battalion then moved across the Orne to the Biéville area and assumed the role of lorried infantry. On the 6th, they advanced south towards Vire where they were ordered to force a bridgehead over the river. In three-quarters of an hour's hard fighting, 'B' and 'C' Companies got across. Casualties were suffered, there were thick woods on either side of the road and the light was failing; nevertheless the position was consolidated and news came that the expected heavy counter attack was no longer a threat, so the advance continued. The 2nd Battalion was the only force employed in an attack towards the main road running east from Vire: a railway was the first objective. 'D' Company was to advance on the left and 'A' on the right, with 'C' and 'B to follow through and exploit as far as possible. There was nobody on either flank when the word was given to advance. A concentration of enemy shells on 'A' Company Headquarters delayed the advance and 'D' Company was held up for a while as the enemy held a sunken road. However 'A' Company pushed on. The Germans, who had few men, were entrenched on rising ground beyond the railway, with many automatic weapons. On 'A' Company leaving the cover of woods, they came under tremendous fire. It was impossible for the British to get their guns in position to return fire and, eventually, under cover of smoke, they had to retire. Meanwhile, one platoon of 'D' Company reached the railway under cover of some buildings but could not move and the rest of the company came under heavy mortar and machine gun fire from the left flank. Finally the company was ordered to withdraw and it was hoped that the platoon that was across the railway could get back under cover of darkness, but it was looked for in vain.

The Battalion then marched to high ground east of Vire on the extreme right of the Second Army. Contact was maintained with the enemy by patrols south-east of Vire, often in daylight, and the Germans were hit hard. On the 6th August, the Battalion proceeded east to just south of Viessoix, later going to Tinchebray and Landisacq and a position south of Flers. Much time was spent in training, especially in river crossings, but on the 29th August the Battalion made one of the longest moves in its history when it went from Flers across the Seine to Vatimesnil, a distance of about 140 miles. More training followed, then, on the 14th September, the Lincolns advanced again - over the Somme, through Mons, Waterloo and Louvain, then over the Albert Canal to an area south of Lille St. Hubert. Two days later 'A' Company was sent to occupy the village of Caulille.

As the bridge over the Escaut Canal at Lille St. Hubert had been demolished, the 3rd British Infantry Division had to force a crossing of the waterway and make good the road to enable the engineers to bridge the obstacle. It was difficult as the banks of the canal were steep and 10 feet above the surrounding country. Furthermore, over the bank, a concrete wall fell 4 – 6 feet to the water. At 11.55 p.m. on the 18th September, the divisional artillery fired concentrations on the enemy positions on the far bank. German mortars replied. At midnight, the first boats hit the water: 'D' Company on the left, 'C' on the right. 'A' followed 'C' and, when across, fanned out and protected the right flank. 'B' Company was held in reserve. The pioneer platoon built two rafts to ferry transport over. The first two companies were across by 12.15 a.m. on the 19th despite heavy fire from small arms and a 20mm. gun. Just before retiring, the enemy set fire to a house on 'D' Company's front and the flames, fanned by the wind, leapt up and illuminated the whole crossing. At 2.15 a.m., all the rifle companies were across and digging in. 'B', 'C' and 'D' Companies and Battalion Headquarters consolidated the village of Broek. 'A' Company was in difficult wooded, marshy country to the right and still in contact with the enemy, who were gradually worn down, and all essential transport was across. The Battalion had acquitted itself well in a short but difficult operation.

The Lincolns moved forward, first to a large monastery east of Achel and then to Hamont. On the 26th September, they crossed the border to Deurne in Holland, moving on to Oeffelt, where they stayed until the 11th October, and received reinforcements, including a contingent from the Bermuda Volunteer Rifles. The next day the Battalion was part of the forces which advanced to clear some woods and capture the town of Venraij. The Lincolns were to pass through the first wood after it had been captured by two other battalions, cross a stretch of open ground (including a water obstacle about which little was known), and clear the second wood. The first part of the operation went so slowly that the Battalion was not called into action on the 13th, which pleased the superstitious!

A strong patrol carried out a reconnaissance. At first light, 'B' Company was to advance and enter the wood covered by 'A' Company, who would then follow. However, the defensive fire of the German artillery and mortars became so heavy that the order was given to retire. It was decided that, with the support of the whole of the divisional artillery and a troop of tanks to bolster the right flank, a full-scale battalion attack should go ahead at 3.30 p.m. 'D' Company would advance on the left and 'A' on the right, followed by 'B' and 'C'. The British barrage came down at zero hour and the attack began. There was more intense fire from the enemy than before but the Battalion simply pressed on although there were many casualties. Eventually the wood was reached and cleared. Schu mines were everywhere. The Lincolns dug in after giving one of the most magnificent examples of courage and determination in the Regiment's history. Casualties were 4 officers killed and 3 wounded, 24 other ranks killed and 111 wounded.

The 2nd Battalion moved back, on the 16th October, to the area from which they started and four months elapsed before they encountered the enemy again in a similar manner. The men were engaged in patrol and sentry duties, constantly moving short distances in awful weather. On the 20th November, they went to Veulen and later began the 'Watch on the Maas' until relieved on the 7th February 1945. After just over two weeks' rest at Wilsele, they proceeded east, on the 24th, and crossed the Maas at Gennep to take part in Operation Veritable. The Division's task was to clear the enemy from a wooded belt of soft ground with inadequate tracks and a few second class roads and capture the villages of Kervenheim and Winnekendonk - an advance of some 7¹/₂miles. The attack began on the 27th February, with 'B' Company on the left, 'D' on the right. 'A' and 'C' passed through and the first objectives were taken with little opposition. Many Germans surrendered. Incessant rain made movements off the roads a nightmare but, by the 1st March, 'A' Company had cleared and consolidated the factory area at the north end of Kervenheim and secured a footing astride the main road from Udem. The next day, 'A' and 'C' Companies easily completed the capture of the village. When a supporting squadron of tanks came up, the Battalion proceeded to attack Winnekendonk. There was 1200 yards of open ground to be crossed after leaving the neighbouring woods before the cover of buildings could be reached. The Battaiion went forward under heavy machine gun, mortar and shell fire, and the light was fading fast but, amidst strenuous fighting, the tanks and infantry entered the village. The next day they captured Winnekendonk: one of the Lincoln's finest actions of the war. Many congratulatory messages were received, but casualties were 16 killed, 65 wounded and 6 missing.

The Lincolns remained in the village for 10 days and, on the 13th March, went to take over a sector of the Rhine, first at Hochend and later at Obermormter. The Battalion crossed the river at Rees, on the 28th, where the bridgehead was shallowest. The Lincolns took part in an attack by two battalions which each had the objective of gaining and holding a bridgehead over the river Aa. They were to hold the line of the Haltuicker Bach while engineers constructed a bridge over the river. 'D' Company crossed in assault boats and pressed on in spite of casualties from spandau fire. 'C' followed. 'A' crossed third and fanned out to the left. Once they were clear of the bank, resistance eased. The operation was an unqualified success. After a few days' badly needed rest, the Battalion moved again, on the 2nd April, to Groenlo. They then progressed to Sublohne via Enschede, Oldenzaal and Nordhorn.

The Battalion was loaned to the 185th Brigade in the centre of Lingen for street fighting in the dark. The enemy had no intention of retreating and often circled back at night behind 'A' and 'B' Companies. 'C' Company was to the right of 'A' as they edged their way through house by house. In the light, the next day, the Lincolns could see what they were up against. With tank co-operation, they were able to make rapid progress and, by early afternoon, 'C' Company had even captured the road junction south west of the town. The Battalion's next task was to assist in opening up the axis Lingen – Plantelunne. The enemy had taken such a beating in Lingen they put up little resistance and 'C' Company reached its objective in thirty minutes. The Battalion moved to Polle Estringen Rottum, Osterkapeln and Barnsdorf on the Osnabruck – Bremen road. Here they protected the left flank of the 7th Armoured Division until the 17th April. The Brigade then attacked Stuhr, Moordeich, Mittelshuchting and Kirchhuchting. 'A' Company was in the lead. It was a long and gruelling day with hard fighting even though the Germans were deficient in artillery. Each company went into action in turn and the enemy retreated. The Battalion captured Kirchhuchting, on the 20th April, taking over 250 prisoners. This brought the total of Germans captured by the Brigade, for the month, to 1000. The Lincolns' casualties on the 19th/20th were 10 killed and 19 wounded.

The 9th British Infantry Brigade opened the Divisional attack for the capture of Bremen at midnight on the 24th/25th April. The 2nd Battalion was ordered to capture the Focke Wulfe works. After heavy fighting, 'B' Company then 'C' Company established themselves at strategic points on the northern edge of the objective. 'A' and 'D' came to take over. 'B' and 'C' moved south to complete the operation by 5.30 p.m. The Lincolns' casualties were 4 killed and 4 wounded.

The 26th April was the last day the Battalion was in action, clearing their area and taking prisoners. On the 27th, they moved to Delmenhorst, 5 miles west of Bremen, and on the 7th May, proceeded to Lengerich, 10 miles south west of Osnabruck, where they heard the war had ended.

Chapter 16
THE 4TH BATTALION IN NORTH WEST EUROPE

Following their two years training in the United Kingdom, the 4th Lincolns sailed from Newhaven on the 9th June 1944, as part of the 49th (West Riding) Division. The crossing to Normandy was uneventful and, the next day, the landing-craft bumped over the sandbanks and up the beach. Battalion Headquarters with 'A' and 'B' Companies disembarked while the craft commander muttered 'and now I've got to get the bloody thing off again.' On the 13th, the Battalion, up to strength in manpower and virtually complete with vehicles, was ordered to the area Tilly-sur-Seulles - St. Pierre. The Lincolns were evacuated during a bombardment by the Tactical Air Force and then sent back to where they had been. During the ensuing nights, some vigorous patrolling was carried out to Les Hauts Vents and the Parc de Boislande. On the 15th June, 'A' Company with a carrier-mortar group was ordered to reconnoitre St. Pierre and, if the enemy was not in occupation, to hold the village until further orders. However, part of the carrier platoon, on entering St. Pierre, came under fire from German anti-tank weapons supported by infantry as the enemy was in force at Fontenay and ready to counter-attack any attempt to occupy St. Pierre. The Commanding Officer of the Lincolns, Lieutenant Colonel Peter Barclay, received information from Brigade Headquarters of the enemy's strength and withdrew his men.

Patrolling continued and it became evident that only a full-scale assault would dislodge the enemy from his position which ran through Tilly, Fontenay-le Pesnil and high, thickly-wooded country to the south and east. A two-brigade advance was decided on, using 146th and 147th Brigades on the right and left respectively. The 4th Lincolns, in 146th Brigade, were to capture Bas de Fontenay and, as their right flank would be open, it was from this direction that a counter-attack might come. The success of the whole divisional plan depended on the Battalion taking and holding their objective.

On the 25th June, 'D' Company attacked on the right, 'A' Company on the left, while 'C' Company and a squadron of tanks protected the exposed right flank: 'B' Company was in reserve. Smoke from bursting shells in the valley, through which the companies advanced, cut down visibility. Not only was it difficult to distinguish one group of men from another, but the smoke made it almost impossible for commanders to keep control by shouting. 'A' Company suffered casualties and became slightly disorganised so Lieutenant Colonel Barclay sent his reserve company through them. 'D' Company advanced successfully and the remainder of the Battalion reached its objectives. Heavy and accurate enemy shellfire was then brought down on 'C' Company's area and, as observation improved, on other parts of the Battalion. However, thanks to support from 185 Field Battery, the expected counter-attack did not materialize. About noon, the 1st/4th King's Own Yorkshire Light Infantry passed through. This, the Battle of Fontenay, cost the 4th Lincolns 14 killed and 64 wounded. 80 enemy dead and 53 prisoners were counted and the material captured included 9 half-tracks, a Mark IV tank, some anti-tank guns and a large pile of small arms. The Divisional Commander, Major General E.H. Barker, commented that 'the Battle of Fontenay was the 4th Lincolns' battle.'

On the 27th June, 'A' Company forestalled the Germans in the occupation of La Grande Ferme, a stout old building between Bas de Fontenay and Tessel Bretteville, that would have made a formidable enemy strongpoint. 'B' Company resisted stubbornly when the Germans attacked in Tessel Bretteville on the 1st July and a counter-attack by 'C' Company was successful. Patrolling was constant and vigorously carried out with the inevitable casualties until the Battalion was relieved on the 11th July. The Lincolns went forward to Tessel Wood on the 16th and occupied Vendes without resistance, following which they were relieved again. On the 26th, the Battalion moved to Démouville, east of Caen, and, five days later, to Sannerville where they relieved the 2nd Lincolns.

Although harassed by artillery and mortar fire, the 4th Lincolns found that the enemy was weak but mosquitoes proved a major trial. On the 8th August, the Battalion moved to Sollers, then Bourguébus and Star Wood, where they spent four days. The next day, they went to Conteville; on the 15th, to Billy and took Airan by assault on the 16th, which also saw the capture of a usable bridge further along the main road. The 18th August was a day of long marches. The Battalion found the swiftly-running River Vie, with high, slippery banks and swollen with recent rain, a serious obstacle. Crossing this by bridges, heavy enemy fire forced the Battalion to withdraw and the advance was not resumed until the 21st. 'C' and 'B' Companies crossed the River Touques and, during the night 23rd/24th August, the Germans withdrew and the Battalion concentrated in the area of Le Brueil-en-Auge. On the 24th, reinforcements arrived as the Lincolns were greatly below strength; 'A' Company, for instance, totalling only 44 all ranks. On the 28th, the Battalion reached the Seine at Quilleboeuf. After some brisk fighting, the Lincolns crossed the river by Royal Engineers' ferries at Caudebec on the 1st September. This passed off without mishap but one company had to paddle with shovels in the absence of oars. The transport went by the nearest road bridge, which was at Rouen.

Le Havre had been bypassed in the swift advance of the Allied armies across France but the stretched lines of communication and the needs of the civilian population made it imperative to capture another major port in addition to Cherbourg. As an essential preliminary to the attack on Le Havre, the Lincolns captured the important outpost of Gainneville on the 2nd September. Le Havre was heavily bombed after the German Commander refused to surrender. The infantry assault began on the 10th September and, after the King's Own Yorkshire Light Infantry had subdued stubborn enemy resistance south of Harfleur, the Lincolns entered the town against comparatively light opposition. The specialist armoured vehicles of the Royal

Engineers were a great assistance. The road bridges over the railway and river were found to be very badly damaged, partly by bombing but mainly due to demolition. However, a route for the renewed advance was discovered on low ground between the main road and the river. On the 12th September, the main assault on Le Havre went in and a series of determined attacks by the Battalion overcame the opposition despite some enemy strong-points. About 500 prisoners were captured by the Lincolns, whose casualties were 13 other ranks wounded.

The 4th Battalion moved back to the area of St. Aubin - Routot for four days' training and recreation. After originally being ordered in the direction of Dieppe, the Lincolns were sent to the neighbourhood of the Albert Canal on the 19th September, and they crossed the Belgian border on the 22nd. Preparations made the next day to force a crossing over the canal were cancelled when it was learned that the enemy had withdrawn. Instead, fresh orders arrived for crossing the Antwerp-Turnhout Canal.

Three crossings were to be made by the different battalions of the Division. The Lincolns were to establish a bridgehead in the area of the bridge crossing the main road. All bridges had been blown and all barges sunk on the north side of the canal. The flat landscape offered little natural cover and bends in the canal gave the enemy great scope for enfilade machine-gun fire, so it was decided to carry out a night crossing. It began at one minute past midnight on the 24th/25th September; assault boats had been carried to the canal bank in intense darkness and absolute silence. Four hours later, the bridgehead was firmly established and the Engineers had a bridge in use two hours after that. Of the three attempted crossings, only that of the Lincolns was successful, and soon armour was pouring over the bridge. The Battalion was relieved and ordered to push eastwards along the northern bank of the canal.

After little more than three-quarters of a mile, the Lincolns re-established contact with the enemy around Bersée. The Battalion, less 'A' Company protecting the left flank, was compelled to concentrate and form a strongpoint in some brickworks. 'A' Company became cut off and had to abandon their vehicles, some carriers and anti-tank guns. However, splendid support gunnery enabled 'A' Company to fight its way back to the rest of the Battalion, which it rejoined next morning. Enemy resistance near the canal bank was ended by a sweep by 'C' Company west and north of the Battalion perimeter when a flame-thrower mounted on a Bren carrier played a major role. 'A' Company carried out a successful action against another enemy force before the Battalion was ordered to move eastwards behind the Polish Armoured Division on the 2nd October.

After a successful attack on some factory buildings south-west of Ravels, the 4th Lincolns pursued the enemy as far as Chapel St. Jean. On the 4th October, the Battalion advanced with a squadron of tanks from the 27th Canadian Armoured Regiment under command. Good progress was made for three miles but, with enemy resistance stiffening, the Lincolns settled down for the night in an all-round defensive position. It was then learned that their vigorous thrust had drawn enemy reinforcements south from Tilburg and the Battalion was ordered to withdraw to the area of Nieukirk on the Belgian-Dutch frontier. A strong German counter-attack was launched two days later. This was a very tough action but the Lincolns held on, assisted by tanks, artillery and mortars, until they were relieved in the afternoon.

The Battalion advanced to the Poppel area on the 8th October and had a relatively quiet week at Baarle Nassau on the Dutch border. On the 19th, the Lincolns came under command of the 2nd Canadian Armoured Brigade. Patrols to a depth of several thousand yards were common and made hazardous by the close country, the unmarked tracks and dry sticks that crackled underfoot. On the 20th, Field Marshal Sir Bernard Montgomery told the Commanding Officer 'I am constantly hearing of the fine achievements of your Battalion.' Three days later, the 6th and 27th Canadian Armoured Regiments were placed under Lieutenant Colonel Barclay's command and these, with his own Battalion and a Belgian detachment, became known as 'Impforce'. The Lincolns had received much-needed reinforcements during the previous fortnight and were up to 75 per cent. of their full establishment.

A successful advance was made to Breda, when over 180 prisoners and many weapons were captured. The Battalion's casualties were amazingly light, only 11 wounded and 2 missing since leaving Baarle Nassau. 'Impforce' ceased to exist on the 31st October and the Lincolns returned to the 146th Brigade. The weather was vile; wet and windy, and the countryside deep under floods; the straight, muddy roads were flanked by deep ditches filled with water. An attack on Willemstad, the Germans' only remaining strongpoint south of the River Maas, was made on the 7th November in torrential rain and a howling gale. However, it was found that the enemy had escaped across the river unobserved. The Battalion's next action was the capture of Maasbree on the 22nd, although bad weather and boggy ground limited the support that could be given by tanks. Patrolling continued vigorously and prisoners captured by 'C' Company gave the positions of the enemy's battalion and company headquarters. The Battalion's pioneers were also able to get precise information of obstacles and anti-tank defences. This, together with the clearance of minefields, proved a great help to the 15th (Scottish) Division in their attack on Blerick.

Part of 'A' Company carried out a well-planned raid on an enemy position at Hout Blerick, inflicting a loss of 4 killed, 2 wounded and 12 prisoners without sustaining any casualties themselves. On the same day, a patrol cleared a locality, 1000 yards to the west. The Battalion reached Nijmegen on the 2nd December and Ressen, under 147th Infantry Brigade, on the 14th. The main problem was flooding and a two-hourly check was kept on the rise and fall of the water level. Towards the end of the month, the Lincolns moved to Haalderen. Vigorous patrolling and sniper activity were carried out. The weather rapidly deteriorated, a fine, cold spell giving way to sleet and snow. The crackling of the ice could be heard from afar in the stillness of the night and no white camouflage suits were immediately available.

On the 12th January 1945, the Battalion moved to west of Bemmel, where they carried out aggressive patrolling, until they were relieved later in the month. In February, the Lincolns went to Valburg where the land in front of the new position was flooded, so standing patrols were established in available buildings and boat patrols instituted. The Battalion was relieved again on the 12th March.

The Lincolns went into action on the 2nd April in dull, windy weather with intermittent rain, and captured Angeren and Huissen despite casualties inflicted by Allied aircraft. The next day, 'C' and 'D' Companies crossed the Rhine near Loovier and patrols from the latter Company penetrated as far as the Ijssel. This was followed by the assault on Arnhem. Two river obstacles, the flat country before the town, the high ground behind it and strong defences made this a difficult task. Another brigade established a bridgehead over the Ijssel south-east of Arnhem, then the Lincolns passed through on the 13th April, and, helped by Royal Engineers assault vehicles and flame-throwing carriers, mopped up a factory in the town and seized the high ground on the far side. The Battalion had a very hard fight but their success contributed to the capture of Arnhem and also the Rhine crossing. This contrasted with the lack of success in the airborne Battle of Arnhem in September 1944. The Lincolns took 234 prisoners in two days at a cost of 5 killed and 49 wounded.

The Battalion was at Wageningen on the 4th May when news arrived that all enemy troops in north-west Germany, Denmark and Holland had surrendered unconditionally. The 4th Lincolns moved to Utrecht and then Maarssen where they disarmed German troops and collected enemy equipment and war material. Occupation duties in Germany followed, including being the first Line Regiment to take over guard duties at the Nuremberg Trials. In the spring of 1946, the Battalion moved to Gevelsberg, where it was disbanded.

Battle Honours and Decorations

The Lincolns lost over 1,000 all ranks and gained 47 Battle Honours in the Second World War. Members of the Regiment won numerous awards including 2 Victoria Crosses, 15 Distinguished Service Orders, 13 Distinguished Conduct Medals, 46 Military Crosses and 81 Military Medals. Over 300 officers, N.C.O.s and men were mentioned in Despatches, many more than once.

On the 10th December 1946, King George VI, in recognition of its services, was graciously pleased to authorize the Regiment to be known by the style and title of 'The Royal Lincolnshire Regiment'.

Chapter 17

POST WAR PEACEKEEPING - THE FINAL PHASE

The Regular Army was reorganised after the Second World War, one result being a pruning of infantry units to find men for the armoured and technical corps that had come into being during the conflict. The number of Regular infantry battalions was cut, but, to avoid them being altogether disbanded, one battalion of each regiment was placed in 'suspended animation' as a cadre. It was to remain dormant for a period of years until it came to life again at the expense of the other Regular battalion. In the case of the Royal Lincolnshire Regiment, it was the 1st Battalion that went into 'suspended animation'.

The Labour Government, which came to power in July 1945, had no alternative but to keep conscription. Initially, it wanted a term of one year but by the time the National Serviceman, as he was called, had completed his basic training and been sent by troopship to some far-flung part of the world, it was almost time for him to be discharged. The term of National Service was, therefore, lengthened, first to eighteen months and then, in 1950, to two years. National Service had an immense social impact. Lincolnshire boys left home, many for dangerous active service in Malaya and elsewhere, and returned two years later men. At the time, many counted the days to 'demob'. However, in later years, most looked back on that period of their lives with affection, admitting that they learned the value of comradeship and teamwork in difficult times – as well as much about themselves.

When the war in Europe ended, the 3rd Division, including the 2nd Lincolns, was selected to garrison Berlin. However, this was changed and the Division was chosen to take part in the assault on Japan. The Japanese surrender interrupted these plans and the Division was sent to Port Said in October 1945. By the middle of December, the Battalion was concentrated in Palestine, at Pardess Hanna midway between Tel-Aviv and Haifa, for internal security duties as relations between Jews and Arabs had rapidly deteriorated since the end of the War.

Roadblocks were manned every third night to enforce the curfew regulations, and two companies were always standing by at short notice to deal with any emergency. The Battalion remained in the Pardess Hanna area until April 1946, when they went to the Canal Zone. They moved to Jerusalem later in the year, where they took over guard duties at the King David Hotel, the General Officer Commanding's house and other important buildings. These guards permanently absorbed two companies; in addition, two roadblocks were manned and foot patrols found by day and night in co-operation with the police.

In June 1947, the 2nd Lincolns were transferred from the 3rd Infantry Division to the 1st Armoured Division. After training in Transjordan from the 20th September to

25th October, the Battalion returned to internal security duties in Palestine, which grew daily more onerous and thankless as the general situation deteriorated. On the 12th May 1948, the Lincolns left Palestine in a three-day move to Gothic Camp, El Ballah, near the Suez Canal.

In the immediate post-war years, infantry regiments were grouped, mainly on a territorial basis, officers and men interchanging between the regiments in the group according to the needs of the service. Thus, in 1947, The Royal Lincolnshire Regiment was included with the Royal Warwicks, Royal Leicesters and Sherwood Foresters in the Midland Brigade. Originally, Primary Training Centres were established at Regimental Depots for basic training, but, in the Spring of 1948, due to shortage of manpower, the Centres were closed down and the duties of recruit training for all Midland Brigade Regiments were undertaken by the 1st Royal Warwicks at Budbrooke Barracks, Warwick.

In view of the importance for County Regiments to maintain a regimental home in their own county, Regimental Depots were revived. This was largely on a care and maintenance basis and with no training responsibilities. At Lincoln, in addition to Battalion Headquarters, room was found for other units and the vehicles and carriers of the 4th Battalion (T.A.). Colonels of Regiments were given the choice of either the selected battalion remaining in suspended animation, the amalgamation of the 1st and 2nd Battalions or the disbandment of one of them. In the case of The Royal Lincolnshire Regiment, the decision was made to amalgamate the two Battalions. This took place at El Ballah in Egypt on the 28th October 1948 when the 2nd Battalion paraded on the arrival of personnel from the 1st Battalion. The last occasion on which a similar event took place was at Malta in 1816.

On the 5th January 1949, the newly reconstituted 1st Battalion was despatched to Aqaba, as part of 'Oulton Force', at the request of the Transjordan Government, to forestall the possible occupation of the port by Israeli troops. Lieutenant Colonel R.H.L. Oulton was the Commanding Officer of the Battalion at that time. The occupation was successful and no hostile incident occurred. Six months later, the Battalion returned to Egypt.

In the spring of 1947, the Territorial Army was reconstituted and the 4th and 6th Battalions of the Regiment were resurrected and included in the 49th (West Riding and Midland) Division. Recruiting for the rank and file was slow, partly due to war weariness and, in 1950, it was decided to amalgamate the two battalions, due to the manpower needs of other newly formed T.A. units in Lincolnshire. Thus the 4th/6th Battalion The Royal Lincolnshire Regiment, T.A. came into being.

The 1st Battalion was ordered to Aqaba for a second time in May 1951 but, apart from 'C' Company, returned to Egypt in October when the security of the Suez Canal became threatened. The Lincolns reached Port Said on the 14th October and were accommodated in 156 Transit Camp on the east bank of the Canal. Rioting was reported at Ismailia and hostile crowds gathered in Port Said. The Egyptian authorities had become uncooperative and were refusing free entry or exit for Service and NAAFI vehicles from the docks area, which was then taken over by 'A' Company. There was much terrorist activity against British troops. On the 19th November, the Egyptian police in Ismailia and Arishia were disarmed without incident. Those relieved departed for Cairo where they were decorated and promoted for gallantry, but the Battalion began to suffer casualties.

Sniping against British troops continued in 1952 and, on the 19th January, there occurred the 'orange-barrow' explosion. At noon, an Egyptian brought a barrow load of oranges to a post at the YMCA Bridge where fire had previously been exchanged across the Sweet Water Canal. After two and a half hours selling oranges to the men, the Egyptian left the barrow, saying he would fetch some eggs from the other side of the canal. Shortly afterwards, the barrow blew up. Heavy fire from the north bank of the canal hampered the evacuation of the wounded. Fire was returned and the Lincolns, supported by armoured cars and Centurion tanks, restored the situation by dusk. In the explosion, the Battalion suffered 4 wounded, 2 fatally. The Lincolns had a supporting role on the 25th January in Operation Eagle, the disarming of the Egyptian police. The latter resisted and there was considerable firing throughout the day before they surrendered. Casualties were incurred on both sides but none by the Lincolns. Ismailia remained quiet for several days, but the repercussions of 'Eagle' included serious rioting in Cairo and a declaration of Martial Law by the Egyptian Government. Vigilance and guard duties continued to be the Battalion's lot for several weeks. In March and April, the Lincolns left for England. They had served abroad continuously for twenty-two years.

The 1st Royal Lincolns proceeded to Goslar, as part of the British Army of the Rhine, in early July 1952 and to Berlin on the 12th April 1954. The following year, they returned to England and embarked by sea for Malaya on the 19th July, with the advance and rear parties leaving by air twelve days later. After a week settling in at Singapore, the rifle and support companies moved to Kota Tinggi, Johore.

The murders of Europeans in Malaya led to operations against the Communists that began in June 1948 and lasted until July 1960. Initially, the Lincolns spent three weeks in jungle training. This took the form of patrolling, jungle navigation, immediate action drills, ambushes and occupying jungle bases. The emphasis was on action at platoon and section level. At the conclusion of the training, each company carried out a two-day jungle exercise. Various courses, peculiar to Malayan conditions, were also attended. These included a fourteen-day jungle cookery course, a dog-handler course of six weeks' duration, a water-duties and a jungle hygiene one.

The Lincolns moved to West Pahang and formed part of 28th Commonwealth Infantry Brigade, which was to be the strategic reserve for the theatre. Battalion Headquarters and Headquarters Company were at Bentong, 47 miles north-east of Kuala Lumpur, Support Company at Bentong airstrip, 'B' Company at Raub, 'D' Company at Benta, 'A' Company at Sabai and 'C' Company was split between Tekal and Kerdau. Some extremely truculent communists in Johore caused a redeployment and 'A', 'B' and 'D' Companies went to new locations between 70 and 80 miles east of Bentong. Battalion HQ and HQ Company moved 50 miles to Temerloh.

Rifle platoons spent most of their time in the jungle moving either on foot or by helicopter and carrying rations for short periods. Longer periods meant the airdrop of supplies from Valetta aircraft. For administration, convoyed transport or armoured 3-ton lorries used the roads. There were Auster light aircraft for reconnaissance. The rifle companies were dispersed up and down 50 miles of single-track railway on which they had their own armoured train. The police lent their armoured rail trolleys, which had diesel engines and a Browning machine gun, for urgent journeys between companies. Operations in each area were controlled by a District War Executive Committee. The Lincolns had 39 officers, including those attached to them, 10 of these were National Servicemen and a further 5 had short-service commissions. By February 1956, the Battalion's strength had grown to 1200, a large percentage being National Servicemen.

Quite soon, all companies were scoring minor successes. On the 25th September, 11 platoon of 'D' Company made the first capture of communist terrorists (CTs). A 5-man patrol forced the surrender of a party official and his bodyguard who were armed with an M1 carbine, a .38 pistol, a grenade and 79 rounds of ammunition. The day before, clothing, ammunition and equipment had been found and, subsequently, with mine detectors, 6 buried shotguns and a rifle were unearthed. During November, two drafts, numbering 80 in all, arrived for the Battalion. About 60 families came out at Christmas and lived in private accommodation in Kuala Lumpur, as there were very few quarters. Husbands could expect about four days a month at most with their families and around 45 single men got away each week for rest and recreation in Singapore.

In October/November, 'A' Company took part in a large-scale operation, about 10 miles from Triang, searching for CTs. Lieutenant Mike Rushby set a record by taking out 3 platoon of the Company for 21 days, staying on himself for a further 7 days with 4 men. The difficulty of distinguishing a communist terrorist from a harmless estate worker was demonstrated when a 'B' Company patrol came across 4 men cutting wood. Having been warned that Malays were clearing the jungle for planting rubber, the patrol did not open fire. The men made off and, next morning, a hideout for 3 terrorists was found within 100 yards of the scene. An opportunity missed?

The Battalion killed its first terrorist on the 9th January 1956 following a tip-off from a communist who surrendered in the previous month. This information also resulted in the capture of clothing, food, medical supplies, printing equipment, documents and weapons including a Luger and a Lewis gun. Patrolling was never ending. The Battalion Newsletter of that January stated: 'One is continually impressed by the guts and cheerfulness of the ordinary soldier but the patrol leader requires all this and much more, too. It is no small demand to ask a young man of 19 or 20 to take two or three other men out into the jungle alone, patrol a difficult and possibly dangerous area and navigate his way back. There are no landmarks, no signposts, no roads, none of the normal means for finding one's way about to which civilised people are used'. Massive firepower was not effective in this campaign: the Lincolns, like other British soldiers, had to live and fight in the jungle for long periods, relying on rifles and light machine guns plus an extremely high standard of minor infantry tactics. Silence, as in the famous advance at Sobraon in 1846, was vital in the jungle.

In March 1956, the Battalion received their first FN rifles. These were automatic assault rifles of the kind developed by most nations after the Second World War when the Germans used the Sturmgewehr version of this weapon to great effect. The British Army adopted the Belgian FNFAL (Fabrique Nationale Fusil Automatique Légère) rifle known as the 'FN'. In April, part of the Lincolns moved to Negri Sembilan, south of Pahang. The Newsletter reported that operations in Malaya as a whole saw communist terrorists 'eliminated' at under 30 a month. As far as the Battalion was concerned, the success rate was one elimination for every 5,000 man-days of patrolling and ambushing. There was a great deal of very hard work over extremely long hours. Duties included clearing helicopter landing zones and providing small garrisons to back up the police in denying the terrorists food supplies from villagers, by doubling up with the police on gate duty and searching the rubber tappers, patrolling and setting ambushes round the perimeter wire at night and assisting with the rice escort. Villages were wired in to protect the inhabitants and to deny supplies, especially food, to straggling terrorists in the jungle. The protected village was a concept of General Sir Gerald Templer and, by encouraging and looking after the loyal Malays, played an important role in the battle for hearts and minds. The Military Cross was won by Lieutenants Peter Surtees and Malcolm Taylor for actions on the 9th May and the 23rd October respectively.

At the end of November 1956, the Battalion less 'B' and 'C' Companies moved to Perak. The remaining companies joined their comrades after Christmas. Lieutenant General Sir Roger Bower, General Officer Commanding Malaya Command, stated that the Regiment 'is certainly one of the best operational units in this country and they have a very fine record in Negri Sembilan...when the Battalion moved...I had a deputation of the unofficial members of the State War Executive Committee asking that I would allow the Regiment to stay in Negri. For all sorts of reasons, this was impossible, but it does show the degree of confidence that the Regiment has established amongst the leading planters and civilians of all races in the state'. It is believed that Sergeant George Bench, Lance Corporal Clive Henson and Private Roger Powell of the Regiment were the first British personnel to receive awards from Negri Sembilan.

The Battalion, less 'B' and 'C' Companies who remained with 26 Gurkha Brigade, was sent to join the Commonwealth Brigade in the Sungei Siput area towards the end of 1956. However, centenary celebrations in Georgetown led to a Battalion Tactical Headquarters and one company being kept on stand-by in Penang from the 4th to 17th January 1957. 'D' Company reported in the Newsletter that the operational area in Perak was completely different from its previous one. There were tin mines and rubber plantations surrounded by mountains containing terrorist hideouts. Living in the lowland area were some 30-40,000 inhabitants 'mainly apathetic, terrorised or

143

actively anti-government'. The locals provided the terrorists with intelligence and food. Control of the latter was always a major activity and men on duty at one gate alone, in conjunction with the police, had to search 2,000 tappers going out to work each morning.

The loss of experienced National Service drafts and the issue of the 7.62mm. self-loading rifle led to a two months re-training period. After this, patrol work continued and, between the 31st May and 21st June, operations reached battalion-sized dimensions. Captain Peter Walter was awarded the Military Cross for an action on the 2nd June. The importance of the Lincolns' activities was shown by the size of the support they were given; a troop of King's Dragoon Guards, who patrolled roads and manned ambushes at night, artillery from 'A' Troop 105 Field Battery Royal Australian Artillery and two 3.7 inch medium AA guns of the 1st Singapore Regiment Royal Artillery, and air cover by helicopters, Valettas and Austers.

On the 24th July 1957 came a joint announcement from the respective Colonels of the Royal Lincolnshire Regiment and the Northamptonshire Regiment that, on account of reorganisation of the Army, the two Regiments were to be amalgamated 'on a date between 1960 and 1962'. Meanwhile, the Battalion continued its operations in Malaya, and although the country became independent on the 31st August, this made little difference to the campaign. However, it gave 'B' Company the opportunity to claim the last 'kill' of a communist terrorist under British rule, two hours before independence. August also saw the end of Support Company, whose members were posted to Headquarter Company or to rifle companies. HQ Company absorbed the Battalion training wing at the same time. This reorganisation was in line with a lower establishment.

Operations continued at high intensity and, in October 1957, Privates D. T. Thompson and D. Jack were the first men of the Lincolns to be killed in action during the campaign. Lieutenant Colonel Frank Goulson was appointed an Officer of the Order of the British Empire on completion of his tour of command that month. Following operations between November 1957 and January 1958, Major G.D. Cole was awarded the Military Cross. Corporal 'Bobby' Shaftoe was given the Military Medal for displaying leadership and vigour of the highest order during hard and arduous patrolling. The Battalion made its seventh major move since arriving in Malaya, when it went to Johore at the end of February. The Newsletter stated that the 40-50 terrorists in the area 'have hardly been disturbed for a very long time' and had 'all the advantage of knowing the marshy and belukar-covered country'.

The western half of Johore contained the Muar district terrorists in its jungle and hills and the eastern half the Batu Pahat or 'Yong Peng Bandits' amongst swamp and rubber estates. Patrols and ambushes were carried out and information of varying usefulness was obtained from communists who surrendered. An ambush was carried out by the Mortar Platoon under Lieutenant John Wooddisse on the 25th March on the Kanka estate near Muar. This led to material progress in the operations against the terrorists in that part of Malaya. The Battalion strength was diminished in April as no more reinforcements arrived. This resulted in men from Headquarter Company being sent to rifle companies for occasional duties. Every day, 2 men left camp very early to bolster police patrols engaged in searches and the vital food checks. The terrorists in the jungle had many sympathisers in the Yong Peng and Cha'Ah area. The Battalion's final engagement at Yong Peng on the 10th May decimated the last fighting terrorist platoon in the area. The Mortar Platoon was operational for 45 days out of 60 from the 7th March 1958. In a final list of awards for Malaya, Lieutenant Colonel Tony Innes was appointed an Officer of the Order of the British Empire and Corporal Alan Bond was awarded the Military Medal. On the 25th July, the Regiment, reduced to 500 all ranks, embarked at Singapore for Mombasa, Kenya. It had the unique distinction of taking part in the first and last military operations in Malaya during British rule. The Lincolns who served in the campaign against the communist terrorists from 1955 to 1958 were worthy successors to those who had fought in Perak in 1875-76. It is said that 85% of the Regiment in the 1950s were National Servicemen. The defeat of the terrorists in Malaya was one of the British Army's finest achievements after 1945 and the Lincolns played a notable part in this.

Mombasa was reached on the 4th August but the Battalion was diverted to Aden, where it arrived on the 9th, as a tactical reserve for operations in the Arabian Peninsula. Hard training and acclimatisation to the heat and sand, but no active service, took place. The Battalion embarked for England on the 10th September and, by the end of November, had moved to Germany. The final parade of the Lincolns prior to amalgamation with the Northamptonshire Regiment, on the 1st June 1960, was held at Minden, West Germany on the 21st April. In a Special Order of the Day, the Regiment's Commanding Officer, Lieutenant Colonel Tony Innes, said: 'In this the 275th and last year of the Regiment you may take pride in the fact that you have been the worthy successors of all those who have served before you'. The title of the combined Regiment was The 2nd East Anglian Regiment (Duchess of Gloucester's Own Royal Lincolnshire and Northamptonshire). This became the 2nd (Duchess of Gloucester's Own Royal Lincolnshire and Northamptonshire) Battalion, The Royal Anglian Regiment on the 1st September 1964 and 2nd Battalion, The Royal Anglian Regiment in 1968. The Amalgamation Parade took place at Watchet, Somerset, on the 30th June, 1960 in the presence of the new Regiment's Colonel-in-Chief, Her Royal Highness the Duchess of Gloucester.

Change had also befallen the Territorial Army in the 1950s when it acquired a secondary role in support of the Civil Power. Training at one camp in three was spent mainly in learning the skills of fire fighting, light rescue and first aid in addition to purely military training. In the 1960s, the T.A. was comprehensively reorganised and ceased to exist as a separate army. Categories of Territorials were created and 2 units came out of the 4th/6th Battalion: 163 (Movement Light) Squadron, Royal Engineers (TA) and a Category II unit with a role in support of the regular army which became a company of the 5th (Volunteer) Battalion The Royal Anglian Regiment. The name of the Regiment lived on in a TAVR Battalion, the Royal Lincolnshire Regiment (T), with a role in support of the Civil Power. This unit was disbanded in 1969 retaining a cadre for future expansion, which came the following year when the 7th Battalion The Royal Anglian Regiment (V) was formed. Two companies carried the subsidiary title 'Royal Lincolnshire' and wore the badge as collar dogs.

EPILOGUE

The Royal Lincolnshire Regiment served its country valiantly for 275 years. Its soldiers fought in Europe, Asia, Africa and America. They earned 131 Battle Honours and other distinctions, from 10 Victoria Crosses to the Regiment's Royal prefix for outstanding services in the Second World War. In the British Army it is the Regiment, with its distinct identity, characteristics and traditions that is the focus and inspiration for its members. Whether marching with Marlborough to the Danube or advancing at Sobraon, suffering the heat of the desert or the cold of mountain winters, the Lincolns always played their part. As will be evident from this history, a change of name does not signal the end of the story. The customs and traditions of The Royal Lincolnshire Regiment are preserved in the 2nd Battalion of The Royal Anglian Regiment and the County's soldiers continue to serve in that Regiment and the Territorial Army.

When the Duke of Wellington was asked by Thomas Creevey about the chances of defeating Napoleon, he pointed to a British soldier and said, 'There, it all depends on that article whether we do the business or not. Give me enough of it, and I am sure.' The Lincolns were wonderful examples of British soldiers and always a great credit to their County.

Appendix 1
TIMELINE

Year	Event	Monarch

Monmouth's Rebellion

| 1685 | Raising of Earl of Bath's Regiment | JAMES II |

War of the Grand Alliance

| 1692 | Steenkirk: first action of Regiment | WILLIAM & MARY |

War of the Spanish Succession

1704	Blenheim	ANNE
1706	Ramillies	
1708	Oudenarde	
1709	Malplaquet	
		GEORGE I

Numbering of Regiments of Foot

| 1751 | Designated 10th Regiment of Foot | GEORGE II |

American War of Independence

1775	Lexington Common	GEORGE III
1775	Bunker Hill	
1776	Fort Washington	
1777	Brandywine	

Naming of Regiments of Foot

| 1782 | Designated 10th (North Lincolnshire) Regiment | |

Napoleonic Wars

1801	Egypt. The Regiment was granted the honour of the Sphinx and Egypt which forms the basis of the Regimental badge.
1804	Raising of the 2nd Battalion
1812-1814	Peninsula

Disbandment of the 2nd Battalion

1816   2nd Battalion disbanded and merged with 1st Battalion

GEORGE IV

WILLIAM IV

The Sikh Wars   VICTORIA

1846	Sobraon
1848-1849	Multan
1849	Gujerat
1848-1849	Punjab

Re-Raising of the 2nd Battalion

1857-1858   2nd Battalion raised

Indian Mutiny

1857	Private Kirk won the Regiment's first V.C.
1858	Lucknow

Malaya

1874-1876   Perak and other areas

Formation of the Lincolnshire Regiment

1881   Designated The Lincolnshire Regiment

Nile Campaign

1898   The Atbara
1898   Omdurman

Boer War

1900   Paardeberg
1900-1902   South Africa

EDWARD VII

Formation of the Territorial Force (later the Territorial Army)

1908   Formation of the Regiment's 4th and 5th
            Territorial Battalions

The First World War   GEORGE V

1914   Mons
1914   The Marne
1914,17,18 Messines
1914,15,17 Ypres
1915   Neuve Chapelle
1915   Suvla
1915   Loos
1916,18   The Somme
1918   The Lys
1918   The Hindenburg Line

Action between the World Wars

1919-1921   Ireland
1931-1932   Shanghai
1936   Palestine

EDWARD VIII
GEORGE VI

The Second World War

1940   Dunkirk
1940   Norway
1943   North Africa
1943-1945   Burma

1943	Salerno
1944	Ngakyedauk Pass
1944	Normandy Landings
1944	Fontenay le Pesnil
1944-1945	Gothic Line
1944	Antwerp-Turnhout Canal
1945	Rhineland

Post War Peacekeeping

1945-1946	Sumatra
1945-1946	Palestine
1946	Egypt
1946	Designated The Royal Lincolnshire Regiment
1946-1948	Palestine
1948-1952	Egypt and Aqaba
1948	The two regular battalions amalgamated to form the 1st Battalion
1950	The 4th and 6th Territorial Battalions amalgamated to form the 4th/6th Battalion

ELIZABETH II

1955-1958	Malaya
1960	Amalgamated with The Northamptonshire Regiment to form The 2nd East Anglian Regiment (Duchess of Gloucester's Own Royal Lincolnshire and Northamptonshire)
1964	Redesignated The 2nd (Duchess of Gloucester's Own Royal Lincolnshire and Northamptonshire) Battalion, The Royal Anglian Regiment
1968	Redesignated 2nd Battalion, The Royal Anglian Regiment

1969   TAVR Battalion disbanded retaining a cadre for future expansion which formed part of the 7th Battalion The Royal Anglian Regiment (V) in 1970

Appendix 2
BATTLE HONOURS

Within two clarions, thereon a sphinx, the plinth inscribed 'Egypt', the Roman numeral 'X'.

Blenheim, Ramillies, Oudenarde, Malplaquet, Peninsula, Sobraon, Mooltan, Goojarat, Punjaub, Lucknow, Atbara, Khartoum, Paardeberg, South Africa 1900-02.

Mons, Le Cateau, Retreat from Mons, **Marne 1914,** Aisne 1914, '18, La Bassée 1914, **Messines 1914, '17, '18,** Armentieres 1914, **Ypres 1914, '15, '17,** Nonne Bosschen, **Neuve Chapelle,** Gravenstafel, St. Julien, Frezenberg, Bellewaarde, Aubers, Loos, **Somme 1916, '18,** Albert 1916,18, Bazentin, Delville Wood, Pozières, Flers-Courcelette, Morval, Thiepval, Ancre 1916,'18, Arras 1917, '18, Scarpe 1917, '18, Arleux, Pilckem, Langemarck 1917, Menin Road, Polygon Wood, Broodseinde, Poelcappelle, Passchendaele, Cambrai 1917, '18, St. Quentin, Bapaume 1918, **Lys,** Estaires, Bailleul, Kemmel, Amiens, Drocourt-Quéant, **Hindenburg Line,** Epéhy, Canal du Nord, St. Quentin Canal, Beaurevoir, Selle, Sambre, France and Flanders 1914-18, **Suvla,** Landing at Suvla, Scimitar Hill, Gallipoli 1915, Egypt 1916.

Vist, Norway 1940, **Dunkirk 1940, Normandy Landing,** Cambes, **Fontenay le Pesnil,** Defence of Rauray, Caen, Orne, Bourguébus Ridge, Troarn, Nederrijn, Le Havre, **Antwerp-Turnhout Canal,** Venraij, Venlo Pocket, **Rhineland,** Hochwald, Lingen, Bremen, Arnhem 1945, North-West Europe 1940, '44-45, Sedjenane I, Mine de Sedjenane, Argoub Sellah, **North Africa 1943, Salerno,** Vietri Pass, Capture of Naples, Cava di Tirreni, Volturno Crossing, Garigliano Crossing, Monte Tuga, **Gothic Line,** Monte Gridolfo, Gemmano Ridge, Lamone Crossing, San Marino, Italy 1943-45, Donbaik, Point 201 (Arakan), North Arakan, Buthidaung, **Ngakyedauk Pass,** Ramree, **Burma 1943-45.**

The Awards in bold type are those emblazoned on the Regimental Colours.

Allied Regiments:- The Lincoln and Welland Regiment (Canadian Army), The Bermuda Rifles and the 1st Battalion The Royal Malay Regiment.

The Royal Lincolnshire Regiment was granted the Freedom of the following Cities/Towns:-

Lincoln	8th June 1946
Borough of Cleethorpes	19th September 1946
Grantham	21st September 1946
(Granted to the 6th Battalion The Lincolnshire Regiment)	
Grimsby (Marching Freedom)	11th August 1959

These honours have been transferred to the 2nd Battalion, The Royal Anglian Regiment.

Appendix 3

VICTORIA CROSS WINNERS

The Indian Mutiny

Private John Kirk	4th June 1857	Benares, India
Lieutenant Henry Marsham Havelock	16th July 1857	Cawnpore, India
Private Denis Dempsey	12th August 1857 & 14th March 1858	Lucknow, India

The First World War

Acting Corporal Charles Richard Sharpe	9th May 1915	Rouges Bancs, France
Captain Percy Howard Hansen	9th August 1915	Yilghin Burnu, Gallipoli
Acting Lieutenant Colonel Lewis Pugh Evans	4th October 1917	Near Zonnebeke, Belgium
The Reverend Theodore Bayley Hardy Temporary Chaplain to the Forces 4th Class	5th, 25th, 26th & 27th April 1918	Near Bucquoy & East of Gommecourt France
Lance Sergeant Walter Simpson (Arthur Evans)	2nd September 1918	South West of Étaing, France

The Second World War

Temporary Major Charles Ferguson Hoey	16th February 1944	Near the Ngakyedauk Pass, Burma
Temporary Captain John Henry Cound Brunt	9th December 1944	Near Faenza, Italy

Appendix 4

THE LINCOLNSHIRE REGIMENT IN THE FIRST WORLD WAR

Battles	Date	BATTALIONS OF THE LINCOLNSHIRE REGIMENT ENGAGED										Total Battalions of Linc. Regt. in each Battle
		1st	2nd	1/4th	2/4th (after Jan 1918 4th)	1/5th	2/5th	6th	7th	8th	10th	
	1914											
Mons	23rd-24th Aug	*										1
Le Cateau	26th Aug	*										1
The Marne 1914	7th-10 Sept	*										1
The Aisne 1914	12th-15th Sept	*										1
La Bassée	10th Oct-2nd Nov	*										1
Messines 1914	12th Oct-2nd Nov	*										1
Armentieres	13th Oct-2nd Nov	*										1
Ypres 1914												
Nonne Bosschen	11th-16th Nov	*										1
	1915											
Neuve Chapelle	10th-13 Mar		*									1
Ypres 1915	22nd Apr-26th May	*										1
Aubers Ridge	9th May		*									1
Bellewaarde	16th June	*										1
Loos	25th Sept-8th Oct			*		*				*		3
Bois Grenier	25th Sept		*									1
the Hohenzollern Redoubt	13th-14th Oct			*		*						2
Gallipoli												
The Landing at Suvla	6th-7th Aug							*				1
Chocolate Hill	6th-7th Aug							*				1
Scimitar Hill	21st Aug							*				1
	1916											
Egypt	Feb-July							*				1
The Bluff	14th-15th Feb & 2nd Mar								*			1
The Somme 1916	1st July-18th Nov											
Albert 1916	1st-13th July	*	*					*	*	*		5
Gommecourt Salient	1st July			*		*						2
Bazentin Ridge	14th-17th July	*										1
Delville Wood	15th July-3rd Sept								*			1
Pozières Ridge	23rd July-3rd Sept										*	1
Flers-Courcelette	15th-22nd Sept	*										1
Gueudecourt	25th-28th Sept	*										1
Thiepval Ridge	26th-28th Sept							*				1
The Ancre 1916	13th-18th Nov									*		1

German Retreat to the	1917										
Hindenburg Line	14th Mar-5th Apr		*	*		*					3
Arras 1917											
1st Scarpe	9th-14th Apr	*							*	*	3
2nd Scarpe	23rd-24th Apr							*	*	*	3
Arleux	28th-29th Apr								*	*	2
3rd Scarpe	3rd-4th May	*									1
Roeux	13th-14th May							*			1
Messines 1917	7th-14th June						*				1
Ypres 1917	31st July-10th Nov										
Pilckem Ridge	31st July-2nd Aug		*					*			2
Langemarck	16th-18th Aug		*				*				2
Menin Road Ridge	20th-25th Sep	*									1
Polygon Wood	26th Sept-3rd Oct			*		*					2
Broodseinde	4th Oct	*						*			2
Poelcapelle	9th Oct						*	*		*	3
1st Passchendaele	12th Oct						*				1
2nd Passchendaele	26th Oct-10th Nov	*									1
Cambrai 1917	20th Nov-3rd Dec			*		*					2
	1918										
German March Offensive	21st Mar-5th Apr										
St. Quentin	21st-23rd Mar	*	*	*		*		*		*	6
1st Bapaume	24th-25th Mar	*	*					*			3
The Ancre 1918	5th Apr								*		1
The Lys	9th-29th Apr										
Estaires	9th-11th Apr									*	1
Messines 1918	10th-11th Apr		*								1
Bailleul	13th-15th Apr	*		*		*				*	4
1st Kemmel	17th-19th Apr									*	1
2nd Kemmel	25th-26th Apr	*	*								2
The Aisne 1918	27th May-6th June	*	*								2
Amiens	8th-11th Aug							*			1
The Somme 1918	21st Aug-3rd Sept										
Albert 1918	21st-23rd Aug	*	*					*	*		4
2nd Bapaume	31st Aug-3rd Sept	*	*					*	*		4
Arras 1918											
Drocourt-Quéant	2nd-3rd Sept						*				1
The Hindenburg Line	12th Sept-9th Oct										
Epéhy	18th Sept	*	*					*			3
Canal du Nord	27th Sept-1st Oct	*	*				*				3
St. Quentin Canal	29th Sept-2nd Oct				*						1
Beaurevoir Line	3rd-5th Oct				*						1
Cambrai 1918	8th-9th Oct	*	*		*		*	*	*		6
The Selle	17th-25th Oct	*	*		*			*			4
The Sambre	4th Nov	*	*		*		*	*	*		6

Appendix 5

TITLES OF INFANTRY REGIMENTS

In Text	Later Title
1st Regiment	1st & 2nd Battalions the Royal Scots (The Royal Regiment)
8th Regiment	1st & 2nd Battalions The King's Regiment
10th Regiment	1st & 2nd Battalions The Royal Lincolnshire Regiment
11th Regiment	1st & 2nd Battalions The Devonshire Regiment
15th Regiment	1st & 2nd Battalions The East Yorkshire Regiment
16th Regiment	The Bedfordshire and Hertfordshire Regiment
20th Regiment	1st & 2nd Battalions The Lancashire Fusiliers
21st Regiment	1st & 2nd Battalions The Royal Scots Fusiliers
27th Regiment	1st Battalion The Royal Inniskilling Fusiliers
42nd Regiment	1st Battalion The Black Watch (Royal Highland Regiment)
58th Regiment	2nd Battalion The Northamptonshire Regiment
64th Regiment	1st Battalion The North Staffordshire Regiment
67th Regiment	2nd Battalion The Royal Hampshire Regiment
81st Regiment	2nd Battalion The Loyal Regiment
88th Regiment	1st Battalion The Connaught Rangers

Appendix 6

GLOSSARY

Abatis	A defence formed by placing felled trees lengthwise one over the other, a barricade of barbed wire.
Anzac	Australian and New Zealand Army Corps.
Armoured Vehicles Royal Engineers	Heavy Churchill tanks equipped with a mortar which fired a petard, an explosive filled canister used for demolitions. These vehicles were also loaded with other explosive devices and could carry bundles of wood (called fascines) to fill ditches, 20-foot assault bridges to span obstacles and a 4-inch explosive-filled iron tube called a snake, which could be sent 400 feet into a mine field and detonated for lane clearance.
Basha	A bamboo hut with a thatched roof.
Battalion	A unit of infantry composed of several companies and forming part of a brigade or regiment.
Bivouac	A temporary encampment, usually for the night.
Brigade	An infantry unit consisting of usually 3 battalions and forming part of a division.
Cartouche box	Cartridge box.
Chaung	A watercourse.
Corps	A part of an army.
Curtain	Plain wall of a fortification, connecting 2 towers.
Dervish	A Muslim religious man who has taken vows of poverty and austerity.
Division	A group of brigades or regiments.
Fascine	A long bundle of branches used for engineering purposes and for lining trenches

Field artillery	Light guns and howitzers capable of accompanying the fighting line of an army.
Furlow or furlough	Leave of absence.
Gabion	A cylinder of wicker or woven metal bands to be filled with earth or stones for use in engineering or fortification.
Gorget	The last relic of armour. A metal crescent-shaped plate worn at the throat by officers. The gorget was abolished in 1830.
Grape	Small cast-iron balls grouped several together to make a scattering charge for cannon.
Halberd	A weapon consisting of a long handle ending in a combined spearhead and battleaxe.
Half moon bastion	A fortified outwork shaped like a half-moon or crescent projecting from the main works so as to allow defensive fire in several directions.
Khor	A dry gully.
Kloof	A ravine or declivity on a mountain.
Kopje	A small hill.
Laager	Boer camp marked and protected by a circle of wagons.
Laagered	Wagons formed into a laager.
Lewis gun	A light magazine-fed, gas-operated, air-cooled machine gun.
Matchlock	A gunlock in which a match is placed to ignite the powder, a gun having such a lock.
Maxim gun	A single-barrelled quick-firing machine gun with a barrel surrounded by an outer casing filled with water to keep the parts cool.
Mine	A receptacle containing explosive placed in or on the ground with the purpose of destroying enemy personnel, etc.
Mortar	A short piece of artillery with a large bore and trunnions on the breech for firing shells at high angles.

Nebelwerfer	A six-barrelled rocket mortar used by the German forces in the Second World War.
Palisades	Fences or fortifications formed of stakes driven into the ground.
Parados	An elevation of earth behind a defended place as a protection against attack from the rear; the mound along the back of a trench.
Patrol	An advance detachment of troops sent to reconnoitre the country and gain information about the enemy, etc.
Puttees	A long strip of cloth wound spirally round the leg from the ankle to the knee, worn for protection and support.
Regiment	A body of troops consisting of several companies, troops or batteries.
Sangars	Parapets, breastworks, fortified lookout posts.
Schu mines	Light anti-personnel mines which could be rapidly laid to form an effective obstacle against infantry, cavalry and light vehicles. As they contained only a very small amount of metal, they were difficult to detect with any standard service mine detector.
Shako	A rigid peaked head-dress, cylindrical, conical or bell-topped in shape.
Stand of arms	A complete set of weapons for one person.
Stokes mortar	A weapon to 'lob' high explosive bombs and shells.
Swivels (swivel guns)	Guns or cannons mounted on pivotal rests so as to turn horizontally in any direction.
Vickers gun	A single-barrelled water-cooled recoil and gas-operated weapon, mounted on a tripod with a full 360 degrees traverse.
Zariba	A defensive enclosure of thorn bushes.

Select Bibliography

Belchem, D., *Victory in Normandy*, Book Club Associates, 1981.

Benson, J., *Saturday Night Soldiers,* Richard Kay, 2002.

Bryant, P. *Grimsby Chums,* Humberside Leisure Services, 1990.

Buzzell, N., *The Register of the Victoria Cross,* This England Books, 1988.

Carton de Wiart, Sir A., *Happy Odyssey,* Pan Books Ltd., 1955.

Carver, Lord, *The Imperial War Museum Book of the War in Italy,*
    Sidgwick & Jackson, 2001.

Chandler, D.G., *Marlborough as Military Commander,* B.T. Batsford, 1979.

Chandler, D.G. & Beckett, I.F.W. (Editors), *The Oxford Illustrated History of the British
    Army,* BCA, 1995.

Churchill, Sir W.L.S., *Marlborough His Life and Times,* George G. Harrap & Co. Ltd., 1958.

Colville, J.R., *Man of Valour,* Collins, 1972.

Dewar, M., *Brush Fire Wars,* Robert Hale Ltd., 1990.

Featherstone, D. *At Them with the Bayonet,* New English Library Ltd., 1974.

Featherstone, *D. Victorian Colonial Warfare* – India, Blandford, 1993.

Fraser, Sir D., *And We Shall Shock Them,* Sceptre, 1988.

Gates, L.C., *The History of the First Battalion The Lincolnshire Regiment in India,
    Arakan, Burma & Sumatra,* Lincoln, 1949.

Gates, L.C. (Editor Griffin, J.A.A.), *The History of the Tenth Foot 1919-1950,*
    Gale & Polden Limited, 1953.

Heathcote, T.A., *The British Field Marshals,* Pen & Sword Books Ltd., 1999.

Hunter, A., *Kitchener's Sword - Arm,* Spellmount, 1996.

Keown-Boyd, H., *A Good Dusting,* Book Club Associates, 1986.

Ketchum, R.M., *The Battle for Bunker Hill,* The Cresset Press, 1963.

Lee, A., *The History of the Tenth Foot (The Lincolnshire Regiment),* Gale & Polden, 1911.

Longford, E., *Wellington The Years of the Sword,* Panther Books Ltd., 1971.

Mackesy, P. *British Victory in Egypt,* Routledge, 1995.

Middlebrook, M., *The First Day on the Somme,* Allen Lane, 1981.

Middlebrook, M., *The Kaiser's Battle,* Penguin Books Ltd., 2000.

Moore, G., *The Last Decade, The Tenth Foot Royal Lincolnshire Regiment* 1950-1960,
    G. Moore, 1981.

Pakenham, T., *The Boer War,* Futura Publications, 1988.

Raw, D., *Its Only Me,* Frank Peters Publishing Ltd., 1988.

Rhodes James, R., *Gallipoli,* Pan Books Ltd., 1974.

Robertson, Sir W.R., Bart., *From Private to Field-Marshal,* Constable and Company Ltd.,
    1921.

Rolf, D., *The Bloody Road to Tunis,* Greenhill Books, 2001.

Simpson, C.R. (Editor), *The History of the Lincolnshire Regiment 1914-1918,*
    The Medici Society Ltd., 1931.

Slim, Viscount, *Defeat into Victory,* The Reprint Society Ltd., 1957.

Watson, J.S., *The Reign of George III,* Oxford, 1960.

Wolseley, Viscount, *The Story of a Soldier's Life,* Constable, 1903.

Index

162

164

166